Roman Catholicism
Yesterday and Today

Roman Catholicism
Yesterday and Today

Robert A. Burns, O.P.

A Campion Book

Loyola University Press
Chicago

Loyola University Press
3441 North Ashland Avenue
Chicago, Illinois 60657

Cover design by Beth Herman Design Associates. Cover photograph by George A. Lane, S.J.

Library of Congress Cataloging-in-Publication data

Burns, Robert A.
    Roman Catholicism yesterday and today / Robert A. Burns.
       p.   cm.
    Includes bibliographical references and index.
    ISBN 0-8294-0711-1
    1. Catholic Church—History. 2. Church history. I. Title.
BX945.B79 1991
282'.09'03—dc20
                                            91-41609
                                                CIP

For my "families":
the Burnses, the Costellos, the Gugginos, and the Krewedls

Contents

PART II

Catholicism Today: Key Issues

PART III

The Future: Movements in the Church

Preface

This book has its origins in a course I have taught at the University of Arizona for some twenty years. Those who have enrolled in my class have come from diverse religious and cultural backgrounds. There has been a fairly even mix of Roman Catholic and Protestant students, together with a number of students who have no religious affiliation. Whatever the mix, there has been a shared curiosity about the belief and practice of Roman Catholicism and many questions concerning the nature of the changes ushered in by the Second Vatican Council.

Much of the content of this book began as detailed lecture notes, and therefore it is designed for college and university level programs. It is also arranged in such a fashion as to make it useful for adult study groups—thus, the summaries at the end of each section, the questions at the end of each chapter, the glossary of technical words, and the selected annotated bibliography ("Further Reading").

In putting together a book of this scope, acknowledgment of those whose work I have drawn upon could be almost endless. Hopefully the textual references and bibliographical citations given throughout the book indicate sufficiently my debt to the scholars who have influenced my thinking.

I would like to especially thank Dr. Suzanne Tumblin for her great help in editing the manuscript.

Robert A. Burns

Introduction

Although the Second Vatican Council ended in 1965, there remains much confusion today, on the part of Catholics and non-Catholics alike, concerning the status of Roman Catholicism. A large part of this problem is due to a lack of awareness of the history of the Catholic Church preceding the twentieth century and a lack of understanding of what transpired at Vatican II. The contemporary meaning of the Roman Catholic Church is a recent development of the entire history of Catholicism beginning with the Council of Trent, which was held between 1545 and 1563 as a response to the Protestant Reformation. The Council of Trent set the tone for Catholic belief and practice for the next four hundred years. The first great shift in Catholic self-understanding since Trent came at Vatican II. In an effort to explain the changed circumstances within Catholicism, this study begins with the Council of Trent, traces the events of the following centuries, and finally describes what took place at Vatican II, together with some of the more important directions followed by Roman Catholicism since the close of the council.

Part I will give a brief historical profile of the Roman Catholic Church beginning with the Council of Trent and continuing through the changes that occurred at Vatican II. Attention is directed at the various stages of development in the Church during this period (1563–1962) and on the Catholic effort to maintain Church unity. Included in chapter 1 is a section discussing the Council of Trent and its aftermath. Brief analyses of the relationship between the Church and science, the Church and the state, and the Church and the Bible follow, together with a brief overview of the history of Catholicism in the United States. Chapter 1 concludes with a discussion of some of the key people and events that led to the convening of Vatican II. Chapter 2 is a rather extensive analysis of Vatican II and the direction that it set for modern Catholicism. Chapter 3 is a treatment of the present understanding of the mission of the Church.

Part II analyzes some of the key issues of present-day Catholicism. Chapter 4 is a discussion of Jesus Christ and the manner in which he is understood by modern biblical scholars and theologians. Chapter 5 is a treatment of the Christian moral life and compares the moral teachings of the Church before Vatican II to those of the modern Church. Chapter 6 is a discussion of the sacramental life of Catholicism.

Part III presents an indication of the future of Catholicism as seen through four of the most important movements in today's Church. Chapter 7 presents the history and development of the ecumenical movement in the context of the Church's relationship to other Christian denominations as well as to the other great religions of the world. Judaism, in particular, will be discussed as an example of Catholicism's relationship to the non-Christian world. Chapter 8 investigates the acceptance of the charismatic movement by Catholicism and seeks to understand the meaning of the Holy Spirit for all members of today's Church. Chapter 9 discusses the role of women in today's Church and the implications for the future of the Church that stem from the full participation of women in the life of the Church. The emphasis in this chapter is on the question of the ordination of women to the priesthood. Chapter 10 is a summary of the history of the social justice movement in the Catholic Church during the twentieth century and includes papal teachings, social justice in the United States, and an examination of liberation theology in Latin America.

The epilogue will briefly discuss Catholicism in the year 2000.

A glossary of various technical theological terms follows the epilogue. An annotated bibliography follows the glossary and includes a reading list for those who are interested in continuing their study of any of the major topics found in this book. Finally, a general index is provided for easy reference.

I hope that this book will help bring into focus many of the key elements in the present Catholic reformation. Surely the Church is in a period of reform. One of the most important contributions one can make is to give perspective to a situation that otherwise can be confusing and disturbing. I hope that the historical and theological approach used in this book will provide a better sense of perspective to the interested reader.

PART I

Modern Catholicism:
Background, History, and Development

1

The Collapse of Christendom and the Rise of Modern Catholicism

The Council of Trent (1545–63)

Among the first twenty **ecumenical** councils, beginning with Nicaea in A.D. 325, the Council of **Trent**, which was the nineteenth council, was unquestionably the most important before **Vatican II**—the twenty-first council—in the shaping of Catholicism. In terms of its clarification of Catholic **dogma** and of disciplinary decrees, it did more to refine and articulate the basic **doctrine** of Catholicism than did any other council in the history of the Church. Trent gave such a strong sense of direction that it came as a great shock to Catholics throughout the world when Vatican II so radically changed that sense of well-being and direction and caused what some have termed a "Copernican revolution" in Catholic thinking. Though it is now correct to refer to Vatican II as the most important council in Catholic church history, it stands to reason that it is of equally great moment to comprehend Trent and the Church that it shaped if one is going to attempt to understand the radical nature of Vatican II.

The Council of Trent took place in three sessions between 1545 and 1563 (1545–47, 1551–52, and 1562–63). By the time the first session was called, the Protestant **Reformation** had been underway for over twenty years. By 1545, all of Scandinavia, the British Isles, and much of Germany, Austria, and France had separated from communion with Rome. In effect, Europe was already polarized: certain parts were Protestant and other parts Catholic. There was a Protestant institutional organization, and a whole generation had been raised in this atmosphere. Thus, by the time the Catholic Church convened the Council of Trent, Protestantism was already well entrenched. The question that arises is obvious: Why had the Church delayed so long before convening the Council of Trent in 1545? After all, the Protestant Reformation is traditionally dated from October 31, 1517, when Martin Luther nailed his Ninety-five Theses to the church door at Wittenberg.

The reasons for the delay on the part of the papacy in convening a council were many. Several problems confronted the Catholic leadership. One difficulty was that in the sixteenth century the Vatican owned a great deal of land in France and Germany and **the pope**, as a temporal ruler, felt that his holdings would possibly be jeopardized if a council were called. This worry tied into a second problem, namely, the fear of **conciliarism**. Conciliarism was a residual of fourteenth-century thinking pertaining to the Western Schism, when there had been three claimants to the papacy. Conciliarism maintained that the authority of an ecumenical council transcended the authority of the pope. There were good reasons for fearing that if a council were convened perhaps even the papacy itself would eventually be abolished. Another reason for the delay in convening a council was that the new ideas preached by Luther, Calvin, and others were not initially perceived to be so greatly opposed to traditional Catholic teaching. The ideas of the Reformation were the outgrowth of fourteenth- and fifteenth-century theological discussions on the meaning of **grace**, Scripture, the sacraments, and the role of the papacy in humankind's redemption.[1] A number of earlier attempts at reform had come and gone. But as the sixteenth century proceeded it became clear that what was occurring was not simply reform, but a kind of revolution.

When at last the Council of Trent convened, its decrees became the definitive and authoritative answers of the Catholic Church and countered the teachings of Protestant reformers such as Luther, Calvin, Zwingli, Henry VIII, and their followers. Among the doctrinal teachings special attention was given to certain topics since the Catholic interpretation had been challenged in each of these areas by the emerging Protestant churches. Among these subject areas were the role of the pope, the nature of the **Mass** as a sacrifice, the meaning and number of the sacraments, grace, justification, and the nature of the Church. Generally speaking, Trent's methodology in answering the questions raised by the reformers was simply to restate the traditional doctrine of the Church. No real effort was made to conduct an open dialogue with the Reformation churches by analyzing the theological and scriptural questions that they had raised. It seems, however, that long before the council convened, all that had transpired in the intervening generation had precluded the expectation of dialogue.

What was at stake at the Council of Trent was the doctrinal authority of the Catholic Church. Never before in the history of the West had the teaching authority of the Church been so seriously challenged. During the **Counter-Reformation** period that followed the Council of Trent and, in fact, until the convening of Vatican II in 1962, the validity and necessity of Church authority continued to be the dominant motif in Roman Catholicism. The unity of Christendom had been sundered by the Protestant Reformation and a strong emphasis on Church authority was used to maintain post-Tridentine Catholic unity.

The direction taken at the Council of Trent can be seen in the definition of the nature of the Church produced by St. Robert Bellarmine. Bellarmine typifies the Counter-Reformation position in accepting the notion that the Church is identified with the **kingdom of God** on earth. His idea of a kingdom was used in the sense of a sovereign society, the same kind of society as was found in the Kingdom of France or in the Republic of Venice.[2] In *Disputations Against the Heretics of Our Time* (1586–93), which consisted of three volumes and was the most systematic and cogent defense of the Counter-Reformation, Bellarmine defined the Church in the following manner:

> The one and true Church is the assembly of man, bound together by the profession of the same faith, and by the communion of the same sacraments, under the rule of legitimate pastors, and in particular of the one vicar of Christ on earth, the Roman Pontiff.[3]

This emphasis on the visible aspects of the Church developed, then, not primarily from an attempt to understand the Church from the point of view of its relationship to the kingdom of God, but rather from an apologetic need to answer the reformers. All efforts were expended to present the visible, institutional Roman Catholic Church as identical with the church founded by Christ. It would be an exaggeration to say that no emphasis was given to the internal or spiritual aspects of the Church. Nevertheless, Bellarmine's presentation, which stressed the visible elements of the Church, dominated Catholic thinking until the **encyclical** letter of Pope Pius XII *Mystici Corporis,* which was written in 1943.

The Counter-Reformation definitions of the Church, which were used in Roman Catholicism following the Council of Trent, were basically exclusivistic and static and conceived the Church as a kind of island kingdom that was touched on its periphery by the flow of history but was not, in fact, essentially changed by historical occurrences. The Church was sufficient unto itself—after all, it was identical with the kingdom of God on earth.

To promote unity the Council of Trent issued a series of regulations that were aimed at protecting Catholics from what were seen to be the erroneous teachings of the Protestant churches and of the world-at-large. One such regulation, the *Index of Forbidden Books,* was clearly aimed at ensuring that Catholics would not be touched intellectually by any of the false teachings of the reformers. Catholics were forbidden under pain of serious sin to read the work of these "heretics."

In 1570, in the aftermath of the Council of Trent, Pope Pius V issued a decree that standardized the **liturgy** of the Mass and that was binding on the entire Church. The uniformity of the Mass symbolized the oneness of the Church throughout the world. As a result of this standardization, the Mass entered into a condition of liturgical rigidity that existed for almost four centuries. A living liturgy was replaced by attention to **rubrics**.

Such a uniform interpretation of liturgy is actually unique to modern times. Prior to the Reformation and the Council of Trent, the Church held a much more fluid attitude toward liturgy and dogma. Certainly after the Council of Nicaea in A.D. 325 a tendency had developed to impose one formulation of a particular doctrine for the whole Church. Nevertheless, the conviction that one single formulation of a doctrine could not *fully* describe the entire content of the teaching in question was not forgotten. The same attitude existed in regard to the liturgy of the Mass. In short, until the Protestant Reformation of the sixteenth century, Catholicism was capable of permitting many theologies (short of heresy) and various liturgies without feeling the need for total uniformity. But as a result of the Counter-Reformation movement within Catholicism, the most static period in the history of the Catholic Church began after 1570 and continued until the eve of Vatican II, at which time Pope John XXIII officially declaimed the narrow attitudes that had developed. This explains his call for the council to "open the windows of the Church" so that the fresh air of the Spirit might open the minds of the conciliar fathers to the realization that the Church can be one without being uniform.

During these four hundred years Protestantism was also undergoing a process of narrowing. In their battles for survival, the Protestant churches had been obliged to describe themselves and, in so doing, they often restricted the more vital elements of Luther, Calvin, and other sixteenth-century reformers. As a result, a very narrow Protestant orthodoxy arose in the latter part of the sixteenth and early seventeenth centuries. Today many mainline Protestants are undergoing the same renewal of self-understanding that is taking place in Roman Catholicism as a result of their missionary movement, the contemporary biblical renewal, and a variety of other causes.

Whereas, in the period we have been considering, Protestants and Catholics were hostile to each other, it now appears that Catholics and many Protestants agree that the task of theology is to illuminate the original meanings of the dogma of the Church and to rediscover what may have been lost through definition. Accompanying the need for illumination, there is a need for reformulation as well. One of the major goals of this book is to examine some of the key reformulations of doctrine occurring within Catholic theology today. This examination will attempt to clarify why the past attitude of polemics and hostility between Catholics and Protestants is giving way to an approach of love and fellowship under one Lord.

Another issue that must be addressed in any investigation of this kind, concerns the direction taken at Vatican II. Will this open-minded approach continue, or will there be a return to the theology of the Tridentine period, the period from the close of the Council of Trent in 1563 until the opening of Vatican II in 1962? Only with the passage of time will we have a complete answer. But it is clear that the import of the doctrinal pronouncements of the past councils has been determined by what was new in them and by the redirection that they have given the thinking of the Church. This is clear in the hardening of the polemical position of Roman Catholicism during the period of the Catholic Counter-Reformation following the dogmatic rejection at Trent of the Reformation. Concerning this stultifying tendency, George Lindbeck, a Lutheran and one of the Protestant experts at all four sessions of Vatican II, made an interesting and, it would seem, correct appraisal. He writes:

> But the fundamentally new fact about the council (Trent) was that in it the Reformation had been dogmatically rejected, and this both reflected and furthered a process in which a repudiation of the Reformers' views on justification, faith, grace, and the relation of Scripture and Tradition became far more total and massive than it was at Trent itself. Something like this seems likely to happen as a result of Vatican II—though now, we may hope, in the reverse direction.[4]

Summary

The Council of Trent was held to present the authoritative answers of the Catholic Church to the objections of the Protestant reformers. In order to promote Catholic unity, clear definitions were given concerning Catholic dogma. For example, a definition of the Church's role emerged that stressed its visible institutional structures and identified the Church with the kingdom of God on earth. Because of the narrowness of this definition, Catholicism tended to become exclusivistic in its thinking and static in its world view. The Council of Trent also issued a number of regulations to promote unity. As we have seen, the liturgy of the Mass was standardized and the *Index of Forbidden Books* was issued. These edicts helped maintain Catholic uniformity for the four hundred years after Trent. Great stress was placed on Church authority to maintain this post-Tridentine Catholic oneness.

After Trent: The Church and Science (The Case of Galileo Galilei)

The alienation of science and religion began with the trial and conviction of Galileo Galilei (1564–1642). The historical context of this event must be kept in mind in order to make it understandable.

Unquestionably, Catholicism had been rendered a serious blow by the Protestant Reformation. Catholic unity had been sundered. Now, only seventy years after the completion of the Council of Trent, a great Catholic scientist was claiming that the earth was not the center of the universe as Ptolemy had taught but that the universe was, rather, heliocentric. If Galileo were correct, many feared, his discovery would call into question accepted biblical interpretations. The teaching authority of the Church was again being challenged, or so it seemed to the Catholic **hierarchy**. Those who condemned Galileo believed that if his teachings were allowed to stand, the credibility of the Church would suffer, and perhaps its unity would be rent once again. And so Galileo was condemned. This judgment proved to be a terrible mistake, whatever may have been the motives of the majority of the Roman commission that sentenced him.

The Galileo incident occurred within the context of the highly systematized intellectual world of the thirteenth to sixteenth centuries. There was a tight integration between the understanding of the physical universe and the world of faith—so tight, in fact, that to attack one was to attack the other. This integration was characteristic of medieval theology, which constantly strove toward synthesis. Scholars were not willing to dichotomize existence. As a result, the **cosmology** of the day was worked into the fabric of theology. As a result of the influence of Aristotle's physics and Ptolemy's astronomy, a view of the universe emerged that placed the earth at the center of circling stars and planets.

Galileo was greatly influenced by Nicolas Copernicus (1473–1543) who in his great work *De Revolutionibus Orbium Coelestium* (Concerning the Revolutions of the Heavenly Bodies) advocated the heliocentric universe theory that stated the earth revolved both on its own axis and also around the sun. Copernicus had died in 1543, the year his book was published. Galileo, born approximately twenty years after its publication said, in 1597 in a letter to astronomer Johann Kepler, that he accepted the Copernican explanation. It was to be his lifelong effort to demonstrate the validity of the new system.

In 1610, Galileo published *The Starry Messenger* in support of the Copernican theory. But despite the many discoveries he made with the telescope and reported in the book, he still had no convincing proof that the Copernican system was anything more than conjecture. His observations militated against Aristotle and Ptolemy, but they did not give binding proof of the Copernican system. Needless to say, *The Starry Messenger* brought immediate responses from opponents. In defense of Aristotle and Ptolemy, the university Aristotelians listed a number of what they considered to be serious objections to the theories of Galileo and Copernicus. Three of the more important objections were:

1. A moving earth, in their view, completely contradicted all the then known laws of physics. They were correct. A new system of physics—that would later be developed by Isaac Newton (who ironically was born in 1642, the year of Galileo's death)—had to be established before the theory of Copernicus could be fully accepted.
2. Aristotle himself had said that if the earth moved, stellar displacements or parallaxes would be observable. But none had yet been recorded. This, too, was a solid objection. In fact it was much later—in 1843—that the first such recording took place, when F. W. Bessel determined the parallax of the star 61 Cygni.
3. The most serious objection to the heliocentric model pertained to logical conclusions from the Bible. The critics of the model stated that if the Copernican system were taken as established fact, and not simply as a mathematical device to aid astronomers in charting stellar positions, Copernican astronomy would then contradict the explicit words of Scripture. It was asked, for example, why Joshua would command the sun to stand still if it never moved anyway (Josh. 10:12–13). Also, how could an earth that moved around the sun be reconciled with Psalm 103:5, which says that God "fixed the earth upon its foundation, not to be moved forever"? Finally, it was believed that the sun must move since, Eccles. 1:5, states, "The sun rises and the sun goes down; then it presses on to the place where it rises."

What the opponents of the heliocentric universe were saying, in effect, was that the Church was certainly not going to change its accepted interpretation of Scripture based solely on the mathematical hypotheses of Copernicus and Galileo, notwithstanding the greatness of these men of science.

Six years later, in 1616, the Congregation of the Index in Rome suspended Copernicus's book *De Revolutionibus Orbium Coelestium* until it could be rendered more hypothetical, a clever maneuver since Copernicus had died in 1543. Nevertheless, suitable corrections were made by the Congregation of the Holy Office, and the suspension was lifted in 1620. Even more pertinent is the fact that in the decree of 1616 all books that attempted to reconcile the heliocentric theory with the Bible were condemned outright. As we will see, Galileo flew in the face of this prohibition.

In 1632, Galileo wrote *The Dialogue on the Two Great World Systems.* His main argument, which again supported the Copernican system, was based on a theory of the tides. He felt that tidal motion could be explained only by the movement of the earth. A second line of argumentation was based on the motion of the sunspots. In both arguments, his conclusions proved accurate, but his line of reasoning was faulty. *The Dialogue* met immediately with furious objections, and a special commission was established in Rome to investigate him. Contrary to the decree of the Index of 1616, Galileo had depicted Copernican theory not as a hypothesis, but as an absolute fact. The trial began on February 13, 1633. In defending himself, Galileo would not admit that he had tried to prove the Copernican theory in *The Dialogue* despite the many passages in the book that seemed to indicate that this was his intent. He also pointed out that the book had an **imprimatur**. However, it seemed clear that he had disobeyed the decree of the index as well as the explicit wishes of Pope Urban VIII, who was a personal friend of Galileo.

The commission debated the case. The minority view opposed the condemnation of Galileo, arguing that if he were later proved to be correct the Church would look foolish. On the other hand, if his theory were eventually proven incorrect, the problem would take care of itself. The majority view prevailed, however, and Galileo was condemned as "vehemently suspected of error." *The Dialogue* was banned, a ban that was not lifted until 1822. The majority of the commission evidently felt that too much was at stake not to condemn the astronomer. He had, after all, in their opinion, violated the decree of 1616. As punishment, Galileo was made to kneel before the commission and recant the Copernican system, was given a penance to recite, and was sentenced to prison. The prison sentence was never imposed, though Galileo remained under house arrest at his home in Florence until his death in 1642.

Thus, the first clash between the Church and modern science came to an unfortunate end. Though Galileo had not proven his case according to the accepted scientific theory, a new kind of science was involved. More important, Galileo called for the Church to reexamine its interpretation of various parts of Scripture. The answer given by the ecclesiastical commission was uncompromising and condemnatory. It was the beginning of the estrangement of science and religion that endures to the present day.[5] The Church's approach to the Bible did not dramatically change until Pope Pius XII wrote *Divino Afflante Spiritu* in 1943, encouraging Catholic biblical scholars to use the methods of **biblical criticism** that previously had been forbidden. Using such tools of scholarship could be expected to resolve the apparent clashes between religion and science by replacing literalistic interpretations of scriptural passages with a more appropriate understanding (consider the two creation accounts found in Genesis 1–3). But the mistrust between science and religion, for the most part, has remained inexplicably firm. The Church's attitude toward the Bible will be examined in a later section.

Summary

Less than seventy years after the conclusion of the Council of Trent the unity of Catholic belief was again challenged by the discoveries of Galileo Galilei. If Galileo were correct concerning the Copernican theory, then serious changes would have to be made in Catholic teaching, especially in regard to the Bible. Church authorities feared the unity of the Church might again be jeopardized if this were done. The commission that tried Galileo ruled that he did not have sufficient physical proof for his claims and forced him to recant his teaching. This authoritative condemnation marks the beginning of the split between religion and science that, in many ways, continues to the present time. The condemnation also highlights the role played by the Church in using its authority, rightly or wrongly, to preserve Catholic unity.

Church and State: The Eighteenth and Nineteenth Centuries

A serious challenge to Catholic unity and authority occurred in the eighteenth century in the form of two interrelated movements—the Enlightenment and the French Revolution. The Enlightenment attacked the basis of revealed religion by denying the authority of the Bible and the existence of the supernatural. In an unprecedented way, Enlightenment thinkers substituted the natural for the supernatural and science for theology. Human reason was deified and moral direction was sought by examining **natural law** rather than church teaching. Institutional Christianity was attacked, and the Catholic Church was accused of standing in the way of the new social sciences as well as economics, politics, and critical history. The discoveries made by Copernicus and Galileo inaugurated the scientific revolution, and later breakthroughs by René Descartes (1596–1650), Francis Bacon (1561–1626), and Isaac Newton (1642–1727) suggested that the universe might be subject to the control and domination of human reason.

The French Revolution (1789–99) brought the ideas of the Enlightenment into the political sphere and brought about the final dissolution of the feudal society that had been a constituent element of medieval Catholicism. The revolutionaries overthrew the French monarchy and even attempted to uproot Christianity itself. The political discontent that resulted in the overthrow of the monarchy had been fostered by the stress on the autonomy of reason in the writings of Enlightenment thinkers such as Locke, Montesquieu, and Rousseau, who also felt true freedom demanded a complete separation of church and state. In order to understand why the Catholic Church reacted so negatively to the French Revolution and the idea of political democracy, one need only recall that the Church favored monarchy as the ideal and advocated the notion that Catholicism should be the official religion of every nation.

Modern historians have coined the term *dechristianization* to describe the actions taken against Roman Catholicism by the French Legislative Assembly and its successor, the National Convention. The revolution brought about the death of some priests and the deportation of a great many more. Further, the revolution led to the closing of the churches and unsuccessful attempts to replace such "superstition" with "civic" religion. Worship and the teaching of religion were prohibited.

The Concordat of 1801, which marks the end of the revolution's attempt at dechristianization, guaranteed full freedom for Christians to practice their religion. The extremism of the French Revolution brought back many of the French and other European intellectuals to the basic principles of Catholicism. As a result, the authority and prominence of the papacy reached great heights during the nineteenth century, especially during the pontificate of Pope Pius IX (1846–78). The authority of the Church was seen as the only possible bulwark against the incursions of rationalism and the **modern mentality.** It is against this background that the origins of the conservative (*ultramontane*) and liberal Catholic movements in France must be viewed. A key individual in the development of both movements is Félicité de Lamennais (1782–1854). Throughout his lifetime, Lamennais was deeply concerned with the revitalization of society.

In the first phase of his career, Lamennais was associated with the conservatism of Joseph de Maistre (1753–1821). De Maistre attributed all the evils of the early nineteenth century to the French Revolution, which he felt had begotten an attitude of permissiveness that allowed everyone simply to choose and follow whatever course of life that seemed most pleasing. Against such antinomianism (the belief that faith alone, without moral law, is necessary for **salvation**) he stressed that the only hope for the recovery of society rested in a return to dependence on authority, especially the authority of the Church, centered in the papacy, and the authority of the state, centered in legitimate monarchy. In his book *Du Pape,* published in 1819, de Maistre argued that true liberty could be achieved, not through the popular democracy advocated by those "liberals" who had supported the French Revolution, but through stern self-discipline. He felt that such liberty could be accomplished only by a sovereignty superior to all others, namely, that of the papacy. Lamennais began his career with the same conservative notions as de Maistre, combining **ultramontanism** (dedication to the papacy) with royalism. In his early writings, which were widely read, Lamennais presented an apologetic for the Christian faith. In it he opposed eighteenth-century rationalism, criticized **Gallicanism**, and argued for the papacy as a safeguard of faith. Lamennais endorsed the papacy as a defense against the liberalism that he felt was threatening civilization. For Lamennais, and for a great many people, the papacy symbolized the values of European culture that were being threatened by the liberal ideas that were intent on reshaping the Western world.

When Lamennais realized that the French monarchs, the Bourbons, were incapable of the kind of leadership he had hoped for, he turned against them and attempted to identify the cause of Catholicism, and of the papacy in particular, with the cause of democracy. By 1830 he had come to the conclusion that the Church should be independent of royal control, since he now believed that governmental interference restricted the freedom of the Church. He also argued that the

Church should abandon its traditional policy of seeking to be the official religion of a given country. In effect Lamennais became one of the most influential of the new breed of Catholic intellectuals who sought to make the Church the beneficiary of the new insights that were brought about by the French Enlightenment.[6]

A group of prominent Catholics became part of Lamennais's circle. One of them was the famous Dominican preacher, Henri Dominique Lacordaire (1802–61). A number of other members of Lamennais's group were competent writers who were in basic agreement with his ideas—they all sought to distinguish between what was true and what was false in the contemporary thinking of their day. In October of 1830, they published the first issue of *L'Avenir*. In this journal, Lamennais and his associates delineated their ideas on Catholic liberalism and on the need for Catholic-liberal cooperation. He chose the motto *Dieu et la Liberté*, thus announcing his intention of reconciling the Catholic Church with the idea of freedom. *L'Avenir* lasted for a little more than one year, from October 16, 1830, until November 15, 1831. It was, undoubtedly, one of the most important Catholic journals of the nineteenth century despite the fact it was so short-lived.

The basic thesis of *L'Avenir* was the idea that the Church must accept the various freedoms defended by Enlightenment thinkers if the society of the future were to be shaped by the Church. Thus, *L'Avenir* rejected the divine right of kings philosophy, even though most of the bishops accepted this teaching, and argued on behalf of the sovereignty of the people. The journal also favored freedom of conscience and of religious worship, the separation of church and state, the discontinuation of the financial support of the clergy by the government, and freedom of education, of the press, and of assembly.

For a variety of reasons, including financial problems, it became clear by November of 1831 that *L'Avenir* could not survive. Lacordaire suggested that a personal appeal for help be made to Pope Gregory XVI. This course of action was chosen. The effects were calamitous for Lamennais and his friends since it led to the encyclical letter *Mirari Vos* of August 15, 1832. In this letter, Pope Gregory spoke out in strong support of the union of church and state. Among the errors of the day, he strongly condemned indifferentism, freedom of conscience, of the press, and of speech, and what he thought was a general tendency to accept liberal ideas in an unqualified fashion. In effect, he condemned the entire program of liberal Catholicism.

With *Mirari Vos,* Pope Gregory XVI committed the Catholic Church to the old social structure. This proved to be a heavy burden for the

Church, and at the end of the century even the more progressive Pope Leo XIII (1878–1903) could not wholly overcome this decision. As for Lamennais, the censure by the pope was too much to endure. Although he submitted at first, he later left the Church and became one of its most bitter critics.

In retrospect, Lamennais and his group can be seen to have advocated a number of policies that, in many respects, the Church officially adopted in the twentieth century. These policies gave concrete expression to the Church's problem of adapting to the needs of a new kind of society that had come into existence with the French Revolution. Such adaption came very painfully and was further delayed by the decisions of Pope Pius IX (1846–78).

During the pontificate of Pope Pius IX, liberal Catholics continued to argue for an acceptance of what they considered to be new and valid theological, philosophical, and social insights. But at the official level, Roman Catholicism remained reactionary. Under Pope Pius IX a fortress mentality deepened and an attitude developed that the only hope for the Church was to defend itself against the new ideas and wait for the time when such dangers had passed. This position was intensified, and all liberal groups and tendencies were once again condemned when, in 1864, Pope Pius IX wrote the encyclical letter *Quanta Cura*. Appended to the encyclical was a document entitled *Syllabus of the Chief Errors of Our Times* in which the pope summarized contemporary church teaching against modern errors. The syllabus was based on a selection of modern errors that had been condemned in some thirty previous allocations and encyclical letters during the eighteen years of the pope's pontificate. Some examples of opinions listed as erroneous in the syllabus are:

> Every individual is free to embrace and profess that religion, which, guided by the light of reason, he or she shall consider true.

> Humankind may, in the observance of any religion, find the way of eternal salvation and arrive at eternal salvation.

> The church ought to be separated from the state and the state from the church.

> In the present day, it is no longer expedient that the Catholic religion should be held as the only religion of the state, to the exclusion of all other forms of worship.

The Roman pontiff can, and ought to reconcile himself, and come to terms with progress, liberalism, and modern civilization.

For some Catholics, the syllabus seemed an embarrassing reversal of the pope's earlier espousal of open-mindedness. For others, it appeared as the definitive divorce of Catholicism from modern civilization. And although there was certainly justification for the syllabus—especially the condemnations it contained of pantheism, naturalism, absolute rationalism, and indifferentism—it did seem that the pope had declared war on modern society.

Most important, during the reign of Pope Pius IX, the First Vatican Council was convened in 1870. Many feared that the doctrine of papal infallibility would be defined. Men such as John Henry Newman in England, for example, believed the Church to be infallible, but felt that a definition of the infallibility of the pope would lead toward further Roman centralization and would also tend to atrophy the episcopacy. However, those who opposed the definition were but a small intellectual minority. On July 18, 1870, the conciliar fathers defined, though not unanimously, papal infallibility as a dogma of the Catholic Church. In part, the definition was issued to combat liberalism and, in part, to oppose the rise of the absolute state in Europe.

Ironically, at the time the absolute authority of the pope was declared, the temporal authority of the papacy came to an end. In September of 1870, Victor Emmanuel's Italian army captured Rome. The pope became "the prisoner of the Vatican," and it was not until the Lateran Treaty of 1929 that the question of the pope's temporal holdings was settled with the creation of Vatican City.

The First Vatican Council assured the fortress mentality for years to come. This posture deepened with the condemnation of modernism by Pope Pius X in 1907 in his encyclical letter *Pascendi dominici gregis*. The popes, by means of frequent encyclical letters on doctrinal and social questions, assumed a role of moral leadership virtually unknown in the history of the papacy. Many Catholics believed the teachings found in such documents to be infallible. Although such encyclicals are of great importance, the only teachings since 1870 that were promulgated as infallible are those of the Immaculate Conception of Mary and of her Assumption into heaven. It is only since Vatican II (1962–65) and its stress on the collegiality of the bishops, that Catholics have begun to see the beginning of decentralization of papal power and the increase of responsibility being given again to local bishops and national conferences of bishops throughout the world.

Summary

The French Revolution was generated by the Enlightenment. The revolution attempted to "dechristianize" France and though it failed to do so, it did mark the beginning of political democracy in that country, as well as the separation of church and state. The Catholic Church suffered greatly during the French Revolution. The extremism of this period led many Catholics back to the principles of Catholicism. As a result, the prominence of the papacy and of Church authority reached great heights during the nineteenth century, especially during the pontificate of Pope Pius IX. The authority of the Church was seen by many as the only possible bulwark against the incursions of rationalism and the modern mentality. Thinkers such as Félicité de Lamennais sought to bring the Church to a position of accepting what he and others felt were valid insights of the Enlightenment, but to no avail. Under Pope Pius IX, a fortress mentality deepened, aided by his *Syllabus of Errors* in 1864 and the definition of papal infallibility in 1870 at Vatican I. This attitude remained, by and large, until Vatican II.

The Church and the Bible

The Roman Catholic Church felt that one of the principal causes of the Protestant Reformation was the proliferation of biblical interpretations among theologians such as Martin Luther, John Calvin, and Huldrych Zwingli. Such interpretations led to the formation of many and varied denominations. To preserve Catholic unity the Church insisted that official interpretations of the Bible could only be made by its formal teaching authority. However, Catholics were encouraged to read the Bible daily and to see in the words of Scripture the way to eternal salvation. Yet Catholics, for the most part, seldom read the Bible. Light can be shed on this apparent contradiction by analyzing the history of Roman Catholicism's relationship to the Bible.

Perhaps the most consistently asked question of Roman Catholics concerns their attitude toward the Bible. Other Christians are often puzzled to learn that the ordinary Catholic has such a limited understanding of Scripture. The answer usually given is that Catholics do have an appreciation of the Bible from hearing the Scriptures read and preached at Sunday Mass. Be that as it may, it is still quite true that most Catholics are not familiar with the Bible and many seldom, if ever, actually read the Scriptures. The basic reason for this unfortunate situation is that after the Protestant Reformation the standard means of teaching used by Roman Catholics was a catechism. Such books were based on the Bible and gave the official Catholic interpretations of the words of Scripture. This methodology was used to prevent a private reading of the Bible from turning into subjectivism, an attitude that was feared, as we have seen, because it was perceived as a cause of the Reformation and the proliferation of Protestant denominations. This attitude has greatly changed since Vatican II. Though Catholics continue to depend on church leadership for authoritative interpretations of Scripture, many Catholics have begun to read the Bible daily and bible studies are common in Catholic parishes and among groups of Catholics, often in an ecumenical gathering.

In order to gain a better understanding of the Roman Catholic attitude toward the Bible, a review of its teachings concerning Scripture is necessary. First of all, it is important to recall that the Church as a community predates the writing of of the New Testament. The Christian community produced the biblical books beginning with the First Letter of Paul to the Thessalonians around A.D. 50, followed by Paul's other authentic letters previous to his martyrdom in A.D. 64 under Nero. The Gospels, as we now have them, were written at various times by church members, starting with the Gospel of Mark somewhere between A.D. 65 to 70, followed by the Gospels of Matthew and Luke between A.D. 70 and 90, and finally by the Fourth Gospel, the Gospel of John, between A.D. 90 and 100. Perhaps the last of the New Testament books to be written was the Second Letter of Peter around A.D. 120. The basic source, therefore, of our knowledge about Jesus and his message is the teaching and revelation contained in the Bible, which was written under the inspiration of the Holy Spirit by members of the early Christian community.

The Bible chiefly used by early Christianity was the Greek translation of the Hebrew Bible (the Old Testament). Because so many Jews lived outside of the Holy Land and because the entire Mediterranean region had been absorbed by the Hellenistic Empire of Alexander, the language of the Diaspora Jews was basically Greek; thus, the Old Testament had been translated into Greek in Alexandria, Egypt, in the third century B.C. and is known as the Septuagint (named for the seventy Hebrew scholars believed to have translated it in seventy-two days). Other writings in Greek were added to the original

Greek translation by approximately 100 B.C., including Judith, Tobit, Wisdom, Ecclesiasticus, Baruch, 1 and 2 Maccabees, and parts of Daniel and Esther. When Christianity moved outside of Palestine and into the Greco-Roman world early in its history, Christians continued using the Septuagint version of the Bible. It was this version that was translated by St. Jerome into Latin between A.D. 390 and 405. Jerome's translation, called the Vulgate, slowly won acceptance based on its evident superiority over other translations after Charlemagne's restoration of the Holy Roman Empire in A.D. 800. It predominated in the Western Church, especially due to the influence of Alcuin of York, Charlemagne's leading scholar. The Council of Trent (1545–63) mandated a new and corrected version of the Vulgate, finally published under Pope Clement VIII in 1592–93. The council declared this version to be the authentic text of the Catholic Church. In *Divino Afflante Spiritu* of 1943, Pope Pius XII declared that the authenticity was juridical, not critical. What this means is that the Vulgate is legitimatized by its long use in the Church as free of error in faith and morals and, therefore, is a safe source of Catholic doctrine. But as Pope Pius made clear, its critical authenticity is *not* affirmed in detail, nor even as a whole, except to the degree that it is a substantially faithful witness of the original text.

Protestant Christianity, beginning with Martin Luther and John Calvin in the sixteenth century, did not accept the seven books of the Old Testament that were originally written outside of Palestine (and rejected parts of Esther and Daniel for the same reason). Rather, Protestants accepted the Jewish canon of the Bible, which rejected any works produced outside of the Holy Land and not written in Hebrew. This canon quite possibly originated at a synod of great rabbis at Jamnia about A.D. 90, though it is safe to surmise that Palestinian Judaism had long rejected these seven books as inspired, even though they had been accepted by most of the Jews living in the Greek-speaking diaspora. Martin Luther's translation of the Old Testament used only the Palestinian canon. The seven books were placed in an appendix and are referred to as apocryphal or deuterocanonical by Protestant Christianity.

None of the disputed books contain matters of great doctrinal importance. Certainly there is nothing in any of these works that can or should lead to essential division among Christians. All Christians are in unanimous agreement that there are twenty-seven books in the New Testament. In the past, fear of using a Protestant version of the

Bible, particularly the New Testament, by a Catholic or vice versa was often due, at least in part, to fear of contention in the footnotes. The footnotes in the Catholic version give a Catholic interpretation; those in the Protestant version, quite naturally, a Protestant interpretation. But with the great biblical revival now taking place, the Bible has become a bastion of unity among Christians. Christian scholars of all denominations are working in unison on ancient biblical manu- scripts. They are sharing discoveries in biblical archaeology as well as in the various linguistic breakthroughs of the past 150 years or so. They are also using textual criticism. And they are now in almost unanimous agreement on the basic translation of the Bible. This is certainly true of Roman Catholicism and the mainline Protestant denominations.

This new accord among Catholic and Protestant scholars dates from the nineteenth century, when discoveries were made in the areas of archaeology, history, and language that were shared by all Christians. Clearly none of these resources were available to the Protestant reformers of the sixteenth century or to the Catholic respondents at the Council of Trent. But these rather recent discoveries are deepening our understanding of the Bible. Such studies, and corresponding fields of research, pertain to what is known as biblical criticism. Perhaps this nomenclature is poorly chosen in that it gives many ordinary believers the notion that something negative is occurring when, in fact, biblical criticism's function is to broaden and deepen the Christian world's understanding of God's Word.

Modern archaeology began at the time of Napoleon's invasion of Egypt in 1798. Along with his troops Napoleon brought 175 scholars, artists, and scientists to sketch and study the antiquities of Egypt. The results of their research were published in seven volumes between 1809 and 1822. The most important discovery made by the French in Egypt was the Rosetta Stone. While constructing a fort at Rosetta in the Nile delta in 1799, soldiers uncovered a large black stone inscribed in three languages: hieroglyphic, Demotic (a form of Egyptian script) and Greek. Working from the Greek—which turned out to be a translation of the Demotic and hieroglyphic texts—scholars, led by Champollion, translated the hieroglyphics in 1822. The trilingual inscriptions had been written in Memphis in 163 B.C. to commemorate the first anniversary of the coronation of Ptolemy V. More important, the translations allowed scholars to read the thousands of inscriptions on Egyptian monuments and tablets that had long held their secrets.

These translations helped provide a better understanding of the Old Testament and so deepened an understanding of the Hebrews in their relationship to Egyptian life and culture.

Another important discovery was made by teams of British and French archaeologists toward the middle of the nineteenth century. Among the discoveries made was that of the palace of Ashurbanapal (668–627 B.C.) at Kuyunjik (ancient Nineveh) by Henry Layard of England. In this palace, thousands of clay tablets were discovered written in cuneiform, a method of writing invented by the Sumerians in Mesopotamia during the fourth and third millennia B.C. Cuneiform—so named from the Latin *cuneus,* "wedge-shaped," because the writing consists of wedge-shaped signs—was used for the writing of many different languages of antiquity during the second and first millennia B.C. and was finally displaced by the Egyptian pen, ink, and paper (papyrus) shortly before the Christian era. The tablets found in the Ashurbanapal library contained letters, contracts, dictionaries, grammars, receipts, tables of measures, lists of events, hymns, prayers, religious epics, medical reports, and astronomical and astrological calculations and dealt with almost every field of knowledge known to scholars of that time. The deciphering of cuneiform was achieved mainly by a British army officer named Henry Rawlinson. Between 1843 and 1847, Rawlinson, risking his life, copied Persian and Babylonian inscriptions found on a great rock cliff at Behistun, Persia, which had been placed there by Darius I (522–486 B.C.). He was finally able to interpret their meaning and, thus, the translation of cuneiform. Before these nineteenth-century developments, the chief source of knowledge of the Egyptians, Assyrians, Babylonians, Aramaeans, and many other peoples who had flourished and died in the Near East had been the Bible. This was no longer the case. The Bible was no longer alone in its witness to the past. Before the translation of cuneiform, for example, many parts of the historical books of the Old Testament remained virtually inaccessible. But with these new discoveries, much insight was gained concerning biblical historical references.

In 1928 the discovery and decipherment of the tablets found at Ugarit in modern Syria added further insights. Until the translation of Ugaritic (ancient Canaanite writing in a cuneiform alphabet) we knew of no literary records left by the Canaanites. With the deciphering of Ugaritic, we learned of past myths that dealt with the gods of the Canaanites. Now we realize that after Joshua led the Hebrews into the land of Canaan, the Hebrews borrowed much of their language, music, and poetry from the Canaanites, whose higher culture was imitated by them.

Discoveries have continued into the twentieth century, notably the Dead Sea Scrolls in 1947 and the tablets of Ebla in 1968. Knowledge of biblical references, as a result, continues to broaden and deepen with each new discovery. Forgotten peoples such as the Hittites and the Hurrians, who were previously only biblical names, have come to life. Knowledge of their customs and laws has helped to explain details in the patriarchal narratives. Ancient Canaanite cities, once known only by name, have unfolded before our eyes as cities such as Jericho, Bethshan, Megiddo, and Hazor have been uncovered. Practically every detail of life described in the Bible is now understood as a result of recent scholarship. Not only does this information provide a solid reply to skeptics who have attacked the authenticity of the Bible but, perhaps even more important, it sheds greater light on the richness of God's message.

Together with the discoveries that have been made concerning the Bible in the fields of language, archaeology, and history, there arose the need to interpret the Bible in the light of all this new information. In recent years Christian biblical scholars have used an Ancient Greek term *hermeneia* (interpretation) to describe the process of deriving contemporary meaning from the past. The task of interpreting the Bible is one of achieving understanding by translating its ancient words and ideas into the clarity of one's own language. To accomplish such a task emphasis is placed on a genuinely historical approach to the Scriptures.

Biblical scholars in modern times have distinguished two major types of historical criticism: lower or textual criticism and higher or documentary criticism. Biblical criticism logically begins with the text itself. For example, since the New Testament was written in Greek, it is valid to ask if, at any given point, the English version faithfully renders the most reliable, reconstructed Greek text. This is the work of textual or lower criticism. A scholar in this field must have at his or her disposal the most ancient manuscripts of the New Testament and must also know other languages, such as Syrian and Latin, in which some of the valuable early copies of the text were translated. The scholar, too, must be proficient in the methods of dating manuscripts. By means of the collation and classification of these New Testament manuscripts, a history of the text types is determined and, upon these findings, a critical text is reconstructed.

Recent New Testament scholars have also stressed the importance of another aspect of research that pertains to literary criticism. They study such matters as the genre of a given book, word usage, sentence, and paragraph structure. They acknowledge the presence of confessional or hymnic formulas that are, perhaps, derived from the traditions of the author's community. They also analyze possible interpolations by later editors or scribes. Such observations shed light upon its author's purpose or intention and on the purpose of the editor(s) of the text. Such critical work is not easily distinguishable from documentary or higher criticism, whose role is to define accurately the circumstances under which a book was composed.

Documentary or higher criticism examines questions of the authorship, date, and destination of the various biblical books. The evidence examined is of two types: internal and external. Biblical writing sometimes yields direct or indirect information concerning its origin. In evaluating this internal evidence, the higher critic is like a person working a jigsaw puzzle. He or she attempts to fit the scattered pieces together. External evidence, on the other hand, has several sources. Such evidence, for example, can be discovered in references to the origin of biblical books in ancient Church traditions. Sometimes evidence is found in the use of language that belongs to a particular historical period. Whatever the external source may be, the critic must decide to what extent such circumstantial evidence is reliable. Thus, primary importance is placed upon the internal evidence.

Textual and documentary studies lead logically to the exploration of the historical setting of a biblical work. The appreciation of any ancient book depends upon knowledge of the conditions of its period, and for such information the use of historical techniques is required. Linguistic analysis and archaeology are also necessary since they enable the expert to, at least partially, reconstruct the background of a particular book. Such information helps to gain a better understanding of biblical personalities and events, which are viewed in terms of their own history to avoid modernizing or romanticizing the person or event in question. Fr. Raymond Brown has written an excellent book, *The Critical Meaning of the Bible*, which can be of great value to anyone who wishes to learn more about biblical criticism.[7] Brown describes the methodology used to analyze Scripture together with concrete examples of such research.

Roman Catholicism places great value not only on the Bible but on the role of tradition as well. Unfortunately the meaning of tradition is often misunderstood. One of the great maxims of the Protestant reformers, and of Protestantism to the present day, is *sola Scriptura,* the Bible alone, as opposed to the concept of tradition as a source of belief. Tradition is the manner in which Catholic Christians understand and live the teachings of Jesus Christ. Tradition is derived from the creeds of the Church, its practice of worship, the writings of its great biblical scholars and theologians, and the teachings of councils and of popes. Tradition continues to develop today, as it will in the future, depending upon the understanding of Christ's teachings and their application in the lives of the Catholic world. The Bible alone contains Christ's original teachings, but the tradition of the Church gives Catholicism the advantage of understanding the wisdom of the Holy Spirit, moving and guiding the Church in the course of its history. To ignore such knowledge would allow a spiritual vacuum to develop. Because the Holy Spirit has been with the Church since Pentecost Sunday and will continue to be with the community of Christ until the last day, the Catholic Church feels it is necessary not only to read Scripture under his present direction, but to be guided as well by the movement of the Holy Spirit as it has been manifested in history from the beginning.

Summary

Roman Catholicism has great veneration for the Bible, which contains the Word of God. However, in order to prevent the private reading of Scripture from turning into subjectivism or into the further proliferation of Christian denominations, Catholics defer to biblical experts under the aegis of the formal teaching authority of the Church for the official interpretations of Scripture. After the Protestant Reformation the standard means of teaching by Roman Catholicism was catechism. As a result, most Catholics seldom, if ever, read the Bible. This attitude has greatly changed since Vatican II, and many Catholics now read it regularly and are engaged in bible study classes. In the past two centuries a deeper understanding of the Bible has been made possible by archaeological, linguistic, and historical discoveries, and by the use of biblical criticism. Although Roman Catholicism venerates the Bible as the Word of God, it also holds tradition in high regard since tradition gives the Church the advantage of understanding how the Word of God has been interpreted in the course of its history under the impetus of the Holy Spirit.

The Catholic Church in the United States

In the nineteenth century, the power of the papacy reached its zenith. During the reign of Pope Pius IX, the fortress or defensive mentality of Catholicism reached new heights and remained at that level until the convening of Vatican II. This was true of Catholicism everywhere, including the United States. During the second half of the nineteenth century great numbers of Catholics emigrated from Europe to the United States. The immigrant church in the United States was presented with many problems of which one of the most important was that Catholics were settling in ever-increasing numbers in a nation that many church leaders understood to be Protestant and hostile to Catholicism.

A variety of issues had to be faced by the Catholic immigrants, not the least of which was Catholic education. Various measures were used to instruct Catholics, but the most important vehicle was *The Baltimore Catechism,* which was published in 1885. Written by authority of the American bishops at the Third Council of Baltimore, it became the primary instrument of Catholic education until Vatican II. Once again we see the teaching authority of the Church guiding Roman Catholics. But with the completion of Vatican II in 1965, *The Baltimore Catechism* became archaic. Still, many Catholics do not understand why the *Catechism* has been discarded since, for them, it is a symbol of unity and stability. In order to understand why the catechism has been set aside, a review of its history and an analysis of its format and content is needed. But first, in order to put the *Catechism* in its proper context, a brief summary of the history of American Catholicism is necessary.

In reviewing the history of American Catholicism it becomes clear that Roman Catholics in the United States have often been suspected by European Catholics of being "too American" or "too democratic." On the other hand, American Protestants have often felt Roman Catholics are too "Roman," with their loyalties torn between their citizenship and their church. There is some truth in each opinion. American Catholics have been consistently loyal to Rome, but at the same time they have also been consistently loyal to their country to the extent of often being called super-patriotic. Roman Catholicism, outside of the Spanish territories such as Florida and the Southwest, did not become noticeable in this country until the mid-nineteenth century and, surprisingly, American Catholicism is indeed historically different from Catholicism elsewhere. Yet strangely even Catholics in the United States have little understanding of their own history or of its uniqueness.[8]

The first Catholic bishop in the United States was John Carroll of Baltimore. When he was elected bishop by his twenty-five fellow priests in 1789, there were fewer than 90,000 Roman Catholics in the colonies, most of whom lived in Maryland and Pennsylvania. The increase in the number of Catholics in the United States in the nineteenth century was dramatic. The statistics tell the story:

```
1790 = 35,000
1815 = 90,000
1820 = 160,000
1840 = 1,300,000
1880 = 6,000,000
1900 = 12,000,000
```

This dramatic increase in Catholic numbers greatly alarmed American Protestants. Anti-Catholic groups such as the Know-Nothings, the A.P.A. (American Protective Association), and others were formed. Much discrimination was evidenced in the job market as well as in personal relationships. The immigrant Catholics met many obstacles in their new environment. Since most of them were not well educated and many could not speak English when they arrived in the United States, their priests took on very important functions. They were not only the spiritual leaders of the community, but the social and intellectual leaders as well. A number of bishops in the nineteenth century were **assimilationist** such as John Ireland of St. Paul, Minnesota; John J. Keane of Dubuque, Iowa; John Lancaster Spalding of Peoria, Illinois; and James Cardinal Gibbons of Baltimore, Maryland. They believed the immigrants should become Americanized as quickly as possible. They also believed that American society, far from being a negative force, represented great opportunity for the Catholic Church. Many other bishops disagreed with them and felt the only safe course for the Church was to separate itself from an American culture that was seen as Protestant, hostile, and a threat to the faith of the immigrant Catholics. In the end the anti-assimilationists won out. As a result, church structure in the United States, together with its system of parochial schools, was organized to resist the threats of a culture that was perceived to be hostile to the faith and religious practices of the immigrants. This attitude remained until Vatican II when a greater appreciation of non-Catholics, together with an openness to the world-at-large, became a substantive part of Catholic thinking. The fortress mentality was discarded. At about the same time, the election of the first Roman Catholic president of the United States, John F. Kennedy, in 1960, marked the beginning of the acceptance of Catholics as full members of American society. A great distance had been traveled since the anti-Catholic attitudes of the nineteenth century.

One of the chief instruments of Catholic education during the latter part of the nineteenth century and continuing into the 1960s was *The Baltimore Catechism.* Written in the closing days of the Third Plenary Council of Baltimore in 1884 and published in 1885, the *Catechism* represents, in effect, the theology of the Council of Trent. The first draft was written hurriedly by Msgr. Januarius de Concilio, a pastor from Jersey City, New Jersey, who was serving the Baltimore council as an advising theologian. Some refinements followed, and the first edition of the *Catechism* was published a few months after the council had been completed.

Public reaction to this new religious education textbook was not enthusiastic. In fact, criticism was so persistent that in 1896 the American bishops appointed a committee to revise the *Catechism.* The project dragged on for several years, but with the death of the chairman of the committee in 1903 the work came to a halt. As a matter of fact, it wasn't until 1935 that the revision was again undertaken. The revised edition appeared in 1941 and dominated the religious scene in American Catholicism until Vatican II. There are several reasons why the *Catechism* was allowed to remain unchanged for so long even though from its inception it was recognized to be deficient. The most important reason was the so-called modernist crisis of 1907. Modernism, which was condemned by Pope Pius X, is rather difficult to define, but the modernist crisis concerns the Church's handling of threats posed by secular science arising especially from the work of Sigmund Freud and Charles Darwin as well as from the new, critical biblical studies. Not certain how to deal with these challenges to received faith, Catholicism concentrated on shoring up the traditional formulations of the faith. The continued use of the *Catechism* was a part of this entrenchment. Even with the revised *Catechism* of 1941, very little was changed in the text other than making certain that the language was as clear and precise as possible.

The initial change of policy toward modern science and biblical studies came in 1943 when Pope Pius XII wrote *Divino Afflante Spiritu.*

The modern movement in theology dates from this time and slowly gained momentum until its decisive impact on the proceedings of Vatican II. Because the revised version of the *Catechism* was published in 1941, it was untouched by the modern theological renewal.

One reason why many Catholics were opposed to changes of any kind, and so had enormous difficulty with the new orientations introduced at Vatican II, was that religious education as represented by the *Catechism* tended to give them a Rock-of-Gibraltar concept of their faith. For this basic reason, a number of Catholic adults find it hard to cope with the changes thrust upon them since Vatican II. The question, understandably, is still asked: Why don't we go back to the use of the *Catechism* since it presents such a stable view of the Church?

The answer, of course, is that the cultural frame-of-reference of 1884 contrasts sharply with that of the present day. Communications, transportation, and technology were in their infancy in 1884. Today we are in an electronic age. Space travel is taken for granted. Medical advances have been tremendous. Life expectancy is much longer. Simply speaking, the Catholic worldview has dramatically changed since the *Catechism* was written. The second point is more intrinisic and has two parts: first, the question-and-answer format of the *Catechism* is stultifying, and second, the theology of the *Catechism* is out of harmony in a number of places with the theology of Vatican II.

As to the format, there are three principal difficulties. First, the *Catechism* is presented by means of questions and answers. The answers are often important conclusions, but the manner by which one would arrive at each conclusion is not included in the format. As a result, the meaning of faith tended to become reduced to memorizing statements. Little room was given to question what the catechism taught and any expression of doubt was often treated as though it were an attack upon the faith. Rather than seeing such questioning as a healthy part of faith, the attitude was, by and large, that the questioner was lacking in true docility. The second difficulty with the format is that like all Catholic catechisms written after the Protestant Reformation, it emphasizes what Protestants deny (e.g., the infallibility of the pope) and plays down what Catholics and Protestants hold in common or deals with the subject in a different fashion (e.g., the Bible). Though biblical texts are given at the end of each chapter of the *Catechism* and within given chapters as well, the fact remains that very little real encouragement was given to Catholics to make the Bible a daily part of their personal lives. This was an effort, in part, to undercut the reformers' emphasis on the private interpretation of Scripture. Authors of the *Catechism* feared that to encourage such reading of the Bible would lead to anarchy or, at least, to further divisions among Christians. As a result, most Catholics today feel very removed from any strong personal knowledge of the Bible, though many are taking steps to overcome this deficiency. The third difficulty regarding the format is that its message tends to be given in terms of obligation. In other words, it is overly authoritative. That the Church has authority is certainly part of basic Catholic belief, but in new books of religious training, the modality of Christian love and the concomitant desire to serve the Lord is now seen as a much healthier basis of communication and decision making.

As to the theology of the Church there are a number of important changes since Vatican II that differ from what is presented in *The Baltimore Catechism*. Several examples will suffice since we will discuss the overall changes in the theological direction of the Catholic Church in the following chapters. One dramatic change pertains to the nature of the Church. The *Catechism* defines the Church narrowly in Roman Catholic terms, whereas Vatican II makes clear that Orthodox and Protestant Christians are truly members of the Church and will be saved, not *despite* the fact that they are Orthodox or Protestant, but *because* they are, in reality, members of Christ's body. The *Catechism* also discusses states of life: the single state, the married state, and the religious state. The married state is seen to be lower than the priesthood, for instance. But Vatican II teaches that all Christians are called to the fullness of love. Whatever place one has with Christ is not dependent on his or her "state of life," but rather on a loving relationship, or lack thereof, with Jesus Christ. In regard to morality, which will be treated in greater detail later, the *Catechism* tends to present moral considerations in legalistic terms, whereas the attitude flowing from Vatican II is that moral considerations must be understood from a more life-centered and interpersonal viewpoint.

For all these reasons—the changed worldview, the problems with format, theological advances—*The Baltimore Catechism* is no longer a useful tool for religious education.

Summary

Roman Catholic teaching authority was presented with a new problem due to the waves of Catholic immigrants entering the United

States beginning in the mid-nineteenth century. In order to give their people solid teaching, the American bishops authorized the writing of a text that became known as *The Baltimore Catechism*. Though the *Catechism* had flaws, it became the chief teaching instrument for American Catholics. It presented a stable view of Catholicism and became one of the primary symbols of the pre–Vatican II American church. Because of the vast theological changes made at Vatican II, *The Baltimore Catechism* is no longer accurate in many areas and so has been discarded by all but the most conservative Catholics. New works have been produced and are being used across the United States. But it must be remembered that *The Baltimore Catechism* served a very useful purpose for the immigrant church in that it provided American Catholics with the basic answers that they needed to understand and maintain their faith.

People and Events Leading to the Second Vatican Council

Throughout the first half of the twentieth century Catholic scholars continued to make important discoveries in biblical and theological research. Biblical studies have already been discussed. Here we will deal primarily with theological advances. Because of the strong conservatism of the Church, most Catholics knew very little about either biblical or theological innovations. Church authority was content to maintain the status quo, as had been true since the Council of Trent. This attitude did not prevent Catholic scholars from continuing their work. They were greatly aided in their efforts when Pope Pius XII published the encyclical letter *Divino Afflante Spiritu* in 1943. In this letter, Pius XII encouraged Catholic scholars to make use of discoveries in archaeology and linguistic analysis, and he supported their use of the historical-critical method. The pope's directive had a great impact on theologians as well as biblical scholars. But in 1950, Pope Pius XII published another encyclical letter, *Humani Generis,* that effectively reversed the openness of *Divino Afflante Spiritu* and plunged the Church into another period of deep conservatism that lasted until the beginning of Vatican II. It is clear that Pius XII felt that the Church was not ready for the new biblical and theological discoveries. An understanding of the events and of some of the more important Catholic theological scholarship in the decades preceding Vatican II, including the decade of the 1950s, provides necessary insights into the reasons why Pope John XXIII felt compelled to mandate an ecumenical council in 1960. Vatican II ended the conservative period that began with the Council of Trent and continued, for all practical purposes, until 1962.

When Angelo Roncalli was elected pope in 1958 and chose the name John XXIII, it seemed most unlikely that his reign as pope would produce any revolutionary changes in the life of the Catholic Church. He was not an original thinker, nor was he a creative theologian. And he was seventy-six years old when he was elected to the papacy. So it came as a shock to all when, in 1960, he called for an ecumenical council to be held. It had been ninety years since Vatican I and few, if any, observers of the papacy expected such a bold undertaking from Pope John. The pope was well aware of the authoritative reigns of his predecessors, Pope Pius XI (1922–39) and Pope Pius XII (1939–58), but in the first two years of his pontificate he became absolutely convinced of the need for change. The best solution seemed to be calling together bishops from throughout the world to discuss the needs and concerns of the whole Church. Thus, he convened Vatican II. As Pope John's career is examined, we can see the reason for his perceptiveness and concern. Perhaps the most important factor is that Angelo Roncalli did not spend his whole career in or near Rome, but had a much broader experience. His own background had taught him that the centrality of the Roman Curia and its denial of many modern influences was too narrow and shortsighted. Early in his career, Roncalli had worked in the Curia but, in 1925, he was appointed apostolic visitor to Bulgaria. Nine years later he became apostolic delegate to Turkey and Greece and for the next ten years he was in very close contact with Eastern Orthodoxy as well as with the Moslem world. Most helpful to Pope John was his tenure in France as apostolic representative from 1944 until 1953. During this period he was impressed with Cardinal Suhard's priest-worker experiment program, which attempted to win back to the Church many who had left the practice of their faith. Priests took jobs in factories, offices, and other workplaces in order to get to know the people and to be known by them. The effort was not without its successes, even though the movement was finally disbanded. Even more noteworthy, Pope John had been exposed to many of the new biblical and theological ideas that were unfolding in France at that time. When he called for an ecumenical council he was well aware of those theologians and biblical scholars who would make an impact on the council. In addition, from 1952 until his election as pope he was the permanent Vatican observer to UNESCO (United Nations Educational, Scientific, and Cultural Organization). This relationship with the United Nations further deepened his understanding of world problems and, correspondingly, of the Church's role in the world-at-large. Finally, in 1953 Pope Pius XII named him a cardinal and made him Patriarch of Venice.

In his opening speech at Vatican II on October 11, 1962, Pope John spoke encouragingly in support of the new biblical and theological ideas and the need to reform the Catholic Church. Two days later Cardinal Lienart of Lille, the second oldest of the cardinals, objected, amid loud applause, to the predetermined membership of bishops on various commissions; his objection was accepted and elections to the various commissions were held a few days later. This event set the council firmly on a path of openness and helped ensure its success.

That openness had been foreshadowed for the council in the writings of theologians throughout the twentieth century. Between World War I (1914–18) and World War II (1939–45), the Church lived under the impact of a strong conservatism and under the power of new movements: liturgical and ecumenical as well as biblical and theological. One of the most important contributing factors in the movements toward change was the use of historical criticism by Catholic scholars. Historical criticism is a relatively late development in the history of Christian theology and was first used by Catholic scholars, in any notable fashion, during the twentieth century. The historical-critical method attempts to discover the original formulation of a belief—and the motives and forces, whether personal or social, underlying that belief—and the part it plays in the development of a particular dogma. Pope John XXIII, in his opening address to Vatican II on October 11, 1962, said that the Church must employ the best methods of research and use the literary forms of modern thought in order to distinguish between the substance of a particular dogma and the way in which it has been presented. What is involved in such an investigation is referred to as the development of doctrine.

Development of doctrine never means the abandonment of doctrine or the substitution of a new doctrine for an older one. Genuine development always proceeds along consistent lines. It is growth from a partial to a fuller vision of truth, so that what has been believed continues to be believed, though with greater clarity and depth. What is implicit in faith, but not fully realized because of historical obstacles, becomes clearly understood as emanating from the gospel message by means of better scholarship and historical perspective. Such methods of research had been used previous to Vatican II by a number of prominent Catholic scholars.

As early as the 1920s attempts to develop a new synthesis between Roman Catholicism and the non-Catholic world had begun to develop. Among the writers in the early period of the twentieth century one of the most influential was Romano Guardini (1886–1968), who taught philosophy of religion and the Catholic worldview at the University of Berlin. Guardini laid the foundations for the liturgical reforms that were initiated at Vatican II. He also helped prepare for a new Catholic approach to the problems faced by humankind in the technological world of the twentieth century.[9]

Another early giant in France was Jacques Maritain (1882–1973), who devoted much of his writing to the effort of reconstructing and update Thomism, which refers to the philosophy of St. Thomas Aquinas (c. 1225–74). Thomas wrote commentaries on the complete works of Aristotle, and in his *Summa Theologica* he used Aristotelian philosophy to support the basic teachings of Catholicism. The work is the greatest synthesis of faith and reason produced by the medieval world and certainly is the best example of scholastic theology. Thomism was revived in the sixteenth century and used, with limited success, by the Catholic Counter-Reformation. Pope Leo XIII in the encyclical letter *Acterni Patris* in 1890, declared St. Thomas the patron of Catholic theology and stated that there was one adequate philosophy, to the exclusion of all other philosophical schools, and that philosophical system was Thomism. However, often those who were Thomists tended to lose sight of the creativity of St. Thomas Aquinas, and they merely repeated his teachings rather than updating and relating his thinking to twentieth-century problems.

Jacques Maritain was successful in attacking some of Thomism's most dated and sterile aspects, though he was met with great resistance in many quarters. Maritain was professor of philosophy at the *Institut Catholique* in Paris from 1912 to 1933. He came to the United States after the outbreak of World War II and continued his work. He died in 1973.[10]

Two other prominent writers in Germany in the first half of this century were Erich Przywara and Otto Karrer. Przywara was a Jesuit priest, who, in a number of books published over a forty-year period, pointed out some of the weaknesses of modern Thomism's didactic approach to theology. He provided new theological insights and a new anthropology that led to and encouraged fresh concepts. Karrer derived his inspiration especially from the writings of Cardinal John Henry Newman, the great English convert to Catholicism in the nineteenth century. Karrer especially strove for a loving relationship among the divided Christian churches and was a pioneer in the ecumenical movement among Catholic thinkers. It was because of the work of men such as Przywara and Karrer, groundbreaking work that was both daring and dangerous at the time, that Vatican II was possible.[11]

The work of thinkers and theologians such as Guardini, Maritain, Przywara, and Karrer were carried on by some outstanding writers in the next generation. In Germany such work was done by the brothers Karl and Hugo Rahner, both Jesuits; and by Hans Küng, Joseph Ratzinger, and Johann Metz. In France there were the Jesuits Henri de Lubac and Jean Danielou, the Dominican Yves Congar, and Cardinal Suhard. One of the best known theologians of the Catholic renewal is the Dutch Dominican, Edward Schillebeeckx. These writers, among others, produced the greatest revolution in theology since the Protestant Reformation. Their works and ideas spearheaded the changes effected at Vatican II.

Henri de Lubac published several books with Congar and Danielou in the *Una Sanctum* series that Congar had begun in 1937. These works helped to promote, among other things, the ecumenical movement. The doctrine of grace was a favorite topic of these French theologians and de Lubac, in particular, contributed new insights to this doctrine as well as to ecclesiology (the study of the nature of the Church) and pastoral sociology. During World War II de Lubac came into contact with many communists and came to understand their humanistic atheism. His books on Proudhon, Feuerbach, and Marx were the products of these encounters. Henri de Lubac was one of the first Catholics to take a serious interest in these modern forms of humanism. The Catholic-Marxist dialogue that continues in earnest today in France and elsewhere in Europe certainly derives much of its impetus from the energy and involvement of de Lubac.[12]

Yves Congar had a deep interest in ecumenical relations that, in turn, inspired his revolutionary thinking about the role of the Church in the modern world. He was also greatly concerned about the position of the laity within the Catholic Church since he believed that they had been placed in a role of obedience and docility, but not one of leadership. One of his most famous books, *Lay People in the Church,* written in 1953, dealt with this problem and helped influence progressive thinking on this topic at Vatican II.[13]

Fr. Karl Rahner was one of the greatest theologians in twentieth-century Catholicism. The quantity of his writings is prodigious, and their substance is impressive. Though there is nothing of the revolutionary spirit in his makeup, he was a prominent contributor to the recent, rather incredible changes in Catholic thinking. One of the reasons Rahner has been so successful is his sense of Catholic tradition. In the best possible way, his approach was conservative. His thinking, as a result, never strayed from the historical path of the Church. This enabled him to defend his positions whenever they were attacked and helped him to influence many who might otherwise never have modified their attitudes or who would not have been willing to see that there is and always has been a development in Catholic thinking about its dogma. Many of his finest essays appear in the multivolume *Theological Investigations*.[14]

In the United States, Fr. John Courtney Murray, S.J., made important pre–Vatican II contributions in his writings on the relationship between church and state and on the correlative question of religious freedom. His work appeared in scholarly articles in the journal *Theological Studies*. In these articles he subjected certain traditional Catholic teachings, especially those of Pope Leo XIII on the relationship of church and state and on religious freedom, to historical and theological reinterpretation. Murray did not argue that Pope Leo's teaching was false, but that it was archaic. Because of these views, Murray was not invited to the first session of Vatican II, but he was invited to the final three sessions of the council. The contributions of this noted theologian are examined in chapter 2.

As we have seen, Pope Pius XII published *Humani Generis* in 1950, and the remainder of his pontificate was one of strong conservatism. It would seem that he began to fear that the new trends in theology would hurt rather than aid the Church. *Humani Generis* forthrightly opposed the new ideas. This is seen in the subtitle: "Concerning false opinions that threaten to undermine the basis of Catholic teaching."[15] The pope named and condemned, among others, the following new trends: existentialism, historicism, the urge for innovations, the false theory of evolution, the Catholic feeling of inferiority regarding modern sciences, the tendency to minimize the differences between the churches, and philosophical relativism (i.e., the notion that there was a need for any other philosophical system other than Thomism). Earlier in the same year the pope had infallibly defined the Assumption of Mary into heaven, although this had long been a strong Catholic belief, and there was no real need for such a definition. What Pius XII was doing, in the hope of reversing the new trends, was asserting his absolute authority over the life of the Church. But the new theological thinking continued, albeit quietly, and erupted forcefully with the appearance of Pope John XXIII in 1958 and the convening of Vatican II in 1962.

Summary

A great deal of serious theological research took place among Roman Catholic scholars during the first half of the twentieth century. However, most Catholics were unaware of such studies since the theologians promoting new ideas were not given approval by church authorities who felt their main obligation was to maintain Catholic unity and stability. New ideas might cause confusion. Indeed confusion did result when these ideas came to public awareness through the teachings of Vatican II. Pope Pius XII had shown a new openness to the demands for change in his encyclical *Divino Afflante Spiritu,* published in 1943, when he encouraged Catholic scholars to make use of the new discoveries in areas such as archaeology, language, and in historical-critical thinking. But Pope Pius XII returned to a strong conservative stance in 1950 with the publication of the encyclical *Humani Generis.* However, the need for change was great. Recognizing that the Church must adapt to present needs and to the discoveries of its scholars, Pope John XXIII called for the convening of Vatican II.

Study Questions

1. Why was there such a long delay (1517–45) in the convening of the Council of Trent?
2. Why is the Council of Trent so important in the overall history of modern Catholicism?
3. Why was the Enlightenment opposed to Christianity?
4. How did the French Revolution affect Roman Catholicism?

5. What was the main thrust of Félicité de Lamennais's thinking? Why was his thought condemned by Pope Gregory XVI?

6. What was *The Syllabus of Errors?* What effect did it have on Roman Catholicism? Why did papal authority become so prominent under Pope Pius IX?

7. How have archaeological and historical discoveries increased our present understanding of the Bible?

8. In Catholic teaching, what is meant by *tradition?*

9. Why was *The Baltimore Catechism* written? Is it still a useful teaching device?

10. Describe some of the Catholic writers whose scholarship contributed to the convening of Vatican II.

11. Why did Pope Pius XII write the encyclical *Humani Generis?*

2

Vatican II

Introduction

The effects of Vatican II are still being assimilated by Roman Catholics. Many agree intuitively with the openness of spirit that the council engendered. Some do not. In this chapter an examination will be made into some of the key insights of the council in order to gain perspective on the direction taken by the Church at Vatican II.

Before proceeding further a background question should be answered. Catholics and Protestants alike often ask about the authority of conciliar statements. This is a rather complex problem. Vatican II, in contrast to all previous ecumenical councils, refrained from formally specifying any of its teachings as dogma in the full sense of the word. Nor were any anathemas or condemnations directed toward anyone who rejected its teachings. However, many of its teachings are presented in such a fashion that they appear to have the force of dogma, at least in the sense that no responsible Catholic theologian would publicly deny them as the teachings of the Church. For example, the decisions in favor of religious liberty, the collegiality of bishops, and the priesthood of all believers would clearly appear to have such authority. Other teachings are also binding in various degrees. There are sixteen documents from Vatican II, and they are referred to as either a constitution, declaration, or decree. Generally speaking, the constitutions, especially what are called dogmatic constitutions, have the highest authority.

Declarations and decrees stand on a lower level (though *The Decree on Religious Freedom* is found in a declaration). Perhaps it is most helpful to say that the doctrine of the council, though in most instances presented as pastoral directives and as guidance for the Church, is official church teaching and is to be followed by Roman Catholics.

A review of the documents of Vatican II reveals that its constitutions, decrees, and declarations are concerned mainly with the nature of the Church. The council was called by Pope John XXIII not to refute error or condemn heretics, but basically to reform the Catholic Church. As St. Augustine, Martin Luther, and so many other theologians have noted, *Ecclesia semper reformanda est* (The Church must always be reformed). Reform was clearly the purpose of the council. In this sense, the council maintained a unity of theme—the reform of the Church—that no previous council ever had.

What is especially noticeable about Vatican II is its tendency to give preference to historical truth without straining theoretical or speculative truth. Edward Schillebeeckx in his book *The Real Achievement of Vatican II* observes that perhaps the essential problem at the council was that so many conservative bishops in attendance were unable to see that "the essence of the Church can never show up other than in historical forms."[1] And yet the council, in its final decrees, presents an image of the Church as intimately involved in history. History is not understood merely as the disturbances of the times that flow past the Church without touching it. Rather, the very essence of the Church is understood as involved in these historical events. In *The Dogmatic Constitution on the Church,* the Church is no longer simply equated with the kingdom of God on earth, as it had been previous to the council. It is seen instead as the "budding and beginning of the Kingdom."[2] Thus, the conceptualization of the Church is no longer seen as being divorced from history, an island kingdom, as it were, forever undisturbed by history. Now the Church is seen as intimately involved in history and as having a mission to make Christ known in history in all of its dimensions.

The Church no longer accepts the view held by the Greek philosophers who taught that the fundamental structures of the physical world are unchanging and that there is no real history of development. Among the ancients, even the Stoics—who did hold that changes occur—believed that the changes were cyclical. Historical categories are now used, and it is maintained that human reality must be understood in dynamic terms with attention focusing on the role of the Church as a historical institution within God's total historical plan. The earlier description of the nature of the Church formulated at the Council of Trent, which described the Church as relatively static, is rejected as inadequate throughout most of the conciliar documents. As we shall see, understanding the Church as a historical institution leads to a much more dynamic conceptualization of the mission of the Church.

Vatican II: The Beginning of the Beginning

Despite the many new attitudes expressed at Vatican II, it becomes apparent in reading the documents of the council that there is a juxtaposing of the new with the more traditional notions of the nature of the Church. This ambivalence allows for quite divergent readings of the theology of the council. For example, the second chapter of *The Dogmatic Constitution on the Church*, entitled "On the People of God," was deliberately placed before the chapter entitled "On the Hierarchy." This emphasis on the entire "People of God" would lead one to believe that the distinctions so strongly maintained between clergy and laity would be subsumed within the one "People of God." But, as we shall see, an ambivalence remains. Although the constitution marks a real breakthrough, it reverts to a more traditionalist position, using standard imagery, in its description of the hierarchy.

What one must remember while studying the documents of Vatican II is that they are compromise agreements on the part of the bishops of the world. Thus, they must be seen as interim documents. In this light, the tensions between the old and the new in the conciliar documents become more understandable as does the reason why Karl Rahner refers to Vatican II as the "beginning of the beginning." [3]

It seems reasonable to predict that the new theological emphases in the documents of the council will continue to predominate as we move toward the close of the twentieth century despite efforts made from time to time to return to preconciliar attitudes. Such a prediction is based both on the nature of ecumenical councils and on the history of past councils.[4]

Much give and take occurred at Vatican II. New ideas were not forced on any of the bishops, and so, no schism resulted. Rather, compromises were reached that have allowed for a healthy development and assimilation of new emphases in the period following Vatican II.

When theologians refer to that which is "new" flowing from Vatican II, they do not necessarily mean that a truth is being proposed for the first time. It would be difficult to determine what might be called "new" in that fashion. A sense of tradition and continuity was maintained, together with an understanding of the fact that there is a development and enriching process at work in the Church's comprehension of the Christian truths. The council also brought to light realities and truths that simply were not operative facets of the everyday thinking of Catholicism. Perhaps the most important theme emerging from Vatican II is the idea that the framework within which the Church is understood is historical and dynamic, rather than ahistorical and static.

Summary

The documents produced at Vatican II were compromise agreements and contain a mixture of new and more traditional ideas. Yet none of the teachings of Vatican II are completely "new." They present either a deeper understanding of existing teachings, or they bring to light ideas that simply were not operative facets of contemporary Catholicism.

A Summary of the Documents of Vatican II

Sixteen documents were issued at Vatican II. Of these, four are referred to as constitutions; namely, those dealing with the Church, the Church in the modern world, the sacred liturgy, and Divine Revelation. The first two will be examined in this chapter. *The Constitution on the Sacred Liturgy* will be treated in Part II when the sacraments are discussed. *The Constitution on Divine Revelation* will be examined in Part III in tandem with the analysis of the ecumenical movement.

There are also three declarations. One of these, *The Declaration on Religious Freedom* is discussed in this chapter. A second, *The Declaration on the Relationship of the Church to Non-Christian Religions,* is discussed in Part III in conjunction with *The Decree on Ecumenism,* and the third declaration, *The Declaration on Christian Education,* deals with the internal problems of Catholic education and does not break any new ground. Strong emphasis is placed on the need for parochial education.

Vatican II also produced nine decrees. It will be helpful to give a brief summary of each.

1. *Ecumenism.* This is a major resource for ecumenical activity. Possibilities of shared love with other religious groups are open now in a manner that simply did not exist before Vatican II. This decree, and **ecumenism** generally, will be treated in some detail in Part III.

2. *The Eastern Catholic Churches.* This decree considers the relationship of Roman Catholicism to the Catholic churches in the eastern world that are in communion with Rome but do not use the Latin rite. These churches are often referred to as the Uniate churches. The rites of these churches are again approved in this decree, guidelines are given concerning sharing in common worship between the Uniate churches and the Eastern Orthodox churches (which are not in communion with Rome), and honor is paid to the patriarchs of the Uniate churches.

3. *The Church's Missionary Activity.* In this decree new freedom is given to bishops in mission areas and more discretion is allowed to make local decisions without first having to consult with Rome. This document is an aspect of the process of decentralization of power that was begun at Vatican II. Closer cooperation is urged between Roman Catholics and other Christians in the mission fields, an attitude that flows from *The Decree on Ecumenism,* which had been accepted previously by the council. As a result, joint translations of the Bible, common use of physical facilities, and many other ecumenical breakthroughs have taken place in missionary areas.

4. *The Bishops' Pastoral Office in the Church.* This decree explains some of the ramifications of the council's teaching on the collegiality of the bishops. Bishops are encouraged to take a greater part in the life of the universal Church as well as continue their role as chief pastor of their individual dioceses. Bishops' conferences for a given

area are encouraged to deal corporately with mutual problems of that region. These directions have been implemented since Vatican II with some measure of success.

5. *The Ministry and the Life of Priests.* This document describes the role and function of the priest. The ordained priesthood is seen within the context of "the priesthood of all the faithful." Dialogue with bishops and the laity is encouraged. It is stated that bishops should gladly listen to their priests and, in turn, priests are encouraged to listen willingly to the laity. As with the other directions given at Vatican II, this teaching has been well adhered to in some dioceses, but not quite so well in others.

6. *Priestly Formation.* Although this document is by no means revolutionary, it clearly directs attention to the education of priests and the need for some restructuring of seminary training. For example, it encourages greater emphasis on the study of Scripture, a fuller understanding of Protestant Christianity and Eastern Orthodoxy, and a better use of the disciplines of sociology and psychology. Within this decree, there is an implicit recognition that seminarians should have more contact with the society to which they will minister, rather than being isolated from the world throughout their seminary training, as has more or less been the rule in the past.

7. *The Appropriate Renewal of the Religious Life.* In this decree a number of suggestions are made concerning the reform and updating of religious orders even though the implementation of these ideas is basically left to the leadership of the various religious communities. Among other directives, it is stated that the religious habit (mode of dress) may be adapted to modern conditions as each group decides is fitting. It is also observed that true renewal will come from the interior rededication to Christ and to the spirit of the founders of the various religious orders in the Church. The decree points out that the life of denial is not so much a denial *of* the world as it is denial of self *for the sake of* the world.

8. *The Apostolate of the Laity.* This decree, which provides for a fuller participation of the laity in the life of the Church, received its impetus from the teaching on the role of the laity in *The Dogmatic Constitution on the Church.* Even though this document does not represent a radical change in teaching it does provide for the elevation of the laity from a second-class status to a much more active and respected role in the life of the Church. This decree surely provided the necessary beginning for further lay participation that occurred

after Vatican II such as the role of the laity as eucharistic ministers, lectors, or members of parish councils.

9. *The Instruments of Social Communication.* Those who have studied the documents of Vatican II generally agree that this decree, which deals with the use of the mass media, is the least satisfactory of the sixteen documents produced at Vatican II. Perhaps its greatest importance lies in the fact that the use of the mass media is officially recognized as an area in which the Church has been deficient. Certainly, since Vatican II, greater use of the mass media has been made although there is always room for improvement.

Summary

Of the sixteen documents produced at Vatican II, four are referred to as constitutions, three are called declarations, and nine are labeled decrees. All of these documents, however, contain the authoritative teaching of Roman Catholicism. A brief summary of the nine decrees are given in this section. A fuller analysis of the constitutions and declarations will be presented in later sections of the book.

The Dogmatic Constitution on the Church

The most important of the sixteen documents produced at Vatican II was *The Dogmatic Constitution on the Church*. In many ways it is the hinge upon which the rest of the documents turn. Understanding the constitution, however, is contingent upon a knowledge of the background against which it was produced. The original draft of the constitution, with its traditional Counter-Reformation approach, was rejected shortly after the council amid charges that it fostered the vices of juridical institutionalism, **clericalism**, and **triumphalism**. The bishops appointed a committee that provided a new document, the text of which was then discussed, refined, and finally accepted by the conciliar fathers. In the constitution, as finally approved, there are three important concepts that merit consideration: (1) the Church as the mystical body of Christ, (2) the Church as the People of God, and (3) the Church as an eschatological institution.

The Church as the Mystical Body of Christ

The first breakthrough of lasting consequence from the apologetic stance concerning the nature of the Church within Roman Catholicism was made in the nineteenth century by the theologian Johann Adam Moehler of the University of Tübingen and later the University of Munich. In a book called *Symbolism,* published in 1832, Moehler brought to light the interior aspect of the Church and recognized the importance of the idea of the mystical body as expressing the unity of Christ with his members in the Church. Another German, Matthias J. Scheeben, writing in the second half of the nineteenth century, also probed the mystical aspect of the Church's life in *The Mysteries of Christianity.* Such investigations were deterred by the condemnation of modernism by Pope Pius X in 1907.

In the 1920s, under the impact of Pauline studies, the body of Christ concept was made the starting point of a new ecclesiological development. For example, in 1924 Karl Adam used the symbol of the Church as the body of Christ as the guiding theme of his book *The Spirit of Catholicism.* His writing was very influential. Then, in 1943, Pope Pius XII confirmed the appropriateness of the term *mystical body of Christ (Mystici Corporis).* He pointed out that the Church is not constituted as a unique and preeminent society from its visible nature alone. Rather, the Church, as an invisible body by reason of the supernatural life shared among its members in Christ, is on a level of supernatural existence far superior to that of the visible Church. However, to a certain extent the teaching of *Mystici Corporis,* by identifying the mystical body of Christ exclusively with the Roman Catholic Church, tended to strengthen the traditional view of the Church as a juridical institution. The acceptance of all Christians as members of the mystical body of Christ occurred at Vatican II. The eighth paragraph of *The Dogmatic Constitution on the Church* states the principle:

> The Church constituted and organized in the world as a society, *subsists in* the Catholic Church, which is governed by the successor of Peter and by the bishops in union with that successor, although many elements, of sanctification and truth can be found outside of her visible structure. [emphasis mine][5]

The council decided to use the phrase *subsists in* instead of *is. Is* would refer only to Roman Catholicism and would have thus excluded Eastern Orthodoxy and Protestant Christianity. Amazing as it now seems, long discussions occurred at the council to determine what words to use. *Subsists in* clearly suggests that others besides Roman Catholics are members of Christ's mystical body. This membership is further discussed and enlarged upon in *The Decree on Ecumenism* and *The Declaration on the Relationship of the Church to Non-Christian Religions.*

The Church as the People of God

By 1950 many theologians were using the phrase *People of God* to describe the Church. They eventually combined this image with the mystical body of Christ. The People of God metaphor clearly referred to the visible aspect of the Church. The visibility of the Church was now seen primarily in the assembly of Christ's people, and not solely in the pope and hierarchy. This view certainly does not deny the basic role of the pope and the hierarchy in the Church; instead it identifies the hierarchy as *part* of the Church's visible structure, rather than identifying the hierarchy *with* the visible structure.

Of itself, the image of the mystical body did not express the linear notion of the Church as a historical institution founded by Christ and moving through history. This temporal aspect is accounted for with the use of the People of God image. Fr. Yves Congar points out that it is necessary to combine the two images. One without the other fails to do justice to the nature of the Church. To discuss the Church only as the People of God tends to obscure, if not to omit, the divine aspect of the Church. In the second chapter of *The Dogmatic Constitution on the Church,* an excellent explanation of the integration of both images is given.

The Church as an Eschatological Institution

The Church is also seen as Christ's "pilgrim" people. This concept is discussed in chapter 7 of the constitution. The pilgrim aspect refers to the Church as eschatological. The word *eschaton* means "the last thing" and in Christian usage refers to Christ's Second Coming. Early Christians, as is seen in St. Paul's two letters to the Thessalonians, expected the imminent return of Christ, so much so that some had left their jobs in anticipation of Jesus's return. But this hope had waned by the beginning of the second century. Then the idea of the kingdom of God was identified with the Church on earth. Even the Protestant reformers took no serious exception to this traditional teaching. But biblical scholarship, beginning with the Protestant scholar Johannes Weiss's, *The Teaching of Jesus on the Kingdom of God,* written toward the end of the nineteenth century, established that the Church is not completely identified with the kingdom of God. Rather, the Christian community lives in tension between the "already" and the "not yet." The kingdom has begun in principle in Jesus and so continues in the Church, but the kingdom will not arrive in its fullness until the Second Coming of Christ.

In 1965 the great German Catholic biblical scholar Rudolf Schnackenburg wrote *The Church in the New Testament.* He observes that the Old Testament image of a wandering people crossing the desert under the leadership of Moses becomes the New Testament analogy for the people of the New Law, who already experience the fullness of the promise, yet still have not reached their goal and require divine aid. Thus, the eschatological notion of the kingdom, begun with the Incarnation of Christ but not yet fully attained, is obtained in the New Testament. Such a vision of the Church is stated in very dynamic terms. The kingdom of God, then, is a future that confronts us in the present, while the Church is understood as a sacramental sign pointing to the coming kingdom.

To understand the meaning of the Church it must be seen from the perspective of God's total work in history. The Church is understood as the official presence of the grace of Christ in the public history of the one human race. Thus, the Church is a sacramental sign of the grace won by Christ and offered to all persons throughout history, even though the great majority of them do not belong to the Christian church.

Rudolf Schnackenburg helps clarify the idea of the Church as a sacramental sign that points to the kingdom of God. In his book *God's Rule and Kingdom* (1963), he suggests that the term *the reign of Christ* be applied to the present, the age between Christ's resurrection and the end of the world, when the kingdom of God will begin. He also believes that the Church should be distinguished from the reign of Christ. The "reign of Christ" embraces the Church but extends to all humanity as well as the entire cosmos. But Christ's reign is realized in a special way in the Church. The Church is the key instrument of Christ's reign, and the present location of that reign's more perfect realization. By the very fact of being the enduring presence of Christ in the world, the Church is his fundamental **sacrament**.

A new definition of the Church thus emerges from Vatican II. The Church is the messianic pilgrim people of God, the primary sacrament of Christ's grace. Its mission is to be the anticipatory sign of the kingdom that has begun in Christ and will be completed with the transformation of the physical universe by the eruption of the kingdom of God into history. The role of the Church is to bring the individual member of society into relationship with the final destiny of humankind, with the kingdom of God. This is accomplished in communion with Jesus in whom the kingdom of God is already present. In its mission, which we will discuss later, the Church proclaims the knowledge of Jesus' universal significance as the revelation of God in the midst of history. By its sacramental community with Jesus, the Church makes it possible for contemporary society to share in the hope for the ultimate fulfillment of humanity. Thus, the Church must realize its eschatological attitude in the midst of the world if it is to be an effective sign. The awareness of this eschatological attitude led to the document *The Pastoral Constitution on the Church in the Modern World.*

Summary

The Dogmatic Constitution on the Church is the most important document produced at the council and serves as a hinge upon which the other documents turn. The Church is no longer completely identified with the kingdom of God in the way it had been since the Council of Trent. Rather, the Christian community lives in tension between the "already" and the "not yet." The kingdom has begun in principle with Jesus and continues in the Church, but the kingdom will not reach its fullness until the Second Coming of Christ. Nor is the Church totally identified with Roman Catholicism, but "subsists in" Roman Catholicism. This term suggests that other Christians are also truly members of the Church. The Church is on pilgrimage toward the Second Coming of Christ and is involved in history. The role of the Church is to serve as the sacramental presence of Jesus Christ in the history of the human race. Thus, the Church must represent Christ to the world in the present yet must also point to the Second Coming of Christ when the kingdom of God will be manifested in its fullness.

The Pastoral Constitution on the Church in the Modern World

The Pastoral Constitution on the Church in the Modern World was not anticipated before the council began since the Counter-Reformation definition of the Church was still operative. As we have seen, that definition was rather exclusivistic and static and conceived of the Church as an island kingdom touched on its periphery by the flow of history, but not in fact essentially changed by historical occurrences. Vatican II, however, revised that perception of the Church. As the People of God on a pilgrimage toward its goal, the Church is the sacramental sign of Jesus *within* history. If this is so, the question naturally arose, how does a Christian relate to present history, to contemporary society, to the modern world? *The Pastoral Constitution on the Church in the Modern World* was drafted in order to give Christianity a sense of direction in relationship to the world-at-large. This document does not pretend to be a final answer to all of the questions addressed, but it is a good beginning.

The Pastoral Constitution on the Church in the Modern World is the longest of the documents produced at Vatican II—an unexpected occurrence since no previous schema was prepared—but the range of questions in need of an answer was so broad that the length of the constitution could have been anticipated. The constitution, to a great extent, borrows from two encyclicals of Pope John XXIII, *Mater et Magistra* (1961) and *Pacem in Terris* (1963). Thus, the document represents Pope John much more directly than does any of the other conciliar documents.

The constitution, rather than showing hostility to the modern world as had so often happened in previous church statements, gives a highly positive evaluation of progress in all realms, not only ethical, social, and political, but also economic, aesthetic, scientific, and technological. For example, the constitution states that modern development, despite its dangers, brings:

> a more critical ability to distinguish religion from magic . . . (and) superstitions . . . purifies religion and extracts a more personal and explicit adherence to the faith (art. 7).[6]

The constitution also states that:

> The triumphs of the human race are a sign of God's greatness and the flowering of his mysterious design (art. 34).[7]

The autonomy of earthly affairs . . . is not merely required by modern man, but harmonizes with the will of the Creator (art. 36).[8]

The Church recognizes that worthy elements are found in today's social movements (art. 42).[9]

Similar praise is lavished on scientific and technological (art. 57), cultural and aesthetic (arts. 60 and 61), and economic (art. 63) advances.

The constitution is framed in a context that does not conceive of salvation in terms only of the individual, but rather in terms of humankind as a whole and of the entire cosmos as well. Its thrust is that Christians should concentrate on devoting their energies to the world in which they live and that, by doing so, they serve God just as genuinely as when worshiping him in church. As a matter of fact, the duty of Christians in no way decreases, but rather increases the weight of their obligation to work with all people in constructing a more human world.

For when, by the work of his hands or with the help of technology, man develops the earth so that it bears fruit and can become a dwelling place worth of the whole human family . . . he carries out the design of God. Manifested at the beginning of time, the divine plan is that man should subdue the earth, bring creation to perfection, and develop himself (art. 57).

One difficulty with the constitution is that it is written almost entirely by Westerners, and so world history tends to be seen too exclusively from a Western point of view. It tends to identify the history of the human race with a set of Western values such as technological and democratic ideologies. A dialogue with representatives of what might be called the Eastern mindset as well as Third World nations would have tempered this approach. Such dialogues have been undertaken, to a certain extent, in the years following Vatican II.

When all is said and done, what is most important to remember about *The Pastoral Constitution on the Church in the Modern World* is that with its corporate view of the human race former problems are posed anew and in new terms. The individual Christian is not seen simply in a one-to-one relationship with God, which had often been the approach of earlier Roman Catholic theology. Rather, a person's relationship with all human beings, Christians and non-Christians alike, is seen as central and as having many implications for the meaning of Christian life. With such an approach, a Christian is freed from any ghetto mentality and is challenged, as a Christian, to become involved in the mainstream of human affairs. This is an invitation that, to any thinking person, is both exciting and, at the same time, the cause of some anxiety. But certainly it is a call to a fuller and more challenging kind of Christian commitment and service than that previously practiced.

Summary

The Pastoral Constitution on the Church in the Modern World is the result of the changed perception of the nature of the Church at Vatican II. As the sacramental sign of Christ within history, the Church must relate to the world-at-large. This constitution describes the world in positive terms and encourages Christians to devote their energies to the society in which they live and to work with all persons, Christians and non-Christians alike, in constructing a better and more loving environment. To do so is to serve God. A corporate view of salvation is presented in this document. Not only as individuals, but as parts of the whole, Christians are encouraged to become involved in the mainstream of human affairs. One difficulty with this constitution is that it sees world history too exclusively from a Western point of view and tends to identify the history of the human race with a set of Western values, such as technological and democratic ideologies. Since Vatican II, however, this problem has been remedied to some extent by dialogue with what might be called the Eastern mindset as well as with Third World nations.

The Declaration on Religious Freedom

The Declaration on Religious Freedom can be understood as a genuine expression of the overall intent of the council to address itself with renewed vigor to the fundamental questions of modern humanity. As Jerald C. Brauer, the noted church historian and professor at the University of Chicago, observes:

> The Council, under the guidance of John XXIII's basic insight, correctly analyzed the central issue as that of modern man retaining his essential

humanity in the midst of a highly developed technological society. The concern of the Council was to speak for the Church to the whole world, to all men, and not simply to the faithful. A profound effort was made through all the schemata to point to the uniqueness, the dignity, and the glorious possibilities of mankind as seen from the perspective of the Christian faith. *The Declaration on Religious Freedom* was part of that effort; thus it ought not to be judged in and of itself, but only in relation to the total work of the Council. [10]

The initial text of *The Declaration on Religious Freedom* consisted of chapter 5 of *The Decree on Ecumenism.* There are close interrelationships between these documents and *The Declaration on the Relation of the Church to Non-Christian Religions.* The basic interrelationship perhaps lies in the fact that Vatican II stressed the importance of true dialogue with fellow Christians and with non-Christians as well. But dialogue cannot be carried on between individuals or groups unless each side takes the other side seriously and assumes there is some truth in the other point of view. Genuine dialogue, in other words, presupposes a condition of religious freedom.

The Declaration on Religious Freedom is a distinctly American achievement that had the strong backing of many American bishops. The influence of Fr. John Courtney Murray, S.J., was notable. Thomas Love, one of the guest observers of the Secretariat for the Promotion of Christian Unity at Vatican II, made the following comment on Murray's significance:

> He was the chief architect of the document; he wrote a profound background paper for the Council Fathers on the problem of religious freedom; he carried on correspondence with some of those who opposed the revised texts; he appeared on a panel sponsored by the bishops of the United States for the press. . . . His profound knowledge of the central problem was persuasive; his manner and humor in verbal articulation were unmatched.[11]

Because Murray's role in shaping this declaration was central, we may better understand the problem of religious freedom as it was confronted at Vatican II by reading his account of it in "De Libertate Religiosa: An Interpretive Analysis" (The Problem of Religious Freedom).[12] The essay presents a description of the traditional and of the more progressive view, of church-state relations within Roman Catholicism. Murray's aim was to establish dialogue between the two positions since he felt that meaningful dialogue with those outside the Catholic Church was impossible until a unified position was reached within the Church. As a representative of the progressive point of view Murray had long been engaged in debate on this problem. In the United States his major opposition came within the pages of the *American Ecclesiastical Review.* The chief antagonists and defenders of the traditional position were Joseph Fenton, Francis J. Connell, and George Shea.[13] They held that in principle the state must recognize the Roman Catholic Church as the true church and should worship God according to the rites of the Catholic Church. In practice they admitted that the separation of church and state may be tolerated where the recognition of the Catholic Church is morally impossible. Murray, who was greatly influenced by the American constitution and the American experience of the separation of church and state, argued that such separation should be accepted in principle and not merely tolerated. Historical consciousness is clearly one of the keys to Murray's thought. A second key is found in Murray's concept of the Church, which was much broader than the beliefs of Fenton, Connell, or Shea—and certainly much less defensive.

In considering *The Declaration on Religious Freedom,* many problems and objections will be dispelled if the type of freedom the council is defending is clearly understood. First of all, the council is not directly concerned with humanity's physical freedom, i.e., freedom of movement. However, physical freedom does enter the picture when religious freedom is violated. If a person were to be imprisoned for his or her religious beliefs, then true religious freedom would indirectly call for his or her physical freedom as well. Nor is the council directly concerned with humanity's psychological freedom. Psychological freedom and religious freedom are clearly distinct, albeit, related. The council is concerned with the latter.

The council is not advocating the so-called moral freedom that the liberalists of the nineteenth century claimed for themselves. According to the proponents of moral freedom, there are no moral obligations that bind people in conscience to seek out and obey objective norms of truth and proper conduct. Concerning the old liberalist notion of religious freedom, A. F. Carrillo de Albornoz, who is the former head of the World Council of Churches Secretariat on Religious Liberty, writes:

> The latter (i.e., the liberalists), as Leo XIII pointed out, championed the sovereignty of human reason, which refuses obedience to God's eternal

Reason, declares its absolute independence of God, and sets itself up as the fountainhead and judge of all truth.[14]

Finally, the document is not concerned with the freedom in Christ of which St. Paul speaks. Christ has freed Christians from sin and death. But this freedom exists on the theological level. It is a power that the human race receives through grace. Human authorities are powerless to suppress or restrict it. The freedom of which the council speaks is a reality in the social civil order, an immunity that people enjoy as members of society and that is guaranteed by civil law.

In short, the subject matter of this document is civil religious freedom. The title itself makes this clear: *Declaration of Religious Freedom: On the Right of the Person and of Communities to Social and Civil Freedom in Matters Religious.*[15] The document states:

> The truth cannot impose itself except by virtue of its own truth, as it makes its entrance into the mind at once quietly and with power. Religious freedom, in turn, which men demand as necessary to fulfill their duty to worship God, has to do with immunity from coercion in civil society.[16]

The civil right to religious liberty is meant to enable humanity to act in good conscience. If everyone were allowed to behave according to their consciences, then freedom from coercion must be granted to all citizens without distinctions. This point is brought out in the declaration.

> The right to religious freedom has its foundation, not in the subjective disposition of the person, but in his very nature. In consequence, the right to the immunity continues to exist even in those who do not live up to their obligation of seeking the truth and adhering to it, *and the exercise of this right is not to be impeded provided that just public order is observed.* [emphasis mine][17]

According to the declaration, preservation of public order involves the following needs:

1. to effectively safeguard the rights of all citizens and to settle conflicts of rights peacefully.
2. for adequate maintenance of genuine public peace, which comes about when men live together in good order and in true justice.
3. for a proper guardianship of public morality.[18]

These three elements are the only social values that comprise a just public order. Only the protection of these values—and these alone—can warrant government regulation or restriction of the right to religious freedom. There are no exceptions to this principle. Even if one religion enjoys special constitutional recognition, other elements of the common welfare cannot be brought in to justify limitations on religious freedom. The declaration is clear on this point and states:

> If, in view of peculiar circumstances obtaining among certain peoples, special legal recognition is given in the constitutional order of society to one religious body, it is at the same time imperative that the right of all citizens and religious bodies to religious freedom should be recognized and made effective in practice.[19]

The juridical criteria concerning public order are quite general. The practical problem lies in their application. Murray, in "The Problem of Religious Freedom," argues that the application would never be arbitrary and he lists a four-fold requirement to insure against arbitrary acts on the part of government. He writes:

> In what concerns religious freedom, the requirement is fourfold: that the violation of the public order be really serious; that legal or police intervention be really necessary; that regard be had for the privileged character of religious freedom, which is not simply to be equated with other civil rights; that the rule of jurisprudence of the free society be strictly observed, namely, as much freedom as possible, as much coercion as necessary.[20]

According to the declaration, the dignity of the human person is the most important basis for humankind's civil right to religious freedom. It notes:

> The Synod further declares that the right to religious freedom has its foundation in the very dignity of the human person, as this dignity is known through the revealed Word of God and by reason itself.[21]

The council spelled out the arguments in favor of religious freedom as based on reason as well as arguments derived from revelation.

Overwhelming priority is given to maintaining the dignity of human-kind. As for the arguments from revelation, the **Church Fathers** saw that humanity's dignity, humanity's likeness to God as revealed in the Bible, necessarily called for religious freedom. St. Gregory of Nyssa asserted:

> The use of violence to force acceptance of the Gospel would be contrary to man's dignity; because man's freedom is what constitutes his likeness to God.[22]

Special Problems

Tolerance

Does the declaration seek to promote tolerance? It would seem not. Tolerance means "to bear with patiently." But the declaration and other council documents demand a more positive attitude toward those who do not share Catholicism's religious beliefs, an attitude summed up in the words *Christian love*.

Atheists and Humanists

Does the declaration uphold freedom for the atheist and the humanist? A careful reading of the document could allow that such freedom is at least implied. However, nowhere does it clearly and explicitly impute this right to atheists and humanists. As a matter of fact, Albornoz feels that the overall tenor and substance of the document seems to oppose freedom for such people. If this is actually the case, Albornoz writes that he would be very disappointed since he cannot see any valid reason, in principle, to deny atheists the same civil freedom granted to theists. He goes on to say that the reason why atheists seem to be excluded "may have its origin in the fact that the schema for this declaration was prepared by the Secretariat for Christian Unity, whose outlook was primarily ecumenical. The problem of atheism would not be a central concern for this body."[19] Yet the fact that atheists and humanists are not explicitly included in the conciliar document is to be lamented.

Inner Freedom

The declaration states:

> The common welfare of society consists *in the entirety of those conditions
> of social life* under which men enjoy the possibility of achieving their own
> perfection in a certain fullness of measure and also with some relative ease.
> Hence this welfare consists chiefly in the protection of the rights and in the
> performance of the duties of the human person. [emphasis mine][24]

In this connection it is important to realize that religious freedom
involves more than strict observance of pertinent legal provisions.
Religious freedom should give rise to a moral outlook that goes
beyond the letter of the law. Society must avoid all forms of coercion,
pressure, or persuasion that degrade the dignity of the individual and
make his or her actions something less than human. Many degrading
types of pressure are so subtle that they cannot be proscribed by legal
statutes; for example, when the members of a predominant religious
community apply economic and professional discrimination.

Education of Children

The council states in this declaration: "Parents, moreover, have the
right to determine, in accordance with their own religious beliefs, the
kind of religious education that their children are to receive."[25] This
principle, it would seem, does not really involve a restriction of
religious freedom. It merely transfers religious freedom from the
immature child to the child's parents, who are responsible for that
child before God and society. It would nonetheless be rash for parents
to extend their authority beyond the limits set by their child's
immaturity. To do this would be to violate the child's fundamental
freedom.

The declaration also states: "Besides, the rights of parents are
violated if their children are forced to attend lessons or instruction
which are not in agreement with their religious beliefs."[26] This
principle is recognized in the United States. But in the case of
voluntary prayers and Bible reading in public schools, undue
pressure to participate is a form of discrimination against those
children who, at the insistence of their parents, do not wish to
participate. Hence on the basis of *The Declaration on Religious
Freedom,* it would seem that Catholics should oppose the institution
of such voluntary prayer and Bible reading.

Other Issues

Of the many other problems raised by the declaration, at least two deserve some comment here:

Development of Doctrine

John Courtney Murray, chief architect of this declaration observes that *The Declaration on Religious Freedom* was the most controversial document of the council because it placed in strong relief the issue of the development of doctrine. Fr. Murray says that it was the notion of the development of doctrine, not the idea of religious freedom, which was the real problem for those who opposed this declaration even to the end. He writes: "But the Council formally sanctioned the validity of the development itself; and this was a doctrinal event of high importance for theological thought in many areas."[27]

The Meaning of Christian Freedom

The principle of religious freedom was narrowly limited in the text. But, as Fr. Murray observes, from this text a second great argument will be set in motion—the theological meaning of Christian freedom. He again writes, "The issue of religious freedom was in itself minor. But Pope Paul VI's vision was far reaching when he called the *Declaration on Religious Freedom* 'one of the major texts of the Council.'"[28]

Summary

In *The Declaration on Religious Freedom,* an entirely new attitude of mind on the part of Roman Catholicism was set in motion. The recognition that everyone may truly and publicly express his or her religious ideology and philosophy of life was a radical change from the ideas taught by Pope Pius IX in *The Syllabus of Errors* in 1864. What is called for is not simply toleration for the various beliefs of others, but rather an attitude of Christian love toward different systems of belief. The ramifications of this declaration will continue to be uncovered for many years to come, not only in regard to the development of true civil religious freedom for all, but also in regard to the separation of church and state as an acceptable principle.

Equally noteworthy for the future is that the Church in the declaration officially condemns all discrimination based on race, color, conviction, and national character. Fr. John Courtney Murray was the chief architect of this document. One of this declaration's most important contributions was that it brought about conciliar recognition of the development of doctrine. A possible weakness, however, is that it does not seem to uphold freedom for the atheist and the humanist, even though a careful reading of the document could allow that such freedom is at least implied. But the overall tenor of the declaration seems to oppose freedom for such persons. If this is so, it is lamentable since there is no valid reason to deny atheists or humanists the same civil freedom granted to theists.

The Dogmatic Constitution on Divine Revelation

Another of the crucial conciliar documents discusses the meaning of divine revelation. It also considers the question of salvation, not only of Christians, but of non-Christians as well. This is always a vital question and one that is often debated among Christians. Some Christians, especially fundamentalists and many evangelicals, believe that only Christians can be saved. All others are seen as among the rejected. Roman Catholicism and mainline Christianity, in general, take a much broader view. Though explanations vary, proponents usually agree that, although Jesus is the unique and sole redeemer of the human race, his grace is given not only to Christians, but to whomever he wills, whether they have heard his name or not. In other words, though Christianity is Jesus' primary sacramental witness and his basic instrument of communication to the world, his death and resurrection and the grace therein obtained were given for the whole of humankind. Jesus is not limited in his ability to bestow his grace. *The Dogmatic Constitution on Divine Revelation* formulates answers to fundamental questions about revelation, grace, and salvation. As was true of the other fifteen documents at Vatican II, *The Dogmatic Constitution on Divine Revelation* underwent a number of changes before it reached its final form. On Tuesday, November 20, 1962, at the first session of the council a majority of the bishops voted to reject the original schema, entitled "The Sources of Divine Revelation," which had been drawn up by the preparatory commission. A new text was prepared and presented on April 22, 1963. Following additional suggestions from the bishops and theologians, the schema was again revised and reissued on July 3, 1964. In this form it reached the council floor during the third and fourth sessions for final changes before its promulgation on November 18, 1965. In order to understand the significance of this constitution it will be necessary to consider the notion of revelation that had been traditionally accepted by Catholics and non-Catholic Christians alike.

The Traditional View of Revelation

The traditional view of revelation was formulated with great clarity by St. Thomas Aquinas in his *Summa Theologica* in the thirteenth century. The major division of humankind's knowledge of God was seen to be either natural or revealed knowledge.

Natural knowledge of God was seen as knowledge that the human mind could attain without any kind of divine aid. Under this schema, all the world religions were said to have such natural knowledge. However lofty such knowledge might be, it was still not understood to be of saving benefit. At best, the medieval Catholic and Protestant theologians maintained, such knowledge made one "without excuse" in the eyes of God. Or put in other terms, such knowledge of God was simply not salvational.

But God did not leave humanity in this condition. In addition to the natural knowledge of God, there was also revealed knowledge. The term *revelation* was denied to natural knowledge, for which no supernatural aid was required. Revealed knowledge is truth supernaturally communicated to people; for example, the truth of the Trinity and of the divinity-humanity of Jesus. Such truth is found only in the Bible. The traditional view denied that the Koran, the Tripitka (a collection of the Buddha's teachings), or the sacred books of any other major religions contained revelation.

Three points in particular about the classical notion of revelation should be noted:

1. Generally speaking, revelation was considered propositional, which fit well with the Western propensity for exact definition. *Propositional* means something that can be written and analyzed.

2. Since it was felt that revelation was contained in the Bible, it therefore was "possessed."

3. The line between natural and revealed knowledge merely separated two kinds of intellectual knowledge. Revealed knowledge was an act of God's grace to the individual, who was understood as an incomplete person without such revelation. However, nothing in the natural knowledge of humanity was contradicted by revelation. This notion allowed Catholic missionaries to seek points of contact with other faiths with the assurance that the path to saving knowledge was an unbroken one.[29]

The Modified View of Revelation

With the beginning of the twentieth century, the traditional view of revelation began to change. The effects of nineteenth-century theology, biblical criticism, modern science, and the comparative study of religion played their part in this change. In the modified view, the distinction between revealed knowledge and the natural knowledge of God has given way to the distinction between general revelation and special revelation. Without attempting to be all-inclusive, the modified view can be diagrammed in the following manner:

Revelation (salvation history)

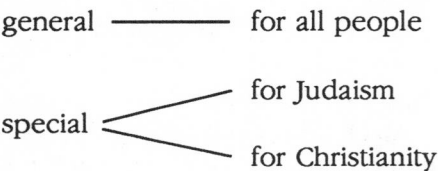

general ———— for all people

special — for Judaism

for Christianity

Christians maintain that in Christ and in the Church revelation reaches its clearest, highest, and most unsurpassable point. In the light of this special revelation in Christ, the notion of a general revelation to all humanity is brought to self-realization as well as the idea of a special revelation to the Jewish people and to others as well. Thus, world religions are now understood to possess revealed knowledge. For example, we find the following statement in *The*

Declaration on the Relationship of the Church to Non-Christian Religions:

Men look to the various religions for answers to those profound mysteries of the human condition which, today even as in older times, deeply stir the human heart: What is a man? What is the meaning and purpose of our life? What is goodness and what is sin? What gives rise to our sorrows and to what intent? Where lies the path to true happiness? What is the truth about death, judgment, and retribution beyond the grave? What, finally, is the ultimate and unutterable mystery which engulfs our being, and whence we take our rise, and whether our journey leads us?

From ancient times down to the present, there has existed among diverse peoples a certain perception of that hidden power which hovers over the course of things and over the events of human life; at times, indeed recognition can be found of a Supreme divinity and of a supreme father too. Such a perception and such a recognition instill the lives of these peoples with a profound religious sense. Religions bound up with cultural advancement have struggled to reply to these same questions with more refined concepts and in more highly developed language.

The Catholic Church rejects nothing which is true and holy in these religions. She looks with sincere respect upon those ways of conduct and of life, those rules and teachings which, though differing in many particulars from what she holds and sets forth, nevertheless often reflect a ray of that Truth which enlightens all men. Indeed, she proclaims and must ever proclaim Christ, "the way, the truth, and the life" (John 14:6), in whom men find the fullness of religious life, and in whom God has reconciled all things to himself (cf. 2 Cor. 5:18,19).

The Church therefore has this exhortation for her sons: prudently and lovingly, through dialogue and collaboration with the followers of other religions, and in witness of Christian faith and life, acknowledge, preserve, and promote the spiritual and moral goods found among these men, as well as values in their society and culture.[30]

This statement marks an authoritative change in approach on the part of Roman Catholicism to non-Christian religions, a change that is found among other mainline denominations as well, such as the Episcopalian church and the majority of Lutheran churches. As long as the world religions were denied the reception of revelation, dialogue was not seen as profitable, since all the legitimate claims of the other participants were denied before the conversation began. Now as a result of Vatican II there is an ever increasing recognition of other religions as communities that the Church can and should enter into dialogue.

Summary

Christian theologians today, other than those who still hold the traditional view, no longer equate divine revelation solely with the Bible or accepted doctrine. Non-Christian religions are understood to be recipients of revelation, too. The highly exclusive medieval view of divine revelation has been superseded. Revelation is now understood to be more than propositional truth. It is now seen to be a divine self-disclosure. God does not merely reveal truths about himself. God reveals himself. In Christ, God communicates himself to the human race. The Church in turn gives witness to and mediates this divine self-communication. Although the Church believes that Jesus is the unique and sole redeemer of the human race, his grace is given not only to Christians, but to whomever he wills, whether they have heard his name or not. In other words, though Christianity is Jesus' primary sacramental witness and his basic instrument of communication to the world, his life, death, and resurrection, and the grace therein obtained, were given for the whole of humankind. Thus, revelation continues to be given by God where and when he wills.

In the last century theological talk of continuing revelation frightened many theologians, but today theologians generally acknowledge that the affirmation of an ongoing revelation in no way weakens the nonrepeatable character of the revelation in Jesus Christ or the basic truths of the Christian faith. This shift in the understanding of divine revelation has been acknowledged and accepted by Vatican II in *The Dogmatic Constitution on Divine Revelation*. An excellent analysis of the meaning of continuing revelation is given by Monika Hellwig in the first two chapters of *What Are the Theologians Saying?* first published in 1970.[31]

Study Questions

1. Are the documents of Vatican II the official teaching of the Catholic Church?
2. How did Catholicism's understanding of history change at Vatican II?
3. Give a brief summary of the nine decrees issued at Vatican II.
4. Give a brief history of the development of the Church's use of the symbols *mystical body of Christ* and *People of God*.
5. Explain the importance of the term *subsists in* as used in *The Dogmatic Constitution on the Church*.
6. How does the definition of the Church that emerges from Vatican II differ from the definition of the Church that stems from the Council of Trent?
7. In what way does *The Pastoral Constitution on the Church in the Modern World* differ from previous church documents concerning the manner in which a Christian should relate to the world?
8. Does the *Declaration on Religious Freedom* basically call for the toleration of belief systems that differ from the teachings of Roman Catholicism?
9. What type of freedom is advocated in the *Declaration on Religious Freedom?*
10. Compare the traditional view of divine revelation with the modified view taught by Vatican II.

3

The Mission of the Church

As seen in the declarations of the Second Vatican Council, the role of the Roman Catholic Church is much more modestly understood today than was true in the past. No longer is the Church of Christ exhaustively identified with Roman Catholicism; it is rather said to "subsist in" Roman Catholicism. The concept of the Church can certainly be rightly applied to those who compose a community of baptized Christians united by belief in Jesus Christ, who live according to the message of the New Testament, who celebrate the sacraments of baptism and the Lord's Supper, and who wish to be regarded by the world as a Christian church.

However, the mission of the total Christian church in relation to non-Christians also seems to be diminished by certain directives issued at Vatican II. Among the statements contained in the conciliar texts, the following seem especially important in reexamining the mission of the Church:

1. Neither the Church, nor "religiousness" itself, is the sole avenue to God. The Church reveres God's grace-filled workings among all humanity, at all times. It respects rather than merely tolerates all people outside the Church, who, seeking the ultimate reality, raise their hearts to the living God, even though they do not always know his name. *The Dogmatic Constitution on the Church* says of atheists, for example, that "whatever goodness or truth

is found among them is looked upon by the Church as a preparation for the Gospel. She regards such qualities as given by Him who enlightens all men so that they may finally have life."[1]

2. Christianity has no monopoly on true religiousness. In *The Declaration on the Relationship of the Church to Non-Christian Religions* it is said that adherents of other religions may be saved, not despite the religions to which they belong, but because these religions can truly mediate, however imperfectly, a knowledge and experience of God. They "often reflect a ray of that 'Truth which enlightens all men.'" Therefore, considering the history of Roman Catholicism, one of the most astonishing statements of Vatican II is that which exhorts Catholics "through dialogue and collaboration with the followers of other religions, and in witness of Christian faith and life, to acknowledge, preserve, and promote the spiritual and moral goods found among these men, as well as the values in their society and culture."[2]

3. The sincere faith-experiences of individual non-Christians are salvational, based on a search for God as expressed by his striving to do God's will as it is known through the dictates of conscience. The mission of the Church seems to be diminished, then, because salvation is conceived not individualistically, but rather in terms of the redemption of humankind as a whole. In order to accomplish this result, God is understood as guiding all the processes of history toward redemption—not simply and exclusively working in and through the Church. The People of God are viewed as only one of the means, albeit the primary instrument, of God's saving activity. As Karl Rahner and others insist, this does not mean there is salvation apart from Christ, since it is precisely the grace of Christ that prepares for the new humanity.[3] But it certainly does mean that redemption is possible for all people, even those who have never heard of the Church or who have explicitly rejected Christianity. This brings us to a discussion of the mission of the Church understood, as it is presently, as the pilgrim People of God who are the sacramental sign to the kingdom which has begun in Christ and will be completed at his Second Coming.

Christians used to think that the mission of the Church was to bring all humankind into the Church some day. In past centuries the principal motive of mission activity, both among Catholics and

Protestants, was evangelical. Saving as many souls as possible from eternal damnation assumed paramount importance since the non-Christian religions were generally considered idolatrous and super-stitious. This motivation was very powerful, and it gave birth to the greatest missionary movement in history. Current Protestant and Catholic theology, with the exception of those who see Christianity from an exclusivistic standpoint, no longer accepts this as proper motivation. Since salvation is not the monopoly of the Christian church, it is clear that the missionary action of the Church must aim at more than conversion and the salvation of individual souls. Thus, the first and immediate task of the Church, as the visible institution of salvation, is to be the presence of Christ among all nations, the sacrament of salvation for those very people who do not visibly belong to the Church. As *The Dogmatic Constitution on the Church* points out, these "messianic people, although it does not actually include all men, and at times may look like a small flock, is nonetheless a lasting and sure *seed* of unity, hope and salvation for the whole human race." [emphasis mine][4] This community of explicit faith, established by Christ for all humanity," is also used by him as an instrument for the redemption of all, and is sent forth into the whole world as the light of the world and the salt of the earth."[5] So the Church is essentially missionary, and her primary concern is to become ever more clearly to all peoples what she is by nature—the sacrament of salvation, signifying the deliverance of all humankind and completing sacramentally what Christ has done "once for all" through his life, death, and resurrection.

The New Testament indicates that the visible Church was intended to be a minority group within the human race. The Church has always been the *pusillus grex,* "the little flock," as Christ referred to it (see Luke 12:20). The first Christians were well aware that they were only a small group in a worldwide empire. The idea of the Church as a "little flock" disappeared when Christianity spread rapidly after Emperor Constantine's edict of toleration in A.D. 313, and the regions to which the Gospel had not been preached remained almost totally outside the Christian perspective. Present-day travel and modern communications have corrected this earlier outlook, and Christianity is once more returning, though not without some difficulty, to an acceptance of the notion that its appeal is and always has been limited in size and outreach.

We should take careful note of the fact that Christ did not send his disciples to convert the whole world to the Church, but rather to teach or make disciples *of all nations* (see Matt. 28:19–20). It would seem that not enough attention has been paid to the difference between the evangelization of nations and the attempt to convert all of humankind. In fact, the injunction to "make disciples of all nations" commands the worldwide proclamation of the Gospel, not the attempt to convert everyone. Such an interpretation seems to be substantiated by an investigation of the writings of the early Church Fathers. In looking at the indices of their writings, one notes an almost complete lack of references to "conversion" in the sense of external conversion to the Church. Indeed, Origen is the only one among the fathers who wrote with concern about the small number of Christians and who pointed out that there were many nations within and without the empire to which the Gospel had not yet penetrated. Although it seems unlikely that the other fathers were unaware of the circumstance, they did not exhort their readers to greater attempts to convert non-Christians, but stressed rather the expansion of Christianity. Thus, a study of the fathers does not lend any foundation to the notion that a total or even general conversion of humankind was deemed necessary in order for the Church to be catholic or to carry out its universal mission in the world. Rather, such a study confirms the theory that to "make disciples of all nations" commands the worldwide proclamation of the Gospel, not the conversion of every individual.

The notion of winning the masses of people to the Church initially arose at the beginning of the Middle Ages when the Church undertook the evangelization and christianization of the Celtic and Germanic tribes of northern Europe. The medieval missionary methodology was not based on Scripture or on early tradition, but on political and social considerations. It was a fact of cultural history rather than of theology. However, it gave rise to a misunderstanding of the mission of the Church that has endured to the present. Thus, in refuting the deeply rooted notion that the Church was obliged to seek the general conversion of the human race, we may see that this is not a repudiation of any former teaching found in the Scriptures or in patristic sources since, in fact, there was no such teaching. It has been merely an assumption, though admittedly a widespread one.

Explaining exactly how the Church was meant to contribute to the salvation of the nations requires an understanding of the biblical idea of representation. The unifying principle that gives salvation history its coherence is that of the representation of the many by the few, and, fundamentally, that of the representation of all by one, namely, Jesus

Christ. The history of salvation, as found in the Bible, develops according to the principle of representation. In the Creation, one man already appears to be the representative of the whole of the universe. Then the people of Israel appear to be the representative of the whole of humankind. Finally, a remnant represents all of Israel. Thus, in the Old Testament, the principle of representation progressively decreases from a multiplicity to the One; that is, Christ. Conversely, in the New Testament the representation broadens progressively from the One to the many. By virtue of the fact that Christ as the One suffers death for the many and that he rose from the dead, it follows that the many are now to represent the One. The apostles represent Christ for the Church; the Church represents Christ for humankind in the form of an eschatological perspective of a redeemed humanity in the future kingdom of God and a redeemed creation of the new earth. In line with this approach, we can say that the Church, under Christ, must effect the application of Christ's redemptive power by representing humankind in its redeemed existence.

There is something reminiscent of the role of Israel in this view. All are called to the coming kingdom, but not everyone is called to bear explicit witness to it. Among each people there is a "remnant" which stands symbolically for others and for humankind as a whole. Like the remnant of Israel, they stand for and represent the totality of the new people of God, sacramentally among nations. St. Paul speaks of the Church as the remnant when he says, "Today the same thing has happened: there is a remnant, chosen by grace. By grace, you notice, nothing therefore to do with good deeds, or grace would not be grace at all! What follows? It was not Israel as a whole that found what it was seeking but only the chosen few" (Rom. 11:5–7). And as Eugene Hillman notes:

> The first advent of the Messiah was through an historical remnant of God's chosen people in the flesh. The Second Coming is through a sacramental remnant of His chosen people in the spirit: those who are called out of every nation to form the new people of God in the visible community of explicit Christian faith and intelligible witness to their belief before all men.[6]

This visible community is the Church, becoming in the extension of different times and places what she is—the "incarnate" sign of Christ's presence among all peoples, signifying and completing symbolically Christ's universal work of salvation, accomplishing sacramentally among each people what he has done historically once for all. Thus, while all humankind is called to salvation, only a remnant is chosen to recognize through explicit faith the historical reality of salvation in Christ. The remnant signifies the vast inner reality of the kingdom of God among men and women. They are the messianic people who, although they do not actually include all people, stand as the symbolic representatives of all.

While the actual number of Christians in the world is very large and continues to increase, their number is actually diminishing when compared to the total world population. However, the important point is that this faithful remnant, this "little flock," is significantly present as witnesses among the nations. Christians must desire and work for the numerical increase of the Church everywhere. The Church, under Christ, must effect the application of Christ's redemptive power by representing humankind in its redeemed existence. To become such a sign, the Church must constantly strive to make itself genuinely representative of humankind in all its ethnic and cultural diversity. Only by incarnating the Word of God among all peoples can the full import of Christ's redemptive work be properly signified.

Eugene Hillman develops such ideas in *The Church as Mission*, which is basically consonant with what we have been saying concerning the role of the Church.[7] But he adds a further refinement of his own, namely, that the establishment of the Church in any particular region is an efficacious sign of the redemption of the particular ethnic-cultural group among which the Church comes into being. Since past, present, and future are all the same in God's eyes, he maintains that this efficacy can extend backward and forward in time, and thus includes the ancestors and descendants of the people presently evangelized. From this he concludes that it is necessary for the completion of salvation history that the Gospel should have been preached among each people at some time before the end of the world, and he implies that once this evangelization has occurred it is relatively unimportant whether a people perseveres in the faith.

The difficulty with Hillman's position is that it gives no explanation of how there can be any possibility of salvation for members of a tribe or nation that became extinct before the time of Christ or before the arrival of Christian missionaries. Furthermore, he seems to make too little of the concern that the Church has always tried to expand its membership within each people and to foster perseverance in the faith once it has been accepted. Nevertheless, Hillman makes clear that the primary mission of the Church is not to convert every individual, but rather to hold up a visible sign of the universality of Christian redemption. What is of chief importance is that the reality of the Church be incarnated in each people to whom the Gospel is preached. Christians, while desiring and working for the increase of the Christian community, should not feel guilty about the failure to win large numbers of converts or worry about the decline of Christianity and its minority status in the world. Rather, Christians should work to see that the Church as sign and witness authentically points humanity to Christ, understood not only in the light of the past, but also in view of the future kingdom of God. To maintain that Christians need not feel guilty about the failure to win large numbers of converts, or worry about the decline of Christianity and its minority status in the world exceeds the teaching found in the documents of Vatican II. However, such a position is made possible by the council's **eschatology** and its abandonment of claims that what is explicitly Christian has a quasi-monopoly on God's saving power.

It is important to emphasize that the mission of the Church is something pragmatic. It is a pragmatic test of explicit Christian faith that is given to some for the sake of actualizing the same grace in others among whom Christ has not been accepted. Paul Tillich, the great Lutheran theologian, makes this point in speaking about foreign missions, when he applies his words to the universal mission of the Church. He writes:

> The action of missions gives the pragmatic proof of the universality of Christianity. It is a *pragmatic proof.* It is the proof, as the Bible calls it, of power and Spirit. It is not a theoretical proof which you can give sitting in your chair, looking at history. . . . Mission is the continuous pragmatic test of the universality . . . of the truth of the Christian assertion that Jesus is the Christ.[8] [emphasis mine]

The Church's mission is a task set for it by the very nature of its vocation as Christ's redeemed community, and in accordance with its position in redemptive history—namely, in the era between the Resurrection and the Second Coming of Christ—the Church functions within that framework and seeks to fulfill the divine plan of salvation. The universality of the Church, therefore, is not promoted on opportunist grounds, but is rooted in its very nature. The Church does not become universal because it engages in missionary activity; rather the Church engages in missionary activity because by nature it is universal.

Both Karl Rahner and Paul Tillich maintain that Christianity is the bearer and interpreter of the final revelation in Jesus as the Christ—final in the sense of the decisive, fulfilling, unsurpassable revelation that is the criterion of all other revelations. They believe, however, that revelatory experiences are universally human and that a revelation once given implies saving power. Thus, Christianity should not deny the validity of other religions. In the encounter with the world religions, for example, Tillich says Christians must not try to make converts, at least as a primary motive, but rather "must drive the other religions to their own depths, to that point at which they realize they are witness to the Absolute but are not the Absolute themselves."[9] Jesus rejected the temptation to be idolized, and this gives Christianity, in principle, the criterion not only against itself, but against all other religions. From a different perspective, Rahner agrees that Christianity should not use the winning of converts as its primary motivation in its encounter with non-Christians, but through dialogue should attempt to aid other religions to discover their depths by making explicit the grace that has already been given for the world, as well as the victory of this grace in the world.[10] Both Tillich and Rahner believe that grace has an inner dynamic tendency to assume historical tangible form in the Christian church, but they are realistic enough to know that for the great majority of humankind this does not always happen, even though justification and salvation are given. However, since they believe that this grace radiates from the historical center of the Incarnation and is assimilated by peoples and individuals in a historical process, and that the grace of God often precedes the explication of that grace through the Gospel, it is thus meaningful to speak of those who live a grace-filled life apart from the Christian religion as "anonymous" or "latent" Christians. Their interpretation has been questioned from various points of view, but it has the merit of upholding the universal effect of the death and resurrection of Jesus Christ.

Christians of the future, as Rahner observes, encouraged by the statement of Vatican II that the Church is "the sacrament of salvation" for all humanity, will know "that the morning light on the mountains is the beginning of the day in the valley, not the light of day above condemning the darkness beneath."[11] They will not anxiously scan statistics to see whether the Church is the largest ideological organization, or whether it is growing proportionately more quickly or more slowly than the world population. They will certainly go out into the world with missionary zeal and bear witness in the name of Christ. They will wish to give of their grace to others since they possess a grace that others still lack—since the explicit self-awareness of grace in the Church is itself a grace. Such Christians will go out into the world serenely and without anguish, knowing that grace can be present and operative to an immeasurable extent in the world without everywhere finding tangible social expression in the Christian church.

Pope Paul VI made a great contribution to the present understanding of the mission of the Church in his letter *Evangelii Nuntiandi* (On Evangelization in the Modern World), which was published in 1975. The letter is technically an apostolic exhortation given in Rome in 1974 on the occasion of the Fourth International Synod of Bishops. The pope states at the outset that the whole mission of Jesus is summed up in his own declaration that he was sent to proclaim the good news of the kingdom of God (Luke 4:43), and particularly to the poor (Luke 4:18; Isa. 61:1). Jesus' evangelizing activities, however, were not restricted to preaching alone. He also proclaimed the kingdom by "innumerable signs: the sick are cured, water is changed into wine, bread is multiplied, the dead come back to life. And among these signs there is the one to which he attached great importance: the humble and poor are evangelized." Evangelization, therefore, means that the mission of the Church is linked with Jesus' proclamation of the kingdom of God, as "liberation from everything that oppresses man, but which is above all liberation from sin and the Evil One." Just as Jesus accomplished this proclamation in works as well as in word, so is the Church called to be a servant as well as a herald of the Gospel.

Pope Paul VI goes on to explain what he means by the phrase "servant of the Gospel." He writes, "Evangelization would not be complete if it did not take account of the unceasing interplay of the Gospel and of man's concrete life, both personal and social." This aspect of the mission of the Church is to help liberate human beings from the evils of poverty, hunger, and sickness and to participate in the struggle for justice and peace. But however closely linked the Church is with human liberation, there are some notions of liberation that are incompatible with the mission of the Church. What is and what is not acceptable will be analyzed in chapter 10, when social justice is discussed.

Summary

In past centuries Christians believed they were commanded to bring the whole of humankind into the Church some day. The principal motive of mission activity was to save non-Christians from eternal damnation. But since it is now believed that God's grace and revelation are given not only by means of the Church but by God himself to whomsoever he wills, the first and immediate task of the Church is to evangelize "all nations" and to be the presence of Christ everywhere, that is, the sacrament of salvation for those very people who do not belong to the Church. The community of explicit faith in Jesus is sent into the world as the "light of the world and the salt of the earth." Though all humanity is called to salvation, only a remnant is chosen to recognize through explicit faith the historical reality of salvation in Jesus. This remnant is the messianic people who, although they do not actually include all humankind, symbolically represent all. This faithful remnant is to be significantly present as a witness among the nations. Thus, Christians must desire and work for the numerical increase of the Church everywhere. To become a sign of redeemed existence the Church must constantly strive to make itself genuinely representative of humankind in all its ethnic and cultural diversity. Pope Paul VI in his letter *Evangelii Nuntiandi* makes clear that the Church must not only preach the Gospel to all nations but must also be servants of the Gospel. This means that the mission of the Church includes not only announcing the "good news" but also assuming the task of liberating fellow human beings from the evils of poverty, hunger, and sickness as well as a call to participate in the struggle for justice and peace.

Study Questions

1. Why does the mission of the Church seem to be diminished by certain directives issued at Vatican II?
2. Did the Church Fathers teach that a general conversion of humankind was necessary for the Church to be catholic, i.e., universal?

3. Is the Church called by the Gospel to attempt to convert everyone to the Christian faith? If so, why? If not, why not?
4. What is the biblical meaning of *representation?* Give examples.
5. Why does Paul Tillich say that the mission of the Church is the pragmatic test of the universality of Christianity?
6. What is the mission of the Church according to Fr. Karl Rahner?
7. Explain Pope Paul VI's basic message in his letter *Evangelii Nuntiandi.*

PART II

Catholicism Today:
Key Issues

4

Jesus

Who is Jesus?

For Catholics, as for all Christians, Jesus is understood to be the Son of God. It is believed that he lived, died by means of crucifixion, and rose from the dead. In doing so he redeemed the world. As a follower of Christ, a Catholic listens to his words through the Scriptures, accepts his teachings, and, through faith, establishes a personal relationship with him. In knowing Christ personally, a life of prayer is of the utmost necessity. But it is also important to learn as much about Jesus as one can: the details and purpose of his life on earth, his preaching, and his miracles. It is vital to obtain the fullest possible understanding of Jesus since the better he is known and appreciated the more he can be fully loved.

It is believed that the crucified and risen Lord is present here and now in the Christian community. Thus, Christ and the Church are inseparable. It is to the Church that one must turn for the fullest understanding of Jesus. If Vatican III were to meet today perhaps the main topic of discussion would address the relevant question, "Who is Jesus Christ for us today?" Since the closing of Vatican II in 1965, it has become clear that all efforts to renew the life of the Church take their strength and inspiration from the depth of the Church's understanding of the nature of Jesus. Vatican II dealt with Christology only secondarily and concentrated instead on Church problems. As we have seen, it produced documents on the Church; the liturgy; ecumenism; relations with other religions; the role of bishops, priests, and the laity; and other church-related topics. And yet the study of Jesus is important not only as a reminder that church doctrines must be subordinated to Christological beliefs, but also to provide grounds for criticising current church life.

During the past twenty years, theologians and biblical scholars, both in academic and popular works, have moved beyond the classic Christology shaped by the councils and creeds of early Christianity. The present studies do nothing to contradict the basic beliefs in Jesus. Rather, they deepen and intensify the Church's understanding of him. Many contributions have been made, but among the most important insights, one area in particular should be noted, namely, the studies concerning Jesus' humanity.

The problems concerning the humanity of Jesus have been due to the stress placed by Christian thinkers on his divinity to the extent that many Christians find it hard to understand Jesus as fully human. In this regard a brief historical review will be helpful. At the Council of Nicaea in A.D. 325 the divinity of Jesus was solemnly defined. This definition was in reaction to Arius who taught that Jesus was not truly divine, but rather a created intermediary between God and humankind. In the next century the Council of Chalcedon, held in A.D. 451, had to meet a different kind of challenge. A priest named Eutyches taught that although Jesus was indeed divine, he was not fully human, but only took on the appearance of being a man. The teaching of Eutyches is referred to as docetism (from the Greek *dokein*, which means "to appear"). In response, the Council of Chalcedon quoted Hebrews 4:15, which states that Jesus is "one who has been tempted in every way that we are, though he is without sin." The council also taught that Jesus is "consubstantial with us according to humanity, similar to us in all things except sin."[1] In other words, Jesus is both true God *and* true man.

Opposition to the belief that Jesus is divine has been more prevalent through the centuries than denial of his humanity, especially among scholars. For that reason the Church has stressed the divinity of Jesus. In doing so, not enough appreciation has been given to the Chalcedonian (and biblical) teaching that Jesus is truly man as well. There has been a tendency to transfer the picture of the glorified Christ back into his public ministry. In catechism classes Jesus was portrayed walking through Galilee or Jerusalem with a halo around his head. Jesus was rarely if ever seen as tired or dirty, annoyed and tempted, indistinguishable in a crowd, or treated as a fanatic. The portrayal was such that it often seemed incredible why all the Jews did not readily accept Jesus as the Son of God. In regard to Jesus' nature, insufficient attention was paid to the many biblical passages that reveal his humanity. Paul, for example, points out in Phil. 2:6–7 that "His state was divine, yet he did not cling to his equality with God but *emptied himself* to assume the condition of a slave, and become as all men are [emphasis mine]."

Scholars are paying attention to this passage that refers to Jesus' *kenosis* (emptying) whereby he emptied himself from a condition in which divine attributes, including omniscience, were fully operative, to a state in which he took on a fully human nature. And yet from the very beginning of his earthly life he was indeed divine as well as human. Therein lies the essence of the mystery of the Incarnation.

Among solidly orthodox Catholic theologians, two basic theories are offered in an attempt to show the relationship between Jesus' divinity and his humanity. A particular concern is the question of whether or not Jesus was limited in his human knowledge, that is, in regard to his own self-knowledge.

Some theologians maintain that because of the **hypostatic union** (the union of the divine and human natures in the one infinite person) or because of special enlightenment given to him by the **beatific vision** or infused knowledge, Jesus simply could not have been limited in human knowledge. Certainly there were no limitations in matters of religion, or the future, or in matters regarding himself. This attitude was long held by Catholicism. In 1907, for example, Pope Pius X maintained that no scholar could teach that Jesus did not have unlimited knowledge.[2] For most Catholics there is an instinctive distaste, therefore, regarding any discussion that maintains that Jesus' human knowledge was in any way limited. It seems to imply a degrading of Christ and certainly violates Catholic sensitivities.

And yet a second theory on the relationship of Jesus' divinity and humanity argues, and offers solid biblical evidence for its reasoning, that neither the hypostatic union nor other possible privileges necessarily granted Jesus extraordinary knowledge. Proponents of this theory tend to attribute to Jesus an intuitive knowledge or immediate awareness of who he was, but they maintain that he had gradually to acquire the ability to express this to himself and then to others over a period of time, not of necessity, but because he willed freely out of love to "empty himself" and truly become a human being. It is at the very core of human experience that one grapples with the question of self-identification and that only through trial and error, often mixed with pain, does an individual really come to terms with a clear sense of his essence. So, too, did Jesus who was human as well as God.

It will be useful to present a few of the many scriptural insights offered in support of the second theory. In regard to Jesus' knowledge of the ordinary affairs of life, there are texts in the Gospels that seem to indicate that he shared normal human ignorance about everyday matters. There are other texts that attribute to him extraordinary and even superhuman knowledge about such affairs. Two texts indicate ordinary human ignorance. In Mark 5:30–33, a woman in a crowd touches Jesus' garments and is healed by his miraculous power. When Jesus perceives that power has gone forth from him, he asks who touched him. His disciples think this a rather foolish question since there was so much jostling by the crowd, but the woman understands and confesses it was she. The narrative seems clearly to presuppose ignorance on Jesus' part regarding who touched him and who was healed. In Luke 2:46–47 Jesus is described in the Temple at the age of twelve astounding the rabbis with his intelligent questions and his knowledge. Then in Luke 2:52 we are told that following this incident Jesus went home with his parents and grew in wisdom, as well as in stature and in favor with God and humankind. The evangelist did not think it was strange that Jesus should ask such questions or grow in wisdom.

In regard to Jesus' knowledge of religious matters, an examination of biblical passages concerning the **Parousia** (Second Coming of Christ) can prove instructive. One question in this regard is whether Jesus claimed to know when the Parousia would occur. A related question is whether or not Jesus expected it to happen in a short time. Jesus gave a variety of answers to this question.

1. *A Parousia in the lifetime of Jesus' audience.* Two famous passages in Mark support this conception. In Mark 13:30 we read: "I tell you solemnly, before this generation has passed away all these things will have taken place. Heaven and earth will pass away, but my words will not pass away." In the context of Mark 13 "these things" include the coming of the Son of Man described in 13:26. This interpretation is augmented by the closely related text of Mark 9:1: "And he said to

them, 'I tell you solemnly, there are some standing here who will not taste death before they see the kingdom of God come with power.'" Again in John 21:22 we find: "If I want him (the Beloved Disciple) to stay behind till I come, what does it matter to you?"

2. *A Parousia delayed and preceded by apocalyptic signs.* That Jesus mentions many apocalyptic signs before the Parousia surely gives the impression that it is not coming soon. In Mark 13, Matt. 24–25, and Luke 21, the signs that, according to Jesus, will precede the Second Coming are: false messiahs, persecution, war, and cosmic cataclysms. There are also several verses that refer to a delay of the Parousia without referring to apocalyptic signs, e.g., Matt. 19:11, 24:48, and 25:5.

3. *A Parousia the time of which cannot be foretold.* Several verses make clear that the disciples cannot know when the Lord is coming since it will be like that of a thief in the night or the unexpected return of a master, e.g., Matt. 24:42–44, Matt. 24:50, and Matt. 25:13. Even more important is Mark 13:32, which states, "But as for that day, or hour, nobody knows it, neither the angels of heaven, nor the Son; no one but the Father."

Jesus' teaching, then, concerning the time of the Parousia is confusing. Epistles in the New Testament, especially 1 and 2 Thess., show that Christians of the first century remained somewhat confused about the question of the Parousia. Since it is not reasonable to assume that Jesus knew when the Parousia would occur but chose for some mysterious reason to express himself obscurely, one is forced to accept Jesus' admission in Mark 13:32 that he did not know when it would occur.

Another important question is whether or not Jesus thought of himself as the **Messiah.** Surely the early Church believed he was the Messiah, the Christ. But as for Jesus' use of this term the problem is more difficult than might seem evident to one unfamiliar with modern biblical scholarship. For example, Jesus is enjoined by the High Priest, Caiaphas, in Matt. 26:63–64: "'I put you on oath by the living God to tell us if you are *the Christ* (i.e., *Messiah*), the Son of God.' 'The words are your own,' answered Jesus [emphasis mine]." Jesus does not refuse the title and does not deny his unique role, but his response shows he would not choose the phraseology himself as an adequate designation of his role. In other words the title *Messiah* as it was understood by the Judaism of his day was an inadequate way to give expression to the mission of which he was, by then, fully conscious.[3]

Terms such as *Messiah* are products of the intellect. The Church teaches that Jesus had a human soul and thus a human intellect. Many modern biblical scholars ask if the Church can admit that Jesus' intellect was *tabula rasa* when he was born (i.e., without knowledge). They also ask if it is possible to maintain that Jesus' intellect was not activated by infused knowledge, but by human experiences, as is true of all other human beings. Their response is that scriptural evidence points in this direction. If so it would have taken Jesus time to formulate concepts, and he might have found some of the prevalent ideas of his day such as the notion of Messiah, inadequate to express what he wanted to say. One would then be able to say that his knowledge was limited, but such limitation would not exclude an intuitive consciousness of who he was and of his unique mission to humankind. His life struggle would have been to discover the proper concepts and words to adequately express himself, both to himself and to his followers.[4]

What is being proposed is that Jesus, though "true God of true God" from the beginning of his earthly experience, was also a true human being in the fullest sense of the words. He was not *acting* as though he were a man, i.e., performing a charade throughout his life, but was truly a human being, learning as all people do, while at the same time intuitively conscious of his divinity. Thus in the Garden of Gethsemani, even though by then Jesus was fully aware of his divinity, he was indeed terrified and, thus, experienced the bloody sweat. And on the cross, when he cried out "My God, my God, why have you deserted me?" (Matt. 27:46), he was not simply quoting the first verse of Psalm 22:1 as though calling attention to an earlier prophecy, but he actually *felt* abandoned by the Father. Nevertheless, he submitted himself to his Father's will. Such an evaluation of the Gospel evidence, if correct, does nothing to detract from the dignity of Jesus. If anything it shows just how loving God is to become fully human in all ways except sin, and it allows Christians to identify even more perfectly with Jesus as a brother who took on the nature of humankind and willingly submitted himself to the trials and tribulations of the human condition. From the Christian perspective, in reaching out to Christ one really does touch a brother, but in touching him one is, at the same time, touching and being embraced by God himself. With such an understanding, Christianity also avoids any danger of making Jesus appear as some kind of mythical, divine being. All danger of docetism can be laid to rest when one takes the Scriptures as seriously as possible and teaches that Jesus was not only truly god but was also truly a human being, just as human as any one of us. Such an understanding can help deepen one's personal relationship with Jesus and, at the same time, can have a great effect on Christian moral life.

Summary

Since the divinity of Jesus has met far more opposition through the centuries than has the fact of his human existence, the Church has placed greater stress on Jesus' divinity. In doing so, not enough appreciation has been given to the biblical teaching that Jesus is truly human as well. There has been a tendency to transfer the picture of the glorified (post-Resurrection) Christ back into his public ministry. Some orthodox Catholic theologians argue that because of the union of the divine and human natures in the person of Jesus, or because of special enlightenment given to him by the beatific vision or infused knowledge, Jesus simply could not have been limited in what he knew, certainly not in matters of religion, or concerning the future, or in matters regarding himself. Other orthodox Catholic theologians argue that Jesus had an intuitive knowledge or immediate awareness of who he was, but they maintain that he had to gradually acquire the ability to express this to himself and then to others over a period of time. This was so, not of necessity, but because Jesus willed freely out of love to "empty himself" and truly become a human being. Solid biblical examples are given to support this theory. If anything, this biblical interpretation shows just how loving God is to become fully human in all ways except sin and allows Christians to identify even more perfectly with Jesus as a brother who took on the nature of humanity and willingly submitted himself to the trials and tribulations of the human condition.

Study Questions

1. Why is it suggested that if Vatican III were to meet today the main topic might be "Who is Jesus Christ for us today?"
2. Explain why the Church stressed the divinity of Jesus rather than his humanity following the Councils of Nicea and Chalcedon.

3. Was Jesus limited in his knowledge in any way? If so, how can he be considered to be divine as well as human?
4. Did Jesus manifest any lack of knowledge regarding everyday matters? Give examples.
5. Did Jesus manifest any lack of knowledge concerning his Second Coming? Give examples.
6. What is meant by *kenosis?*

5

The Christian Life (Morality)

Introduction

Perhaps the most critical area of change stemming from Vatican II is that which pertains to morality. In the past, Roman Catholics were bound to a legalistic type of moral teaching whereby one either followed or did not follow the rules. If not, the confessional was the place where such transgressions were admitted and absolved. However, in many ways, such an approach has been greatly altered. Although Catholics are at least intuitively aware of this new attitude in analyzing moral problems, they are often confused as to why change has occurred, what this new approach actually is, and how its application affects the Christian moral life.

Pre–Vatican II Moral Theology

The Manualist Tradition

At Vatican II the conciliar fathers rejected a special document entitled *On the Moral Order* that had been written by a preparatory commission. It was repudiated, after some debate, because it contained the same kind of legalistic and casuistic approach that had dominated Catholic moral thinking since the Council of Trent. More will be said later concerning the reasons why such an approach is no longer seen as acceptable. Instead of a special document, the council interspersed its teaching on morality throughout the other documents as the need arose. Rather than a blueprint notion of morality, there was a strong insistence at Vatican II on individual responsibility and on the freedom necessary in one's personal response to God. The council also placed great emphasis on human solidarity as well as on the need to respond ethically and responsibly to the world in which we live. This is seen clearly in *The Pastoral Constitution on the Church in the Modern World.* God's call is to be heard at the present time in our daily lives.

Prior to Vatican II, Roman Catholic **moral theology** had been dominated since the sixteenth century by orientations stemming from the Council of Trent. After Trent, the renewal of the Christian life and of the sacrament of penance called for priests to be trained as confessors. The *Institutes of Moral Theology,* the forerunner of twentieth-century textbooks, represented a successful crash program for the training of confessors. Since the end of the nineteenth century there has been a reaffirmation of the methodology of the *Institutes,* which was first produced in the seventeenth century and was perfected during that period by St. Alphonsus Liguori. The manuals of moral theology used in all seminaries in the United States, and still used in a number of seminaries today, were written around the turn of the century. Though new editions continue to be published to update these manuals, the basic approach remains that set down in the earlier *Institutes of Moral Theology*. It will be helpful to recount here some of the basic orientations that dominated Catholic moral thinking from Trent until Vatican II.

Since moral theology was oriented toward the role of the confessor in the sacrament of penance after Trent, the dividing line between mortal and venial sin was seen to be of greatest importance, and this question often became of primary concern to Catholics when faced with difficult moral decisions. It will be shown later why this juridical approach had to be supplanted.

Moral theology during this period also reflected the defensive attitude that characterized Catholic thinking after the Protestant Reformation. For example, if reference is made to the "world" in any of the essays or books written about morality during this period, the reference often is found under the heading "occasions of sin." The "good" Catholic tried to protect his or her faith against the attacks of a "world" that, in general, was seen to be hostile and/or antithetical to the Catholic faith. Catholics in the United States, for example, developed a very negative attitude about public schools. Such institutions were seen to be Protestant and generally subversive to the teachings of Catholicism. This explains why so great an effort was made to develop the parochial school system among Catholics in this country.

Catholics were also strongly encouraged to develop the virtues of loyalty, docility, and obedience. These three traits fall under the typology of "passive" virtues and for most they became the key Christian attitudes. In many Catholic high schools, for example, one would find on the bulletin board the phrase *pro Deo et Patria* (for God and Country). This portrayed the ideal of being loyal both to God (and the Church) as well as to the government. Docility and obedience were strongly inculcated in Catholic schools. One accepted what was taught in a docile fashion and then was obedient to the precepts one had learned. The presupposition was that what was taught was clear and logical and true, and once learned should be followed. To deeply question one's faith was seen as disloyal, unnecessary, and perhaps even dangerous to one's faith. Solid questioning, however, is important, and doubt is a part of faith. Without such questioning and the resolution of doubt, faith is not permitted to deepen and is put in jeopardy of becoming superficial and, perhaps, of being lost. What must be done is to examine constantly the categories of one's thought in order to deepen one's knowledge or faith. From this vantage point we will now present a critique of the manualist tradition and then examine the kind of moral categories that emerged from Vatican II.

Criticisms of the Manualist Tradition

Isolation of Actions

The manualist tradition in many ways was more influenced by the approach of William of Ockham (c. 1280–1349) than by that of St. Thomas Aquinas (1225–74). To say this is unfortunate is a colossal understatement. Ockham was a nominalist philosopher and taught that the only thing that is real is the individual. Such great stress was placed on the individual that terms such as *society*, *universal*, and *genus*, were not seen to represent reality per se. They were only name tags. Thomas, on the other hand, was an Aristotelian and taught that these terms were indeed reflective of reality per se. Suffice it to say that through Ockham's influence an individualistic type of moral teaching arose within Catholicism that concentrated on individual actions, individual dispositions, and individual habits that, for all practical purposes, often became totally disconnected from the circumstances surrounding the actions. To this day there are Catholics who confess missing Mass on Sunday even though there may be extenuating circumstances of which they are aware. They still confess the omission because they continue to focus on the individual action (attendance at Mass) that was not performed. This practice seems incredible to many observers, and indeed it is, but it shows the inability of those who were brought up in the manualist tradition to make a mature moral judgment since emphasis was placed on the performance or nonperformance of an individual action. This attitude, in turn, was greatly influenced by the **legalism** that was a concomitant emphasis in the manualist tradition. Legalism is an overemphasis on the letter of the law to the detriment of the value or values contained in the laws or the observance of a law to such a degree that the spirit of the law suffers or is lost completely.

Legalism

The manualist approach, as seen in the *Theologia Moralis* of St. Alphonsus Liguori, was casuistic, i.e., based on case studies, and was interested in the logical pursuit of exact measurements of individual actions that were subject to minute scrutiny. This tendency begot a legalism within Catholicism that dominated the moral sense of the clergy. Moral decision making, in fact, became severed from the social and psychological circumstances surrounding the action. Such legalistic attitudes also ignored the sense of the whole personality that, as we will see, has now become the basis of ethical discussion among

Catholic moral theologians. But within a legalistic framework, the law often becomes an end in itself, as it did for many Catholics. Jesus himself castigated the Pharisees for teaching the letter of the law as opposed to the spirit of the law. Such is the constant temptation of any legal system, and it has proven to be no less so for Catholicism. Laws that are given to guide believers in their response to God often reach a stage where they defeat their own purpose and become a real obstacle to mature moral growth. Legalism can easily use the law to avoid the complexities of life and the pain of decision making. The law decides all questions in advance; one has only to obey. Younger Catholics will not recognize the impact of this legalistic approach on the Church, but those who are older recall how scrupulously laws were observed, whether they pertained to Mass on Sunday, abstinence from meat on Friday, Lenten practices, or marriage to a non-Catholic. The law simply was to be obeyed, and it is important to recall that such legalism produced highly complex and extremely subtle arguments that often ruled out the ordinary layperson from relying on his or her own conscience and in practice forced them to rely on the judgment of the confessor. Ironically, the law that made Catholics free frequently became a source of constraint. Is it any wonder, then, that Vatican II signaled the death knell for legalism within the moral teachings of Roman Catholicism?

Minimalism

A moral theology that stresses a strict adherence to laws and their observance also produces among many a rather subtle attitude that says, in effect, that if there is no law then the action under consideration is moral or at least morally neutral. This attitude presumes, even if only obliquely, that law is the be-all and end-all of moral decision making. That this is not so should be obvious upon reflection. The limited purpose of law is to point in the direction of true Christian love. But love is so all-embracing that it surely cannot be fully encapsulated under the rubric of law. Yet for those who developed a legalistic mindset, a minimalism in Christian living at times certainly resulted. Christianity and the observance of the law became an equation. As long as one obeyed the law, such as fasting, attending Mass, etc., he or she had done enough. Where there were no laws, however, as, for example, in business dealings, one might well imitate what in fact were nonethical procedures, practices that are "accepted by everyone," even though they are actually hurtful and unloving. A mature Christian morality would discern the values in question and make a decision depending not on whether or not a given law existed, but depending rather on what one perceived as moral or immoral action. With the help of Christ, one decides what must be done. It is interesting to compare former legalistic attitudes toward business procedures with those found in the American bishops' pastoral, *Catholic Social Teaching and the U.S. Economy* (published November 11, 1984), which emphasizes human dignity and values and the need for discernment regarding business dealings.[1]

Too Extrinsic

Simply to obey a law is no guarantee that one is acting morally. Even presuming a law is good, there must be more than the mere observance of that law. According to St. Thomas Aquinas, the obligation of law stems from the connection of the action performed with the value the law embraces. It is not simply enough to observe a law. To do so may mean very little. St. Thomas Aquinas maintains that the routine, mechanical observance of the law is not true Christian moral activity. This hardly seems debatable. But, as in all human endeavors, we are frequently tempted to take the easiest route. In directing people's lives, it is easy to become administrators rather than educators. This is especially true in the case of moral theology. It is easier to make laws than to promote the true and the good. And to many it seems easier to simply follow existing laws than to make a serious effort to analyze the values these laws may or may not embrace. One of the present tasks of moral theology is to educate Catholics to make the intrinsic connection between what they do at any given instance and the moral value of that action, whatever it may be.

Summary

Perhaps the most critical area of change stemming from Vatican II is that which pertains to morality. After the Council of Trent, Catholics were bound to a legalistic type of moral teaching whereby one either followed or did not follow the rules. If not, the confessional was the place where such transgressions were admitted and absolved. Since the confessional was so important in the renewal of the Christian life following Trent, manuals of moral theology were written to train priests as confessors. There are four basic criticisms of the manualist tradition.

1. *Isolation of Actions.* Concentration was so strong regarding individual actions, individual dispositions, and individual habits that for all practical purposes the moral action being considered often became totally disconnected from the circumstances surrounding the action. But such circumstances must be considered in evaluating the morality of an action.

2. *Legalism.* The manualist approach begot a legalism within Catholicism, so much so that for many Catholics the law became an end in itself. Such legalism produced highly complex arguments. As a result, the ordinary Catholic was often forced to rely on the judgment of his or her confessor rather than on his or her own conscience. Such a system became an obstacle to mature moral growth.

3. *Minimalism.* A moral theology that stresses a strict adherence to laws produces among some a rather subtle attitude that allows, in effect, that if there is no law then the action is moral or at least morally neutral. For those who developed a legalistic mindset, a minimalism in Christian living at times resulted. As long as one did what the law required, he or she had done enough. A mature Christian morality would discern the value in question and make a decision based not simply on whether or not a given law existed, but rather on what one perceived as a moral or immoral action.

4. *Too Extrinsic.* Morality demands more than simply observing a law. St. Thomas Aquinas maintains that the routine, mechanical observance of the law is not true Christian moral activity. The manualist approach, since it was legalistic, often did not concentrate on teaching Catholics to make the *intrinsic* connection between what they did at any given instance and the moral value of the action in question.

The Present State of Moral Theology

New Orientations in Moral Theology

The spirit of Vatican II has greatly influenced the present orientation of Catholic moral theology. The council marked the beginning of the end of a morality that was centered primarily around the confessional and that was too individualistic, legalistic, minimalistic, and extrinsic. Certainly morality can no longer emphasize conformity to a static set of laws as if everything were completely settled and spelled out in such norms. What then, precisely, is the present task of moral theology? The beginning of the answer to this question is found in chapter 5 of *The Dogmatic Constitution on the Church* where we are informed that all Christians are called to the fullness of love. It states, "Thus it is evident to everyone that all the faithful of Christ of whatever rank or status are called to the fullness of the Christian life and to the perfection of charity."[2] This statement makes clear that not only priests and religious, but all Christians have the same call to perfection. The task of moral theology thus becomes clear, namely, to show all Christians how to pursue their vocations to holiness *in* the modern world. This can properly be termed an awesome task, but it is of paramount importance for the future of the Church that it be carried out in a loving and clear-minded fashion. The difficulty of this venture is underscored in *The Pastoral Constitution on the Church in the Modern World,* which states, "The split between the faith which many profess and their daily lives deserves to be counted among the more serious errors of our age."[3]

The Christian mission remains always open to approaches that are better adapted to the changing circumstances of our time. When such updating is necessary the Church does not mean to imply that the new approach is radically new. As Pope Paul VI stressed in his first speech at Vatican II on November 18, 1965, *aggiornamento* (updating), does not mean a break with the true tradition of the past. Rather, *aggiornamento* means doing the research needed to separate the true tradition of the Church from the historical and cultural overtones of a particular period and society. Such research has been undertaken by a variety of important moral theologians since the conclusion of Vatican II. The results have been very helpful in broadening the context of moral thinking. The context is no longer individualistic but rather is seen from the perspective of a corporate view of society. We must now examine the orientations that have superseded the legalism and minimalism of the past.

Personalism

Moral theology is no longer considered primarily in the light of conformity of conduct with external laws or norms. Vatican II emphasizes, in a number of ways, that one must find the reason for any moral action within the depths of one's own personality, in one's conscience. The moral life of every Christian consists of the development of his or her conscience. Without such development one remains forever immature. How this can be done, since so many Catholics feel restricted by laws, is a burning question. Nevertheless, it must be done. In this regard, *The Declaration on Christian Education* of Vatican II states, "For a true education aims at the formation of the human person. . . . This sacred synod likewise declares that children and young people have a right to be motivated to appraise moral values with a right conscience, to embrace them with a personal adherence, together with a deeper knowledge and love of God."[4] It is because we value order, stability, and justice that we enact laws that embody such values. The values themselves are of the greatest importance. Laws are secondary to these values. The real authority of a given law rests not with the will of the lawmaker, but with the value implicit in that law. And so Catholics must be able to discern the given value in order to conscientiously give personal acceptance to what is presented. Laws can help us recognize what must be done, but they cannot be the full measure of our personal response. Only a personal response to a given value challenges us at the core of our personality.

A Life-Centered Approach

The new, more intrinsic approach to moral thinking avoids the pitfall traceable to William Ockham and St. Alphonsus Liguori, who divided morality into isolated actions that are seen primarily in relationship to a given law, and not in relationship to the set of circumstances surrounding the action in question. For example, often times a preacher at Mass would warn of the one **mortal sin** that could send any member of the congregation to hell. This sin might be missing Mass on Sunday or on a holy day of obligation, or a variety of other mortal sins. But because of the ongoing dialogue with psychology, sociology, and other related sciences, our knowledge of human relationships is such that we now know the difficulty involved in saying that any one action fully expresses the depth of our personal understanding and response. Because of the present understanding of the ambiguity of external actions, the concept of mortal and venial sin has been rethought. Once mortal sin is understood in terms of the fundamental relationship between a person and God—which consists primarily of a basic orientation, not individual actions alone—the presumptive nature of the older approach to the meaning of mortal sin no longer retains great value or usefulness. New understandings of the meaning of mortal and venial sin, have led, concomitantly, to the reassessment of the meaning and practice of the sacrament of penance.

Sin and the Confessional

There are many practicing Catholics who seldom, if ever, receive the sacrament of penance, which is now referred to as the sacrament of reconciliation. There are many reasons for this. One problem pertains to the manner in which older Catholics received this sacrament in their youth. Often confession was a weekly practice and was done in a rather mechanical fashion. Lists of sins tended to be repetitious and usually of a less serious nature. Added to this was the expectation placed upon a person that demanded that he or she "go to confession" each week. That this was not a pleasant duty can be easily attested. With the changes of Vatican II and the new openness in the Church, the sacrament of reconciliation was one of the first things that many Catholics felt was no longer necessary, though this was not the intention of Vatican II. Changes were needed, however, and have been effected so as to make reconciliation much more meaningful than it was in the recent past. These changes will be discussed in a later section. Perhaps an even more serious problem pertaining to reconciliation is the question of sin itself. For many people in our society, the word *sin* is no longer meaningful or, at least, has lost much of its force. Since this is so, it becomes obvious why reconciliation has lost its impact. We will first examine the meaning of sin as it is understood by biblical scholars and theologians at the present time, including the notions of mortal and venial sin, and then we will examine how the sacrament of reconciliation has been modified since Vatican II.

The Biblical Meaning of Sin

The biblical understanding of sin has been lost to many people for a variety of reasons. For some, past overemphasis on sin has caused them to ignore the concept altogether. This reaction is often coupled with a decline in respect for authority that stems from the decade of the 1960s. Further confusion is experienced due to the effect of psychology, especially of behaviorism and free will. Either free will is completely denied or, if accepted, the idea of sin is greatly weakened or excused due to the effects of heredity and environment. Though such insights should not be ignored, neither should they be used to blunt our consciences. Also, there are a good number of devoted Catholics who seldom, if ever, receive the sacrament of reconciliation because the sinfulness of sexuality was so greatly overemphasized in the past that, once they are married, they think they are "in the clear." One fine practicing Catholic said, in all candor, that the first time he received the sacrament since his marriage was at the first communion of his eldest child. His comment: "Once you're married, what can you do that's *really* sinful?" For other Catholics the idea of sin is ignored because in the past it was presented in too simplistic a manner. Everything was seen in black-and-white terms. This is no longer true, as we shall see. Another reason for the demise of the idea of sin is that too much emphasis has been placed on the individual, and too little attention has been paid to the effect of sin on the community. Sin, even if committed alone, weakens the covenant made between the community and Almighty God, who is Lord of all. There are no "private sins" in the strict sense of the words.

Perhaps the idea of sin has suffered most due to the secularization process. Many now think in such a secularistic fashion that they fail to see that sin involves one's relationship with God himself as well as with his or her neighbor. Sin means that our personal relationship with the transcendent God is somehow violated when we do evil to our neighbor. This is what *sin* means. From the biblical perspective, if an action is not against God, it is not sin. We can speak of it as an evil, perhaps, but not as sin. But since the Second Commandment, "to love our neighbor as ourselves," is a concrete sign of our acceptance of the First Commandment, "to love God above all," both are intimately connected. To do evil to our brother or sister is to sin against God. In biblical religion, morality is inconceivable outside the context of the covenant with God. In the Old Testament the covenant is made by Abraham and renewed by Moses in the name of their people. The Jews, above all, are the people of the covenant. In the New Testament it is through the life, death, and resurrection of Jesus that the new covenant is ratified. Christians are, primarily, the people of the covenant. And sin becomes a violation of this community covenant that not only rejects in some fashion the transcendent God, but also wounds the community in some sense as well. If we cannot see that sin involves both our relationship with God and with the Christian community of which we are members, then it is apparent that there is a dramatic need to redefine the meaning of the word.

The word most commonly used to mean "to sin" in the Bible, *hamartenein,* can more properly be translated as "missing the mark." In the Old Testament, for example, this phrase does not primarily refer to one's failure to fulfill the letter of the law. Rather it points to one's failure to conform to the covenant relationship that God had established between himself and his people. To sin is not simply to break a rule; it is the failure to respond as one should to the love of

God. We see this in the ninth chapter of the Book of Deuteronomy when Moses descends from the Mount carrying the tablets of the Law. He finds the Israelites worshiping a golden calf. In doing so they "missed the mark" of the love by which God had committed himself to them. When Moses breaks the two tablets of Law, it is not simply because his people had broken a law, but because they had broken their personal covenant bond of which the law was only an external expression. The common word for sin in the Bible, then, clearly envisions a relationship of love between God and humankind that is violated. Hence, to speak of sin in only a social context, in a manner that implies that social injustice is sin in and of itself, distorts its biblical meaning.

In the New Testament the authors also use the classical Greek noun *hamartia* and the verb *hamartenein* for sin. The Greek word for sin occurs sixty times in the letters of St. Paul. Among all the New Testament writers, it is Paul who presents the fullest theology of sin. For him, sin is universal. All human beings are involved in sin. It is a condition from which sinful actions originate. It is also a power that has us in its grip. It is not merely an external power, but it becomes part of us, so that we become "the slaves of sin." But we can overcome sin through faith in Jesus Christ, by having him dwell in our hearts, and by his spirit taking possession of us (Rom. 8:1–17). If we fail to understand the dark power of sin in its fullest sense, then we will certainly be unable to understand the meaning of redemption, of Christ's victory over sin. And if this is so, we will also be lacking in the depth of our understanding of the life, the crucifixion, and the death of Jesus Christ. The consequences of such lack of perception will certainly become evident in one's life as a Christian and in one's personal relationship with Christ. Perhaps, unwittingly, many have become victims of what the great Lutheran theologian Dietrich Bonhoeffer refers to as "cheap grace" in his *Cost of Discipleship*.[5] Grace has been won by the victory of Christ over sin, and if we recognize the depth of this statement, then we will realize that imitating Christ's grace is indeed costly and involves dying daily to our sinful self in order to rise in the love of Christ.

The Community (Covenant) Aspect of Sin

One final point about the biblical meaning of sin is important to consider. The conviction of a communal aspect of sin is found in Christianity. For Christians the covenant relationship that is sealed through the blood of Christ on the cross became the foundation of the

Christian community. St. Paul developed this idea in his theology of the Body of Christ, with all the effects this implies on the mutual relationships between members of the community. Because of the excessive individualism of our day, it is very important to accentuate the communal dimension of sin. Individual rights are upheld as the supreme standard for all, and the sole criterion for ethical conduct is the individual conscience. This is commonly stated in arguments used by many who live together before marriage as well as those who support abortion. In the latter instance, the phrase *the mother's right to choose,* is seen by its supporters as an absolute, as though no communal dimension were at stake. But we are "our brother's keeper" if the parable of the Good Samaritan has any meaning and, as Christians, we are interdependent as members of the one body of Christ, just as we are interrelated to all human beings as members of the "family of Adam."

We are, then, called to the love of our neighbor, but this should not be equated with the love of God per se. The love of God implies a transcendent element that makes such love radically different from the love of neighbor. Jesus taught that there are two great commandments: the love of God and the love of neighbor. But they are not of equal importance, and they are clearly two separate commandments, albeit intimately related. In the same way that sin contains a transcendent element, so too does the love of God. God is "wholly other," "numinous." Thus, to love God is radically different than to love one's neighbor. To love the transcendent God requires an act of complete surrender that cannot be demanded by any other kind of love. To completely identify the love of God with love of neighbor would be to deny the transcendent element in the love of God and would reduce God to an unnecessary entity that can result in a secular humanism for many. Though such an attitude can be very benign and loving, it loses touch with and can cause one to deny the existence of the God of biblical religion.

Degrees of Sin

Catholic theology teaches that not all sins are of the same importance. This concept is foreign to most Protestant thinking, which is content to admit that we have sinful natures that have been redeemed by the life, death, and resurrection of Jesus Christ. Through one's faith in Jesus, he or she is "saved" or redeemed from his or her sins. Catholicism agrees with this premise, but feels it is biblically necessary to distinguish between grave and less serious sins. St. Paul speaks of "the slavery of sin, which leads to *death* [emphasis mine]" (Rom. 6:16), a statement that implies a moral attitude leading to a complete rejection of God. This condition of "death" is what Catholicism refers to as "mortal sin." Jesus himself speaks about the blasphemy against the Holy Spirit that will never be forgiven (Mark 3:28–30, Matt. 12:31–32, and Luke 12:10). Surely we have here a reference to a deadly (that which kills the relationship) or mortal sin. This passage does not imply that the saving power of God is limited. Nor does it say that such a sin *cannot* be forgiven. Rather, it says that such a sin *will not* be forgiven. What seems to be at issue here is that those who blaspheme against the Holy Spirit have placed themselves in the position that they are no longer open to the power of the Spirit that is able to save them, since they deny the Spirit even exists, or refuse to turn to the Spirit for forgiveness.

The clearest reference to degrees of sin is found in the First Letter of John. At the conclusion of the letter, when John speaks of the efficacy of prayer, he writes, "If anybody sees his brother commit a sin that is not a deadly sin, he has only to pray, and God will give life to the sinner—not those who commit a deadly sin; for there is a sin that is death, and I will not say that you must pray about that. Every kind of wrong-doing is sin, but not all sin is deadly." (1 John 5:16–17). John does not say exactly what he means by a deadly sin, and he gives no concrete example of what he had in mind. Nonetheless, he clearly indicates a distinction in the gravity of sins that are committed. Catholic moral theologians have tried to clarify the meaning of the deadly or mortal sin with great precision.

At the Council of Trent it was decreed that penitents should confess all their mortal or deadly sins according to the kind of sin involved, e.g., murder, and the number of times such a sin had been committed. But Trent did not specify what constituted mortal sin; thus, it became the work of moral theologians and of canon lawyers to make clear to Catholics exactly what was or was not a mortal sin. This was a burdensome undertaking since to commit a mortal sin was tantamount to bringing about spiritual death. It meant the severing of the bond of love between the sinner and Almighty God. Since spiritual death resulted, this meant that if one were to die in such a condition, he or she would be punished by spending all of eternity in hell.

In analyzing mortal sin great stress was placed on the external action. Certain acts were considered by their very nature to be mortal such as adultery, murder, masturbation, and birth control, among other sins. A mortal sin had to meet three conditions: (1) the action must be, in fact, grave; (2) the person performing the act must be aware of its gravity; and (3) full consent of the will must be given. Thus a mortal sin came to be defined as the transgression of a divine law in a grave matter with full knowledge and full consent. A venial sin, on the other hand was understood to include lighter matter, e.g., anger, lying, gossip, etc. A venial sin could also refer to a grave matter where full knowledge or full consent of the will was lacking. Many older Catholics will remember the sin-grids that were drawn up, which were quite long and contained lists of mortal and venial sins. Since they were so clearly presented as mortal or venial sins, there was little room for discussion. What had to be resolved in order to determine the gravity of the sin—and this, for the most part, was done in the confessional—was the awareness or the degree of consent involved. Such a clear-cut approach helped Catholics to examine their consciences honestly and to make sincere and worthwhile confessions. On the other hand, such concentration on individual external actions did lead many to develop rather scrupulous consciences. They were afraid to "give themselves the benefit of the doubt" on any moral matter and compulsively confessed anything and everything that involved any semblance of sin. For others, because of the heaviness connected with mortal sin, a certain laxity arose toward sins that were understood to be "only venial sins." The approach used in analyzing sin was developed in the manuals of moral theology, which we have already critiqued.

Since Vatican II, mortal sin has been understood from a different perspective than the analytical one stemming from the Council of Trent. No longer is such great weight attached to external action alone. Many Catholic moral theologians, conscious of the ambiguity of external action, view sin in terms of a fundamental relationship between the person and God that consists primarily of a basic orientation, not of individual actions per se. Modern moral theologians are stressing more the basic attitudes that motivate a person in his or her daily living. These are referred to as fundamental options, and they point to the underlying attitudes toward God and humanity that affect moral decisions. For example, if a person has deliberately chosen to live his or her life completely for himself or herself, without regard for God or for fellow persons, then he or she can be said to be in the state of mortal sin. All actions will be affected by this choice. If one's basic choice is for God and others, immoral actions are judged to be venially sinful to the extent that they fail to be in accord with his or her basic choice.

Theologians today, then, are stressing that mortal sin, in the biblical sense, is to choose oneself before God, to make something other than God the center of one's life, whether this be wealth, fame, or sex. This more intrinsic approach to morality tries to avoid the mistake of dividing the moral life into isolated actions that are seen primarily in their relationship to an external law rather than in relationship to an individual's total personality.

Various theologians, conscious of the ambiguity of external action separate from the fundamental orientation of the person in relation to God and neighbors, have introduced a new distinction in the understanding of sin, namely the notion of serious or grave sin as differentiated from mortal and venial sin.

Mortal Sin: A basic choice, **fundamental option**, or general life-direction that chooses self over God. This basic attitude flows from the core of the personality and determines the overall direction of a person's life.

Serious or Grave Sin: An action of a serious or grave nature that does not, of itself, necessarily indicate that the fundamental relationship to God has been broken.

Venial Sin: A sin that involves less serious actions or, if the matter is serious, where there is neither full knowledge or full consent. This is the traditional understanding of venial sin.

In order to understand the difference between mortal sin and serious or grave sin, several examples will be helpful. Let us suppose there are two Catholic men, both thirty years of age, both married, and each the father of two children. Both are members of the same Catholic parish. We will refer to them as Mr. Smith and Mr. Jones. On the same day the following events occur. Mr. Smith has a fight with his wife and leaves his home. He decides to take a ride and ends up at a brothel. Once there, though he had not planned to do so, and has never done so before, he goes to bed with a prostitute. He immediately feels terrible. Is this a mortal sin or a serious (grave) sin? In my opinion it is a serious or grave sin because he has not changed his fundamental option toward God in this one action alone. But it is a serious sin and a clear sign that there is something wrong with his relationship with his wife. Should he go to confession? Again, this would seem to be a very appropriate time to seek the sacrament of reconciliation and, hopefully, to begin to receive appropriate marriage counseling, if not from a priest, then from someone the priest might recommend. Is it necessary to go to confession in this instance? Certainly. But even this question seems to be a residual of the legalistic mindset of the recent past. At least such a serious sin is a clear sign that marriage counseling is needed, and to submit such a sin to the sacrament of reconciliation should be a clear choice for any practicing Catholic.

On the same day, Mr. Jones rents an apartment for his secretary; she becomes his mistress. He is clearly aware that he is violating his marital vows, but he does not care. What is more, he intends this situation to endure not simply for a day but for as long as possible. Is this a mortal sin or a serious (grave) sin? It would seem clear in this case that Mr. Jones has broken his fundamental relationship with God. His basic life-direction has radically changed. This attitude flows from the core of his personality and so determines the overall direction of his life. It is, then, a mortal sin.

In both of the above examples the two men break their marital vows. They are, then, guilty of serious offenses. Grave matter is involved. The difference lies in the fact that one breaks his fundamental relationship with God and the other does not. In the manualist tradition both would be seen to be guilty of mortal sin since the external action is indeed grave. But present moral theology looks not only at the external action but also tries to determine whether or not the individual has made a fundamental option that severs his or her relationship with God.

Perhaps another example will be helpful. Here we will refer to Mr. Brown and Mr. Hopkins. They are also men in their early thirties, fathers of two, Roman Catholics, and members of the same parish. On a particular Sunday neither attends Mass. Mr. Brown fails to do so because he had a terrible fight with his wife the previous evening. On Sunday morning he refuses to go with her to church. But he would refuse to go *anywhere* with her since he's still angry and very upset. Is this a mortal sin? Hardly. It seems rather to be an expression of personal pique at his wife. A bit immature, perhaps, but certainly not the expression of a fundamental change in his relationship with God. It is a venial sin. Mr. Hopkins also misses Mass that day, not because of a fight with his wife, nor out of laziness, but because he has decided that being a Christian interferes with his life-style. He is guilty of many illegal business activities and has decided to repudiate Christianity since it interferes with his life. Missing Mass on this particular Sunday is a sign of a basic decision he has made henceforth to repudiate Christ. Is this a mortal sin? Most assuredly. What must be analyzed, then, is not simply the external action. Both Mr. Brown and Mr. Hopkins missed Mass on the same day. But the underlying reasons for doing so are radically different.

From what has been said, it should also be apparent that moral theology should avoid the mistake of saying that certain positive laws bind "under pain of mortal sin." For example, let us consider the law that states that one must attend Mass on Sundays and holy days of obligation. Mortal sin is not primarily a penalty or a punishment but rather involves the reality of breaking one's personal relationship with God. There are a great variety of reasons why one might not attend Mass on a particular Sunday or a holy day of obligation. It would be better to cast such laws in terms of the greater or lesser importance of a particular action and to stress the positive reasons that underlie the law.

Sin and the Desire for Certainty

For a person living a good, moral life, there arises a desire to know with certainty and to what degree whether he or she has sinned or not. An individual may even desire a new list of sins attached to the traditional threefold division of mortal sins, serious or grave sins, and venial sins. But to attempt to create such lists of sins would be a serious mistake. It would lead to a neolegalistic morality that, in turn, would set an individual on the path to a new system of law and would return once again to a legalistic mindset. This would not lead to moral maturity. The authority attached to law is not simply the will of the lawmaker, but the human value that is involved, whether it be love, justice, or truth. Values are primary. Laws are secondary or derivative. It is certainly true that laws can help us to recognize what God expects of us and can give insights into human values, but they can never become the be-all and end-all of our response or of our responsibility. Laws are important and necessary for the good of society, but an exaggerated emphasis on law can lead to serious deficiencies in a person's understanding of Christian morality. For example, a spouse may feel constantly guilty over having been unfaithful to his or her partner once during thirty years of marriage. And though some sense of guilt is certainly healthy in this instance, that same spouse may feel no sense of guilt ever over the fact that he or she constantly criticizes and makes life most unpleasant for the partner. A real blindness can result since no great "law" has seemingly been violated. Or a priest may feel a grave sense of guilt for not saying his assigned prayers on a given day, but the same man may never feel guilty about his curt and harsh attitude toward his parishioners or toward strangers who may come to him for help, and he may feel no guilt for his failure to keep updated on Catholic theology and ethics. To overemphasize the law tends to reduce morality to obedience and leaves very little room for one's conscience to operate in a healthy fashion and so leaves little opportunity to exercise one's personal responsibility. Thus, although laws are necessary, it is even more important that Christians be educated to respond freely to the important values exemplified in the life and teachings of Jesus Christ.

Moral Instincts

Once moral values are acquired and a person accepts a set of moral principles, some caution must be exercised in order to develop, over and above moral principles, a moral instinct. Some very highly principled people are intolerable. They can be very harsh and judgmental. They can be so inflexible in their behavior that they make life miserable for everyone. Such a person has *the* principle for every occasion, whether you agree or not. The problem with such a person is that he or she acts as though morality is a strict science when, in fact, it is an art. Life is very complex, and the circumstances surrounding the performance of a given action are so variable that a morally rigid attitude can become a serious obstacle to acting in a truly Christian fashion. Moral principles are necessary, of course, but it is essential to realize that they are at best the beginning of an answer to a particular problem and not the whole answer. Moral instincts or, if you will, the promptings of the Holy Spirit, enable us to discern a given situation, to understand the circumstances, to see the various options, and then to intuit which option is best. Such moral instincts presume a person has a set of moral principles, but the same set allows them the freedom of discernment in a given situation. It was to such moral instincts that Martin Luther referred when he said "*pecca fortiter*" (sin boldly). Obviously he wasn't encouraging his listeners to sin. Luther himself had been in bondage to legalism that resulted in a painful period of scrupulosity. Once he was spiritually freed from this condition he became aware that he had been inflexible in his attitude toward the moral life. When he said "pecca fortiter," he was encouraging his hearers to listen to the promptings of the Holy Spirit in a given situation; to discover the possible options; to choose what one considered the best available option; and then to boldly follow his or her conscience. The alternative, as Luther knew from personal experience, was to be so frightened of misusing a moral principle that one was paralyzed in a condition of nonaction. So, boldly trust in your spiritual decision with the understanding that even if events show it was not the best decision objectively, or reveal it to be an incorrect decision, it was still virtuous and pleasing to God. In your freedom, and as a Christian, you did what you thought was best. No one can do more.

Moral principles are acquired from a variety of sources. They can be learned in church, from books, or in the classroom. We can choose our moral principles, and we can justify almost anything we do in the name of some moral principle. For example, there is a principle that says we must be truthful. Consider this case. A man, obviously distraught and looking a bit pale, asks a friend how he looks. In a "truthful" answer the reply might be devastating, all things considered. But if "truth" is embraced by "love," then one's moral instinct will find a kind and uplifting reply, without in any way violating the real meaning of truthfulness.

Moral instincts differ from moral principles in that they cannot be deceived. We can deceive ourselves when we use our conscience, since conscience can be manipulated and confused in applying moral principles. But moral instincts, the promptings of the Holy Spirit, cannot be fooled. They strike at the very essence of the matter and tell us that in these circumstances *this* must be done. To develop such instincts prayer and the deepening of one's relationship with Christ are necessary. The closer one's personal relationship is with him, the healthier one's moral instincts will become. Similar instincts are developed within a marriage. The deeper and more loving such a relationship becomes, the more unerringly do those instincts operate in a wholesome fashion in relationship to one's partner. Where many err in regard to the development of their moral instincts is in their lack of prayerfulness, which is so important in deepening and quickening their relationship to Christ and the Holy Spirit.

The Sacrament of Reconciliation

The removal of sin is a basic concern of religion. In the Old Testament, there are many examples of the Jewish people asking for the forgiveness of their sins. This is still done by the Jewish community on Yom Kippur, the Day of Atonement, a holy day celebrated by a great majority of the Jewish people. On the Day of Atonement, the Bible tells us, a priest placed his hands on the head of a goat and confessed the sins of the community. The goat was then driven off into the desert, symbolizing the removal of the sins of the community and a ritual representation of God's love for Israel. The act of God's forgiveness is emphasized throughout the Old Testament. It is taken for granted that Yahweh is a forgiving God. In Numbers 19:14, God's forgiveness is attributed to his covenant love for Israel. In the Old Testament the forgiveness of sin is seen as a gift of God. Such forgiveness cannot be merited. In Isa. 43:25 Yahweh says, "I it is, I it is, who must blot out everything and not remember your sins." And yet humankind had a role to play. There are a number of examples in the Old Testament of penitential rites associated with the forgiveness of sins. These include confession of sin, fasting, and observing external signs of mourning (see Dan. 9:3–5 and 9:18–19). These symbolic rituals were ultimately performed for the benefit of humanity since it was believed that all sin is punished in some fashion. Thus, fasting or the wearing of sackcloth symbolized the punishment sinners realized was the result of their sins. At times these acts are almost presented as a condition of forgiveness that would be granted only to the extent that they produced in an individual a sense of his or her status as a sinner before God and represented his or her response to the divine offer of forgiveness. A conversion of heart, a true act of repentance, was seen to be necessary. As the prophet Joel states, "Let your heart be broken, not your garments torn, turn to Yahweh your God again" (Joel 2:13).

In the New Testament we read that Jesus died on the Cross for the forgiveness of sins. As a matter of fact, much of his public ministry was devoted to healing and forgiving sins. It is clear that Jesus' forgiving of sins caused great consternation among the Pharisees. They well knew that God alone can forgive sins. In Mark 2:5–7, Jesus declared forgiven the sins of a man who was paralyzed. Some scribes cried out, "He is blaspheming." Jesus went on to cure the paralytic of his illness to show that he had power not only over sin but over the effects of sin as well. It was not a personal sin that had caused the man's paralysis, but rather the paralysis was the result of humankind's fallen nature. Thus, sickness and death are seen to be effects of the state of sin in which the human race presently exists. Jesus was showing he had power over both cause and effect. In the version of the same story found in the Gospel of Matthew, we read of the reaction of those who witnessed what Jesus had done. Matthew writes, "A feeling of awe came over the crowd when they saw this, and they praised God for giving such power to men" (Matt. 9:8).

Catholics believe that the mention of giving such authority "to men" suggests that Matthew is referring to the authority to forgive sins that existed in the Church during the time he was writing his gospel, perhaps about A.D. 70 or 80. Catholic interpretation finds this idea consonant with what Matthew later reports Jesus saying to the Apostles, namely, that whatever they bound or loosed on earth would be so accepted in heaven (Matt. 18:18). Matthew's words are confirmed on Easter Sunday in the upper room when Jesus breathes on the apostles (a sign of conferral of authority) and confers on them the power to forgive sins or to hold sins bound (Matt. 20:23).

All of the passages from the Bible just cited are the basis of the development of the sacrament of reconciliation (penance) within the Catholic Church. From these sayings of Jesus the conclusion reached is that Jesus, who had forgiven sins on earth, continues to forgive sins on earth through the instrumentality of the Church. But, as is the case with so many other aspects of church life, the experience of God's forgiveness in the sacrament of reconciliation had its own historical development. In the first centuries of Christian history, it was left to the decision of individual bishops to determine how the gospel principles of forgiveness would be applied toward their people. Gradually, set forms for the administration of the sacrament were accepted. In the early centuries one could go to one's parish priest to confess grave sins in secret and the priest would determine whether the sins were serious enough to demand a public penance. If so, the penance was given, but absolution was granted only after the penance was completed. Absolution was solemn and was usually conferred by a bishop on Holy Thursday. Such public penances became so severe—e.g., abstinence from sexual intercourse with one's spouse for a year or more, sometimes for life—that people delayed receiving the sacrament until on their deathbed. This attitude of receiving the sacrament only once during one's lifetime became so accepted that a council of bishops at Toledo, Spain, in A.D 589 condemned the repeated use of the sacrament as an abuse. But sometime after A.D 600 the frequent use of confession became a fairly common practice, especially due to the influence of the Church and its missionaries in Ireland.

The Irish church produced penitential books that listed penances for the various kinds of sins. These books were written to aid priests in their role as confessors. Serious sins were met with very difficult penances, at least from a modern point of view, penances that involved rigid fasting or the reciting of long lists of prayer. During this period clear emphasis was placed on the need not only for confession, but for contrition and conversion as well.

In 1215 the Fourth Lateran Council made confession an annual obligation for all Catholics. This is still required but only when one is aware of having committed a serious sin. At the Council of Trent (1545–63), it became mandatory for all mortal sins to be confessed in detail, that is, in kind (e.g., adultery) and in number. In 1576, immediately after Trent, St. Charles Borromeo—one of the greatest theologians of the Counter-Reformation period—maintained that every church should have a confessional box, and this soon became the practice throughout the Catholic world. By the beginning of the twentieth century, confession had come to be seen as a necessary preparation for communion. Though this had not been formally decreed, it had become an almost universal pastoral practice. When Pope Pius X, in 1905, recommended frequent and even daily communion, the pattern of weekly, or at least regular confession, soon followed. There are still a good many older Catholics who think they must receive the sacrament of reconciliation each time they intend to receive communion, though this is not so. For most Catholics, the reception of communion is seen to be not only permissible, but even desirable, as long as they are not conscious of any grave personal sin.

In 1974, Rome allowed new legislation to celebrate the sacrament of reconciliation. There are four types of celebration:

1. Individual confession and absolution. This can be done in the traditional anonymity of the confessional box, or in an enclosed area, face to face with the confessor. Many find the latter much more personal and helpful spiritually.
2. Individual confession and absolution, preceded by a communal preparation that can include Scripture readings and a sermon, and is concluded by a community act of thanksgiving.
3. Communal penance services to promote a spirit of repentance, but that does not include the forgiveness of serious sin. This is still reserved to private confession.

4. A general confession of sinfulness, followed by general absolution, but with the requirement to confess privately at a later time.

These new forms of celebration represent an attempt to revitalize the sacrament of reconciliation. As has been mentioned, many Catholics seldom if ever receive this sacrament today, and Church leaders are striving to help church members arrive at a mature understanding of the spiritual value of the sacrament in today's world. There are a number of theologians who would prefer that actual absolution not be restricted to private confession, but be given in communal penance services as well. They believe this would have a very salutary effect on a large number of Catholics and would still demand sincere contrition and conversion for the sacrament to be valid for a given individual. These same theologians would argue for the continuance of private confession as well as the acceptance of communal services that would grant absolution for even serious sins. They argue that the two forms of the sacrament would be complementary, showing both the role of the individual person and also the involvement of the community in our sinful actions.

Be that as it may, the question "Why go to confession at all?" is still prominent in many minds. After all, since only God can forgive sins, why confess to an intermediary, another human being, a sinner like all of us? Certainly God alone has the power to forgive sins, and no good works on the part of any human being can merit the grace of forgiveness. Surely if we directly turn to Christ and beg his forgiveness, even of a serious offense, he will forgive us. Undoubtedly. Why, then, the need for the sacrament of penance? To answer this question it is important to recall Christ's own words. Pertinent biblical passages have already been referred to at the beginning of this section. All these Scriptures are important in answering the question "Why confession?" This is especially true of Matt. 20:23 in which the apostles (and thus the Church on earth) are empowered to forgive sins. Priests through the centuries have had this power conferred on them at ordination by bishops, who are seen as successors of the apostles, upon whom this power was originally conferred. We read in John 20:22–23: "Receive the Holy Spirit. For those whose sins you forgive, they are forgiven; for those whose sins you retain, they are retained." Why would Jesus give such a commission since he, above all, understands that only God can forgive sins? The Catholic answer revolves around the idea of Christians being a people of the new covenant that was ratified by the blood of Christ. It also is founded on the belief that Christians are all members of the one Body of Christ. He is the head of the body; they are the members. And his word, as understood by the Church, must be obeyed.

It must be understood that the sacrament of reconciliation is only mandatory when a member severs himself or herself from the Body of Christ by committing a grave sin in a knowing and deliberate fashion. To receive the sacrament of reconciliation when no mortal sin is involved, as is often the case, is a devotional action and can be of great spiritual aid, but it is not strictly required. However, in the case of a mortal sin (deadly sin), not only is one's relationship to the head of the body (Christ himself) affected, but so is one's spiritual relationship to the members of the body, the Christian community. The community's love-life with Christ is damaged by the member who breaks his or her covenant bond with him, be it by a deliberate act of murder, adultery, or whatever. The priest, commissioned by Christ through the Church, speaks in the name of Christ and with the power of Christ entrusted to him, not only words of forgiveness and reconciliation with Christ, but of reconciliation with the whole Christian community as well.

It is, practically speaking, impossible to explain to someone who has never experienced the grace of a good confession, the great spiritual satisfaction of the sacrament of reconciliation irrespective of the nature of the sin. The penitent has humbled himself or herself before the Lord and confessed his or her sins in a contrite fashion. In hearing the words of absolution spoken by the priest, there is a beautiful feeling of being touched by Christ's mercy and love, and of being touched, through the priest, by the Christian community as well. Reception of the sacrament in this way furthers the process of daily conversion and can be a tremendous aid to one's spiritual growth. On God's part, the act of forgiveness is instantaneous and a pure gift as is seen in Jesus' parable of the Prodigal Son. For the sinner, the act of forgiveness is but the furthering of a process of reconciliation with one's neighbor. It is here that the practice of asceticism, prayer, almsgiving, and other forms of penance can be of great help. It is through such means that one's conversion to Christ and repudiation of particular personal sins can have its full effect on one's heart, mind, and will.

Ordinary Means of Reconciliation

For some Catholics the impression is still very strong that sins are only truly forgiven through the sacrament of reconciliation. They have been taught that sins can be forgiven by means of a perfect act of contrition, but probably believe that one would practically have to be a saint to make such an act of contrition. And so we are back again to the sacrament of reconciliation as the only sure way to know our sins are really forgiven. But to think in this way is to forget or to neglect the fact that the Church teaches that there are many everyday means of reconciliation. God's grace can come to us in a variety of ways. The process of conversion and healing is furthered by prayer, whether public or private, by fasting, and by giving of alms. One's daily work offered to Christ can serve as a means of reconciliation. Meditation can be most helpful in the battle to overcome sin and to deepen one's relationship to Christ. It is sad that many Catholics seldom avail themselves of the sacrament of reconciliation, but this is often compounded by not making time for prayer, meditation, and performing loving acts for their fellow human beings, all of which can deepen a person's love-life with Christ and thus help overcome sinful tendencies. For many Americans, time has become a real spiritual enemy. They tend to be doers, to be busy about many things. As a result, they get caught up in an activistic pattern and, in some ways, are almost imprisoned by their surroundings. In the same way, noise of many varieties can deaden one's reflective and spiritual powers. Be it the television, radio, music, telephone, or any other form of distraction, all can become obstacles to spiritual development. It is a shame when even the ordinary means of reconciliation become extraordinary, especially since Vatican II clearly teaches that all Christians are called to the fullness of the Christian life and to the perfection of charity.

In discussing ordinary means of reconciliation, it is important to keep sight of the fact that the sacrament of reconciliation is still very important for spiritual development. In this act of confessing one's sins, God's forgiveness reaches a special intensity. Such reconciliation with the Christian community is an outward sign of reconciliation with Christ, and when a priest gives absolution it is the concrete expression of Christ's forgiveness. Such intensification of spiritual existence can be a great stimulus in the process of growing in the Lord and, in many ways, is similar to the relationship of a husband and wife in marriage. There are many ordinary means of expressing love for one another, such as hugs and kisses, words of tenderness, and acts that are emotionally supportive and uplifting. But it is, above all, necessary that such actions be intensified in the act of marriage. It is sometimes forgotten that intercourse between a husband and wife is *the* sacramental act of marriage. Certainly the other ordinary acts of love are necessary in the marital relationship, but they are quickened and deepened by the act of intercourse. To omit making love over a long period of time can be devastating to a marriage. This is obvious to everyone. In regard to the sacrament of reconciliation, the same kind of tendencies, though more subtle, are evident. Christians need to perform daily actions that continue and deepen their love-life with Christ. Occasionally it is very helpful and important to confess those sins that most impede one's relationship to Christ and to neighbor. This is true of devotional confessions as well as confessions of a mortal sin. The sacramental act quickens one's ordinary actions and serves as an important stimulus to living the Christian life, just as the sacramental act of intercourse quickens the daily love relationship between husband and wife and serves as a stimulus to a loving Christian marriage. Unfortunately, many Catholics have repudiated the sacrament of reconciliation due to the distaste engendered in their youth when confession was demanded often and was done in a legalistic fashion. But the Church has changed and so must its members. Catholics must rediscover the deepest truths of their faith, including the purpose of going to confession. If not, they will deprive themselves of a very important spiritual gift offered to them by Christ through the Church. But, above all, it is necessary is to grow in virtue, whether one avails oneself of the sacrament of reconciliation frequently or only very occasionally.

Reward and Punishment in the Bible

Since Vatican II, Catholicism has been concerned with the improving of the world in which we live. No longer can the Catholic Church be accused of an essentially otherworldly approach to human existence. Because of this, the concepts of **heaven** and **hell** no longer carry the same impact. For many adult Catholics the feelings associated with "heaven" and "hell" are not very positive. In the past, heaven was presented as the essence of happiness, but the imagery used to describe it did not always make it appear particularly attractive. The beatific vision, golden harps, and angelic choirs were not easy to identify with. But heaven was greatly to be preferred to hell, which was easier to imagine and was filled with terror. And hell, with all its Dante-like tortures, awaited people who died with mortal sins on their souls. For some, the fear of hell became obsessive, and though this is seldom the case today, the concept of hell is still a motivating factor in the moral decision making of many Catholics.

One of the problems in discussing the afterlife, and in referring to heaven and hell, is that although they are meant as symbols, their descriptions are often taken literally. Metaphors are understood as if they were scientific statements. Likewise, Catholic teaching concerning **purgatory** lends a kind of tangible reality to that state. For many Catholics, purgatory is seen as a kind of hell, a terrible place to be, but tolerable in the sense that it is only temporary and once one's time there is served one will enter heaven for all eternity. And because the symbols of heaven, hell, and purgatory have been understood and described in so literal a fashion, the scientific community easily debunks such ideas. In the ancient world, they were regarded as fixed abodes in a tiered universe—with heaven above, earth in between, and hell below. Purgatory was assigned various possible locations. But with the demise of ancient scientific cosmology and the rise of modern science such a view of the world became scientifically untenable. What has been needed is a rethinking of the intent of these symbols, lest their real meaning be lost. But this task is complicated by the fact that the contemporary world is highly technical and literalistic in its thinking. Many Americans tend to reduce reality to categories they believe science will accept and approve. Literal language designating particular and verifiable objects has become the criterion of all language, even though many modern scientists are clearly aware of the symbolic in their scientific models. Modern humanity still has deep religious longings, but we often lack the sense of the symbolic and poetic that allows us to discover solutions to the questions raised by our spiritual yearnings.

There is still another problem in discussing the concept of hell for many members of contemporary society, including Catholics. The idea that a loving God sentences people to an eternity of torture in hell is a repugnant notion. Why would God create the human race in his own image and likeness and then condemn many of his creatures to such a fate? This question deserves an answer, and that answer revolves around the concept of sin in this life and its consequences in the hereafter. An image that should be eradicated is that of God checking his books to determine what a person's account might be at the time of death, as though some quantitative measure of credits and debits had to be drawn up. Christ knows his own simply by looking at them. In a very real way human beings are continually being offered Christ's grace throughout their lives, and they either accept it or reject it. How they decide is *their* judgment. Whatever punishment one receives is the inevitable result of sin. Sin occurs when a person decides to commit a sinful act and continues as long as one remains in a sinful state. The punishment comes from within oneself in terms of alienation and a loss of integration. On the other hand, a person who is Christ-centered and consciously striving to love others, experiences a continual growth, a process that continues throughout life and after death as well. Jesus' own words greatly aid us in our understanding of punishment for sins. In the Gospel of John 12:47–48 we read, "If anyone hears my words and does not keep them faithfully, it is not I who shall condemn him, since I have come not to condemn the world, but to save the world: he who rejects me and refuses my words has his judge already: the word itself that I have spoken will be his judge in the last day." To put the question of reward and punishment in proper perspective, then, we should not think of the judgment we face at death as though it will be a great shock. We will be seen as we have lived, in love with Christ or in a seriously sinful state, and the rewards or punishments we obtain will be but a continuation of the way we have been living.

At this point it will be helpful to recall the exact teaching of the Catholic Church concerning heaven, hell, and purgatory. Before doing so, however, we should be clear in our thinking. The future life is so radically different from this life that little can be said about it. There is a certain sameness in relation to this life in that here we already live either with Christ (implicitly or explicitly) or in a state of sin. But the future life is also a new creation. The self enters that life, but in a transformed fashion. It should be noted that all descriptions of the afterlife tell more about cultural anticipations than about the nature of the future life. It is far better to trust in the belief that God will take care of his people in a manner far beyond human expectations, than to try to describe what simply is not known.

The Catholic Church is very careful and limited in its teachings about the afterlife. Concerning heaven, St. Paul quotes Isa. 64:3 when he writes, "the things that no eye has seen and no ear has heard, things beyond the mind of man, all that God has prepared for those who love him" (1 Cor. 2:9). These words must be kept in mind in any discussion of heaven. Scripture testifies that all human beings will rise again, as did Jesus. This does not mean that the molecules of our present bodies will be reorganized (since molecules are in a constant state of reorganization). Rather, St. Paul speaks of the "spiritual body" in 1 Cor. 15:31–50 and indicates that we should not think of the resurrection as a return to the bodily existence we now possess. Our present body is but a prefiguration of what is to come. St. Paul writes in 1 Cor. 15:42–44,

> It is the same with the resurrection of the dead: the thing that is sown is perishable but what is raised is imperishable; the thing that is sown is contemptible but what is raised is glorious; the thing that is sown is weak but what is raised is powerful; when it is sown it embodies the soul, when it is raised it embodies the spirit.

St. Paul goes on to say,

> This corruptible body must be clothed with incorruptibility, this mortal body with immortality. When the corruptible frame takes on incorruptibility and the mortal immortality, then will the saying of Scripture be fulfilled: "Death is swallowed up in victory." "O death, where is your victory? O death, where is your sting?"

Those who die in Christ will rise with him, then, to share the everlasting love of his perfected community. What will it be like to live in heaven? We simply don't know. Certainly we are free to believe that nothing of the loveliness we have here on earth will be lost. We can also exclude the notion of any boredom in heaven. Those who enter the kingdom of God's love will be surrounded by loving individuals and share in the infinite love of God. And love dynamically begets love. Thus, if one believes in Christ, in his resurrection and in his promises, it is enough to beget hope in the mysterious kingdom Christ has promised to those who do the will of his Father. But it is also important to realize that through the grace of Christ the kingdom is already within us to be shared with loved ones. Such a belief liberates us from the dark powers of the present age and allows us in hope to love God above all things and to love our neighbor as ourselves out of love of God. This surely is a foretaste of the heavenly kingdom we have been promised.

The official teaching of the Catholic Church concerning hell is quite terse. This may seem strange since there are many references to hell in the Bible as the place of eternal punishment for those who reject

God. Though there have been many imaginative ideas about hell throughout history, the common thread is the idea that the soul not only suffers the pain of physical sensation, but the pain of the loss of God as well. Catholic theologians, since early in church history, described the fires of hell as symbolic of such pain, but sermons often referred to the flames of hell as though they were literal. The horrors of hell were the ultimate threat used to urge one to live a good moral life. Today, it is not the fear of hell, but the love of Christ—seeing him as a savior and a model—that encourages a Christian to live morally. The Catholic Church in its formal teaching states that hell exists as the consequence of one's final personal separation from God, that it begins immediately after death, and that it lasts forever. The Church says nothing at all about the number of people in hell and surely makes no statement about particular individuals, such as Judas Iscariot, being there. Only God can make such judgments. And since we read in 1 Tim. 2:4 that God wills all humanity to be saved, we cannot pretend to know when the possibility of damnation is actualized.

At the present time the concept of hell is undergoing considerable reinterpretation among Catholic theologians. Hell is being extricated from the notions of sulphur pits and lakes of fire (or ice). Two current reinterpretations (and it must be remembered they are just that—reinterpretations) are rather commonly put forth: (1) conditional immortality and (2) the universality of salvation.

Those who hold the idea of conditional immortality maintain that hell implies that those who totally separate themselves from the love of God simply cease to exist at death. The soul is not understood to be naturally immortal and can only gain immortality by means of a wholesome relationship to God. If a person freely chooses against such a relationship then at the time of his or her personal judgment at death, he or she ceases to exist. In other words, the individual is annihilated. The argument for this position is often supported by reference to the image of Gehenna (hell) in the New Testament. Gehenna was the refuse dump in the valley of Hinnom just outside of the walls of Jerusalem. The garbage that was dumped there certainly ceased to exist eventually. It was consumed by a fire "that is not quenched" and eaten by "worms that do not die" (Mark 9:43–48). Other garbage was constantly being deposited, but the point that is stressed is that none of it survived. And so this metaphor for the idea of punishment, Gehenna, seems to suggest that hell symbolizes complete annihilation, not ongoing and eternal torment. Such an interpretation highlights the notion of hell resulting not because of a terrible and harsh judgment by the Almighty and merciful God, but due to the culmination of sin wherein one cuts himself or herself off from the most essential of relationships. This lack of a relationship with the source of one's existence leads to the disaster of annihilation.

A second interpretation of hell is that of universalism, which theorizes that despite sin, all of humankind will finally be saved and enter the kingdom of heaven. Certainly all responsible Roman Catholic theologians insist that anyone who is properly aware of the enigma of human sinfulness must at least grant the possibility that one can eternally separate himself or herself from the love of God. But a number of Catholic writers are quick to remind us that God does indeed will all humanity to be saved. Hans Urs von Balthasar, for example, argues that to affirm dogmatically that damnation is ever actualized amounts to subverting the Gospel and, in effect, to make bad news part of the good news.[6] The Lutheran scholar George Lindbeck observes that apparently many of the bishops at Vatican II agreed with the kind of thinking represented by von Balthasar's opinion since they refrained throughout the conciliar documents from appeals to the hope of heaven or the fear of hell, both of which had been traditionally upheld to encourage good Christian living. Lindbeck notes that this omission disturbed many of the conservative bishops who complained "that the doctrine of eternal damnation was being replaced by belief in universal salvation."[7] Their fear was unfounded since Vatican II did not teach the idea of universal salvation, even though one must admit that the council did emphasize the universalistic motifs in the letters of St. Paul, especially Ephesians and Colossians.

There are a number of criticisms of the teaching of universalism, but perhaps the most serious objection is that it does not deal with the reality of sin. It could be argued further that universalism trivializes the very notion of evil. The universalists respond to this problem in a variety of ways, some more cogent than others. The chief focus of such universalist answers is the overwhelming triumph of the grace won for humankind by the life, death, and resurrection of Jesus Christ. Concerning universalism even Karl Barth, the great Swiss Protestant theologian of the period covering approximately 1920 to 1965, makes some surprising statements. Barth was a very conservative Reformed Church theologian, but concerning universalism he cautions that a person should not surrender himself or herself "to the panic which this word seems to spread before informing himself [or herself] exactly concerning its sense or nonsense."[8] Barth goes on to advise that we should be at least stimulated by passages such as Col. 1:19, which states that God has determined through his Son as his image and as the first born of the whole creation to "reconcile everything in his person." A number of biblical passages are used by Barth and others to make this point. For example, Rom. 8:38–39 is often quoted. It states, "For I am certain of this: neither death nor life, no angel, no prince, nothing that exists, nothing still to come, not any power, or height or depth, nor any created thing, can ever come between us and the love of God made visible in Christ Jesus our Lord." All those who argue on behalf of this position maintain that sin must be taken very seriously, but they argue that because of the infinite nature of God's redeeming grace, we *cannot* completely separate ourselves from his love, even if we attempt to do so.

Fr. Karl Rahner's position on the question of the universality of salvation can perhaps serve as a symbol of the thinking of the more progressive Roman Catholic theologians. He writes, "It would be erroneous, against the Christian faith, and arrogant presumption on the part of the creature, were we to think that we knew that all men are saved."[9] Rahner thinks that every attempt to teach the universality of salvation is fundamentally to assume knowledge that we simply do not have. Everyone must work out his or her salvation in fear and trembling without certain knowledge of salvation. However, Rahner goes on to say that if we forego the theoretical and reflective knowledge of what will be, then:

> We are also called upon to hope, firmly and unshakably, in the hope against all hope for ourselves and others. Then we may also *with hope* read what is written: "God has included all men in the rebellion, in order to include all in his pardon" (Rom. 11:32), even if we must leave it to God in the case of this word, too, how he alone is to fulfill it.[10] [emphasis mine]

Rahner believes that since God has planted this hope, he may also fulfill it. And he goes on to ask "Is something not possible to God even though it is as impossible to man as a camel passing through the eye of a needle?"[11]

Moving away from the question of universal salvation and away from the concept of hell, we can begin to investigate the Catholic Church's teaching on the subject of purgatory. It is a careful teaching. Officially Roman Catholicism holds that those who die in the love of God undergo a purification of any stain of sin that is on one's soul at death. Although most Protestants reject this teaching, some find it to be very important. For example, C. S. Lewis writes:

> Our souls *demand* Purgatory, don't they? Would it not break the heart if God said to us, "It is true, my son, that your breath smells and your rags drip with mud and slime, but we are charitable here and no one will upbraid you with these things, nor draw away from you. Enter into the joy"? Should we not reply, "With submission, Sir, and if there is no objection, I'd rather be cleansed first." "It may hurt, you know." "Even so, Sir."[12]

Catholicism also holds that such souls can be aided by the prayers of Christians, especially by the sacrifice of the Mass. Nothing else is said officially concerning purgatory. There are no church teachings that obligate Catholics to believe anything about the nature or duration of this purification. Whether purgatory is a place, a state, or a process is not part of official teaching. Today opinions vary among theologians concerning the meaning of purgatory. One of the more common opinions among Catholic writers is that purgatory refers to the event that occurs when a Christian dies and then is judged immediately after death. The person being judged sees himself or herself as he or she really is in relationship to the living God and, in so doing, suffers deep humiliation for any aspects of his or her sinful nature not yet repented. Thus, the sins are "purgated," and the individual is invited then into the heavenly kingdom.[13]

The symbol of fire is often associated with the teaching of purgatory and perhaps it is an apt symbol. For example, if a person is caught in a sin he usually blushes. In doing so a person can feel as though his face is "on fire." Seeing oneself as God does surely would produce an analogous result. Certainly this would be true at the time of personal judgment and would cause an individual deep personal anguish. A real purgation would result. Whether such a purgation suffices or a further duration of time would be necessary continues to be the subject of ongoing speculation among thinkers.

The notion of **limbo** baffles many Christians and they often wonder if it is still a part of Catholic teaching. *Limbo* is a technical theological term (Latin: *limbus* [edge]) referring to the state of those souls who are neither in heaven nor hell nor purgatory. Traditionally a distinction has been drawn between the ***limbus patrum*** (the place and state of those who merited heaven before the time of Christ but were not able to achieve it until his redemptive act could be completed) and the ***limbus infantium*** (the place for children who died without baptism before they reached the age of reason).

Historically, neither revelation nor the earliest Christian tradition deals with the notion of limbo. Early Christianity taught that salvation in Christ depends on membership in his Church, which initially begins with baptism. It was only in the early fifth century when **Pelagianism** denied these teachings and asserted in proof of its views that God does not deny access to the kingdom of heaven to unbaptized children that the teaching about limbo arose. It was proposed for the first time by St. Augustine (d. A.D 430). His teaching about limbo went uncontested for centuries. Limbo was understood as being a place of great natural happiness, but one where its inhabitants were denied the vision of God, which took place only in heaven. Since infants were unbaptized and hence were not Christians, it was believed that they lacked the necessary grace to go to heaven. But since they had committed no personal sin, Augustine and those following him felt God would not subjugate them to the pains of hell. It was in this manner that the notion of limbo arose.

St. Anselm of Canterbury in the twelfth century and, later, the great thirteenth century scholastic thinkers such as St. Thomas Aquinas and St. Albert the Great, and Catholic thinkers up until the time of Vatican II, all firmly agreed with Augustine in his notion of limbo. In present-day theology the existence of limbo is questioned by many, including some distinguished theologians and historians of dogma, and there is a great deal of discussion as to whether the assumption behind the teaching of limbo (namely, that the persons in question are excluded from heaven) is in fact a theologically unchangeable one. Those who believe the teaching should be discarded appeal in particular to the dogma of God's universal will that all might be saved to determine that the children in question are saved by the blood of Christ.

As regards the present state of research on the question of limbo, it is clear that opinions still vary widely among specialists. However, those who hold the more progressive view regarding the salvation of infants through Christ's atoning death have been able to establish many important points in their favor. The Church's teaching authority has, until now, not officially accepted their viewpoint, but it allows inquiry to continue without hindrance.

From a pastoral point of view, it is important to understand the origin and history of the teaching of limbo, and a pastor should be able to relate this information to his people, especially to those parents of children who have died without receiving baptism. Since there is no definite doctrine of faith regarding such children, parents can surely entrust the eternal destiny of their child to the mysterious but infinitely kind and powerful love of God, to whose grace no limit is set by the earthly circumstances that he, in his providence, has allowed to take place.

Sexual Ethics

Confusion about the meaning of sin today can certainly be blamed to a great extent upon our society's preoccupation with sexuality. It is often the case that when a Catholic (and many other Christians as well) speak of someone as immoral, most often the reference is to the commission of some sexual sin. This is despite the fact that the individual in question may be greedy, violent, unjust, or cruel. But traditional moral teaching paid much more attention to the Sixth and Ninth Commandments than to the others, and the area of sexuality was treated in a predominantly negative fashion. Much of the teaching warned of the dangers of sex and caused Catholics to become extremely cautious when dating. As a matter of fact a great deal of the fear engendered often carried over into marriage, with unhappy results for many. In contemporary society the Manichaean dualism (the belief that the body is evil, the soul is good) that has troubled the human race for about three thousand years is being set aside. For many, sex is no longer understood as something that is dirty or obscene. Rather it is seen to be beautiful, fulfilling, and inter-personal.

At the risk of oversimplification, one can argue that much of the negativity toward sexuality can be traced to the origins of the great world religions during the first millennium before Christ. In places such as India, Persia, and Greece, the world of the body was separated from the world of the spirit and ideas. Authentic existence was believed to subsist only in the world of the spirit or of the Idea, while the material world was often seen as a prison constricting the spirit. From this principle it followed that sex, which is associated with the body, was negative. It is a long journey from the world of Zoroaster, Manes, and Plato to the **Jansenism** taught in the Irish seminaries of the nineteenth century and from there imported to the United States, but the connections are rather clear.

Interestingly, it is difficult to discover many traces of such dualism in the Jewish and early Christian traditions. It is noteworthy that in the Jewish Scriptures the description of the relationship between God and his chosen people was seen as a marital union. St. Paul continued this imagery for the followers of Christ and, in so doing, laid the foundations for authentic Christian sexual personalism. But this insight was rather quickly overcome due to other Pauline statements such as "it is better to be married than to be tortured" (1 Cor. 7:7), not to mention the dualistic influences of the Manichaeans and Neoplatonists and, later, of the Albigenses and Jansenists. Because of these influences, and for a variety of other reasons, Catholicism did not deal well with the positive notion of sexual personalism until Vatican II. Though the Church has adopted a healthier attitude toward sex, it must also be admitted that freedom from guilt and inhibition has been both partial and limited. Fear and anxiety about sex persist and probably always will, since humankind has great problems with intimacy and builds rather strong defenses, both psychic and physical, against it. Nevertheless, it is clear that Catholicism now understands human sexuality as a true gift from God, a gift that is to be relished and enjoyed.

It would be ridiculous to say that the older tradition had no positive and healthy teaching on sexuality. For example, the creation description is very clear: "God made human beings, male and female he created them . . . and God was pleased with what he saw. The man and woman were both naked, but they were not embarrassed" (Gen. 1:27–2:25). The Song of Songs describes the beauty and erotic love of two people, a relationship that was sensuous and passionate. The prophets and St. Paul used the marital relationship as a metaphor of God's love for his people. Other examples could be given, but the point is that the positive aspect of the tradition was never lost. At all times there were many people whose common sense, emotional balance, and solid family upbringing enabled them to understand and live healthy sexual lives. What must be comprehended today is that an understanding of sexual ethics requires a continuity with the deepest and most positive insights the Scriptures and Catholic tradition have to offer, while eliminating at the same time the heresies of **Manichaeism** and Jansenism, which so deeply affected and perverted a true Christian understanding of human sexuality.

Vatican II has changed the essentially negative approach toward sexuality to a considerable degree without substantially changing the

Church's specific teachings. No longer could a Clement of Alexandria compare marital intercourse to "an incurable disease, a minor epilepsy." Nor could a pope, St. Gregory the Great, state that it is as impossible for a married couple to have intercourse without sin as it would be to fall into a fire and not be burned. The documents of the council show a radical departure from previous teachings in that they go beyond the harsh dichotomy between sex primarily for procreation and sex primarily for pleasure. The fundamental importance of the sexual dimension of human personality is explicitly acknowledged. For example, in regard to sexuality, the council stressed the intrinsic goodness of conjugal love, and the goodness of its sexual expression. In *The Pastoral Constitution on the Church in the Modern World* it is stated:

> The actions within marriage by which the couple are united intimately and chastely are noble and worthy ones. Expressed in a manner which is truly human, these actions signify and promote that mutual self-giving by which spouses enrich each other with a joyful and thankful will.[14]

The Council Fathers go on to say that it is a good thing for a married couple to make love. This sexual expression of the couple's mutual love has a value apart from—but not unrelated to—the value of children. And the whole marital relationship "maintains its value and indissolubility even when offspring are lacking."[15]

Vatican II, in agreement with Catholic tradition, also teaches that while human sexuality is a vital part of marital love, that love is essential for the procreation and education of children.[16] The council gave equal status to both the love-union and procreative aspects of sexuality, rather than insisting, as had been the case in the past, upon the primacy of the procreation and education of children. But the council also insisted on the inseparable link between these two purposes. However, the council went on to teach "that certain modern conditions often keep couples from arranging their married lives harmoniously, and that they find themselves in circumstances where at least temporarily the size of their family should not be increased."[17] The council advocated responsible parenthood by teaching that in particular circumstances a couple ought not increase the size of their family. The council is teaching the obligation of responsible parenthood in the context of family limitation. But what means are permissible to bring about the regulation of family size? The council, in fact, did not discuss the question of birth control explicitly, but only in general terms, and this led to a continuance of the debate. The matter was officially resolved with the publication of the encyclical ***Humanae Vitae*** by Pope Paul VI on July 25, 1968, in which he upheld the teaching that artificial contraception is always wrong. In writing this letter Pope Paul was in agreement with the teaching of the encyclical letter of Pope Pius XI ***Casti Connubii*** written in 1930.

The birth control controversy in the years following 1968 has continued to bring great agitation into the lives of Roman Catholics. To many Pope Paul's teaching in *Humanae Vitae* came as a surprise since the papal birth control commission appointed by Pope John XXIII and continued by Pope Paul VI after Vatican II had voted 41 to 9 to change the traditional teaching prohibiting all artificial methods of contraception. The continuing debate pertains not only to the question of sexual morality but to other areas as well, most notably the authority of the Catholic tradition against contraception and the authority of papal teachings. Other important questions focus on the possibility of the development of doctrine or even a change of doctrine. Some moral theologians have argued that acceptance of the official teaching on birth control was seen by many Catholics as primarily a question of institutional loyalty and obedience to papal authority rather than a matter of sexual morality.[18] To advocate a change in teaching did indeed require the proponents of change to show how such an action would be in harmony with Catholic tradition and even demanded by such tradition in the light of the new circumstances of the modern world. An attempt to do so was made by the members of the commission on birth control in their report "The Theological Report of the Papal Commission on Birth Control," published on June 26, 1966. A summary of this report, which was rejected by Pope Paul VI, can be found in James P. Hannigan's excellent work, *What Are They Saying About Sexual Morality?*[19]

In general, Catholic moral theology has approached the question of sexuality in the light of a natural law methodology. In this context, nature means the physical, biological, and natural processes that are common to humanity and to all the animals. The Church's teaching regarding birth control maintains that the biological process cannot be artificially interfered with since to do so is a violation of nature. Those who dissent argue that if procreation were the only purpose of sexual intercourse, then it would follow that the teaching of the Church is correct. But since there is another basic purpose, namely, the expression of and deepening of mutual love, it does not necessarily follow that nature has been violated. The basic argument of those who disagree with the official teaching of the Church is that nature is much broader than the biological functions but must include the totality of the person, that is, every aspect of one's nature, not only the physical but also the social, moral, religious, psychological, and cultural aspects. This basic change in the understanding of the natural moral law is one of the primary grounds for the continuing dissent to *Humanae Vitae* and has led to charges of physicalism and biologism repeatedly made against both the encyclical as well as the more recent (1975) Vatican document, *Declaration on Sexual Ethics*. Fr. Charles Curran's critique of this declaration can be seen as a representative example of such charges. Curran, recently censured by the Vatican, first observes that the methodology adapted in this declaration is basically the same as that used in *Humanae Vitae*. He then writes:

> The Declaration is guilty of physicalism, since it understands sexuality primarily, if not exclusively, in the light of the physical structure of the act itself. Such a defect is clearly associated with the emphasis on the act alone and not on the person. The personal dimension of sexuality, the whole psychological aspect of human sexuality, and human sexual maturity as a goal toward which one strives are all missing. By focusing the ethical analysis unilaterally on the physical act and the faculty, there is little or no room for considerations of the psychological, the personal, the relational, the transcendent and other important aspects of human sexuality.[20]

The continuing debate on the birth control issue is rather clearly delineated. The official teaching of the Church on the one hand, and the reasoning of those who dissent from this viewpoint on the other, are readily understood. Most Catholics in the United States disagree with the official teaching and act accordingly, not as disobedient sons and daughters, but as loving members of the Church who have investigated the matter and have acted in accordance with their conscience. Nevertheless, church teaching can never be taken lightly, and it is important that such teachings on this subject be carefully read and studied. The same kind of careful study is also necessary regarding *The Instruction on Respect for Life in its Origin and on the Dignity of Procreation* issued by the Congregation for the Faith under the signature of Cardinal Joseph Ratzinger in 1987. Perhaps the chief errors made since Vatican II are the lack of easy availability of church documents in many local parishes and the paucity of classes and symposia addressing controversial topics.

Summary

Vatican II marks the end of a period when legalism dominated Catholic moral theology. The difficult task of moral theology today is to teach Church members that *all* Christians are called to the fullness of the Christian life and to the perfection of charity, and to show the various members of the ecclesial community how to pursue their vocations to holiness in the modern world.

The moral life of every Christian consists of the development of his or her conscience. Without such development one remains forever immature. But how this can be done, since so many Catholics have had their consciences restricted by "laws" is a burning question. Nevertheless, it must be done. Laws are important, but the real authority of a given law rests not with the will of the lawmaker but with the value implicit in that law. And so Catholics must be able to discern the given value in order conscientiously to give personal acceptance to what is presented. Only a personal response to a given value challenges us at the core of our personality. In making such a response, the set of circumstances surrounding the action in question must also be considered.

The biblical understanding of sin has been lost to many people for a variety of reasons, and so there is a great need in present society to rehabilitate the true meaning of sin. St. Paul teaches that all human beings are involved with sin. It is a condition from which sinful actions originate. It is also a "power" that has us in its grip. If we fail to understand the dark power of sin in its deepest sense, then we will certainly be unable to understand the meaning of redemption, of Christ's victory over sin.

Catholic doctrine maintains that we live not only in a condition (state) of sin but that there are degrees of sin. Venial sin lessens our love for Christ and his community while mortal (deadly) sin breaks one's relationship to God. Several biblical passages refer to the existence of mortal sin. However, moral theology after Trent weakened the notion of mortal sin by putting too much stress on the external action. Since Vatican II moral theologians have viewed mortal sin in terms not only of individual actions but in terms of a radical change of a basic orientation to God. Mortal sin, in the biblical sense, is to choose oneself before God, to make something other than God the center of one's life, whether this be wealth, fame, or sex.

Once moral principles are acquired and a person accepts a set of moral principles, some caution must be exercised in order to develop, over and above moral principles, a moral instinct. Moral instincts or, if you will, the promptings of the Holy Spirit, enable us to discern a given situation, to understand the circumstances, to see the various options, and then to decide the best option. To develop such instincts prayer and the deepening of one's relationship with Christ are necessary.

The removal of sin is a basic concern of religion. God alone can forgive sin since it is an action committed against him. Catholicism teaches that there are many everyday means of being reconciled to God. Not only should we ask his forgiveness of our sins but the process of conversion and healing is furthered by means of prayer—whether public or private—by fasting, by giving alms, by offering one's daily work to Christ, or by meditation, and in a variety of other ways as well. The sacrament of reconciliation is another means for the forgiveness of sins. Even though this sacrament is only mandatory when one commits a mortal sin, it can be used in a devotional manner in overcoming venial sins. On God's part, the act of forgiveness is instantaneous and a pure gift as is seen in Jesus' parable of the Prodigal Son. On the part of the sinner, this act of forgiveness is but the furthering of a process of reconciliation with one's neighbor and can be greatly aided by the grace of the sacrament of reconciliation.

Since Vatican II the Catholic Church can no longer be accused of an essentially otherworldly approach to human existence. Consequently, the concepts of heaven and hell no longer carry the same impact as was formerly the case. However, the concept of hell is still a motivating factor in the moral decision making of many Catholics. Rather than stressing the idea of reward and punishment in the afterlife, the Church today teaches that moral actions should be performed primarily because of our love of Christ and of our neighbor. Nevertheless, a review of Church teachings on heaven, hell, purgatory, and limbo can be helpful in that we are reminded that the future life is so radically different from this life that little can be said about it. Descriptions of the afterlife tell more about cultural anticipations than about the nature of the future life. In considering life after death it is far better to trust in the belief that God will take care of his people in a manner far beyond human expectations than to try to describe what simply is not known.

A final word must be said concerning sexual ethics. Traditional moral teaching paid much more attention to the Sixth and Ninth Commandments. The area of sexuality was treated in a predominantly negative fashion. Vatican II has changed this approach toward sexuality to a considerable degree without substantially changing the Church's specific teachings. For example, documents of the council show a radical departure from previous teaching insofar as they transcend the harsh dichotomy between sex primarily for procreation and sex primarily for pleasure. The fundamental importance of the sexual dimension of human personality is explicitly acknowledged. In regard to sexuality, the council stressed the intrinsic goodness of conjugal love. A controversy still remains regarding the birth control policy as articulated by Pope Paul VI in the encyclical letter *Humanae Vitae.* Problems also exist regarding the recent teachings of Cardinal Ratzinger's *Instruction on Respect for Life in its Origin and on the Dignity of Procreation.* Such church teachings can never be taken lightly, and it is important that such teachings are carefully read and studied. Perhaps the chief error that has been made in this regard since Vatican II is that church documents, together with classes and symposia on the topics in question, have not been made easily available in many local parishes.

Study Questions

1. What was the manualist tradition? Describe the four basic criticisms of such an approach to morality.
2. Since all Christians are called to the perfection of charity, what is the task of moral theology today regarding the discerning of values? What is meant by personalism?
3. What is the biblical meaning of sin? Has the notion of sin been cheapened in modern society?
4. Why does Catholicism teach that there are degrees of sin? Is there any biblical evidence for such a teaching?
5. In regard to the notion of mortal sin, what is meant by the term *fundamental option?*
6. Is there any difference between a moral principle and a moral instinct?
7. What is the biblical evidence for the sacrament of reconciliation?
8. Briefly describe the history of the development of the sacrament of reconciliation.

9. Can a Catholic grow in virtue even though he or she seldom uses the sacrament of reconciliation? What are the ordinary means of reconciliation?

10. Is the concept of hell a strong motivating factor in the moral decision making of many Catholics? Why? Has this approach changed since Vatican II?

11. What does the Church teach concerning heaven, hell, limbo, and purgatory?

12. What historical factors influenced Catholicism's negative approach toward human sexuality? Did Vatican II essentially change this way of thinking about sexuality?

13. Explain the basis of Catholicism's offical teaching concerning birth control. What is the argument of those who dissent against this teaching?

6

The Sacraments Today

Roman Catholicism believes that the seven sacraments of the Church are key moments in a believer's relationship with Christ. They help one to respond to Christ in a unique manner as well as to be nourished and nurtured by him from the beginning of one's Christian existence to the moment of death. Included in our reflections will be a brief consideration of the history of the sacraments and of the reasons why Catholicism believes there are seven sacraments rather than only two (baptism and the Lord's Supper), which is the teaching of most of Protestant Christianity. Recent changes in the administration of the sacraments, especially those pertaining to the **Eucharist** (Mass), will also be briefly treated.

In the ancient Roman world, the Latin word *sacramentum* referred to the oath of allegiance taken by a soldier when he was inducted into one of the legions of the Roman army. In the early third century the Christian writer Tertullian referred to baptism as a sacrament in order to emphasize the commitment one made to Jesus when one was baptized. By means of the sacraments, a Christian is helped to "put on a new man," that is, take up a new life-style dedicated to Christ.

The Vulgate (Latin) edition of the Bible uses *sacramentum* to translate the Greek word *mysterion* (mystery), a term used by St. Paul in reference to the "hidden plan" by which God intended to save, renew, and unite all things in Christ (Eph. 1:9 and 3:3–9). Early

Christian authors, writing in Greek, often spoke of Christian "mysteries" in relationship to many of the rituals and prayers that were being used by the Church. A special place was given among these mysteries to a series of actions leading to one's final initiation as a Christian. Among these actions were found Lenten instructions, anointing, profession of faith, and finally baptism itself. St. Augustine, who died in A.D. 430 and was the most influential Christian writer of the first Christian millennium, said a sacrament is a holy sign (symbol) through which a Christian perceived and received Christ's grace. He said this sign is made up of two essential parts, a material component (e.g., water in baptism) and the spoken word of conferral (e.g., "I baptize you in the name of the Father, and of the Son, and of the Holy Spirit"). Despite such definitions, Christian writers continued to refer to a variety of other rites as sacraments, including the sign of the cross, the anointing of kings, the reception of ashes on Ash Wednesday, and the Trinity (e.g., in the mid-twelfth century St. Bernard of Clairvaux referred to the Trinity as the mysterious oneness of the three divine persons and as a great sacrament to be worshiped rather than investigated).

Peter Lombard, who died in A.D. 1159, in his famous *Book of Sentences*, which was a standard textbook for Christian theologians until well into the seventeenth century, argued that there were only seven sacraments. St. Thomas Aquinas and most Catholic writers essentially agreed with Lombard's reasoning. In the sixteenth century, Protestant reformers such as Martin Luther and John Calvin argued that, according to the strict word of Scripture, only two sacraments were instituted and ordained by Christ as signs and means of grace: baptism and the Lord's Supper. The Catholic response to the Protestant reformers came at the Council of Trent, which formally defined the seven sacraments: baptism, Eucharist (the Lord's Supper), confirmation, reconciliation (confession), marriage, holy orders, and the anointing of the sick. All were instituted by Christ as sacraments, even though the biblical testimony is not equally clear for all seven. Above all, the Council of Trent's response to the Protestant reformers was a strong statement of support for the sacraments, which contrasted sharply with the eventual Protestant tendency to subordinate the sacraments to the preached sermon.[1]

Modern Catholic theologians such as Edward Schillebeeckx and the late Karl Rahner have applied the term *sacrament* in a wider sense than simply to the seven sacraments.[2] Christ himself, as the

Word of God become human, is understood as the primordial sacrament of one's encounter with God. God's love for the human race becomes visible in Jesus as a great sign, as does God's saving mercy in Jesus's death on the Cross, and his resurrection from the dead.

In addition, the Christian church (which includes all Christians) is understood as the basic sacrament of Jesus. The Church is both sign and cause (as instrument) of the ultimate unity of all things in Christ. And, as is so well pointed out in *An American Catholic Catechism,* the wider use of the term *sacrament* is an indication that the sacraments of the Church are being understood less as detached events of grace between God and humankind than as meaningful moments within God's plan of salvation.[3] The sacraments are rites of incorporation in which Christ draws men and women more fully under the influence of his redeeming grace and his saving mission. The sacraments are indeed events of grace, integrated into the life of Christians, in which the Spirit of God is imparted by the Lord who is ever sending his Spirit into the world. In the sacraments, incorporation and grace are extended through symbolic or ritual actions of human communication and worship in the Church in the form of initiation (baptism), reconciliation (confession), a community meal (Eucharist), or a marriage commitment. In the sacraments, both the community and individuals give expression to their faith and, under the influence of the Holy Spirit, develop and deepen this fundamental receptivity to Christ's presence and influence.

Catholic doctrine teaches that each of the seven sacraments responds to a deep personal need for Christ's redemptive presence at critical moments in each person's life-history. A succinct analysis of the seven sacraments and the role each plays in one's life is given in *An American Catholic Catechism.* The following passage deserves to be quoted in its entirety.

> *Baptism* envelops the beginning of life in God's loving kindness and stamps it with the irrevocable concern of Christ and his assembled people. As a person approaches maturity, *Confirmation* renews the gift of God's spirit as the source of strength and support in a life of discipleship and service. In ecclesiastical *penance,* we can deal with the cancer of sin and the wounds of guilt and infidelity by approaching the Lord, "a God merciful and gracious, slow to anger, . . . forgiving iniquity and transgress of sin" (Ex. 34:6). When serious illness threatens to engulf us in self-concern, *sacramental anointing* brings God's presence and assimilates us to Christ

who suffered on behalf of many. *Ordination* and *marriage* are sacramental dedications of mature Christians to the lifelong vocations of loving
service to which God calls them.

Our basic problem, however, the one that accompanies us for a lifetime,
is the way we relate to other people. Can we overcome the stifling effect
of self-seeking so as to live in peace with others? Can we grow in prompt
readiness to help and serve the Christ who calls to us through people in
need? Thus, God would have us return constantly to the *eucharistic meal*
where we and those near to us are made one body in Christ and where
we are inserted into Christ's selfless giving of himself on behalf of every
human person. Through the sacraments, therefore, the course of our
personal lives is repeatedly punctuated by God's loving presence at just
the moments of our greatest need of him.[4]

It is clear, then, that in the term *sacrament* there is found the
concrete reality of the life of every Christian. Thus the word should
not be understood only as referring to seven efficacious rites. It should
be taken to mean that the people of God, as an ecclesiastical
community, is transformed into a sacrament. In other words, there is
a visible community of human beings living in actual contact with the
rest of humankind that, through its existential actions, contains,
manifests, and communicates the saving presence of Christ. Such
sacramentality implies that Christians should adopt an attitude that
goes far beyond ritualism or **moralism**. Instead of concentrating
primarily on devotions and religious practices that are simply a means
to an end, Christians should dedicate themselves to the work of being
true and efficacious signs of salvation, a demanding and vital task.

The renewal of the sacramentality of the Church that began at
Vatican II is aimed at helping Catholics to understand the symbolic
value of each sacrament in order to help them become better
witnesses of Christ. For example, confessions are now heard face-to-
face, if one so desires. This format is much more personal than the
anonymity of the confessional, and many find it more spiritually
beneficial. Stress is also placed on the fact that in the sacrament of
reconciliation the priest represents not only Christ but the community
of Christ as well, since all sin is not only against God, but violates the
love relationship of the community as a whole. The marriage
ceremony, always so beautiful, is more so now. Couples have much
more input in the service. They may choose the Scriptures, ask family
or friends to serve as lectors, or select the music. This greatly adds to
the celebration of marriage and manifests in a unique way the

couples' personal relationship with Christ as well as the community involvement of their fellow Christians. Among other things, the newly married couple pledge that they will be true signs of Christ. This personalism and sense of community is also found in the baptismal rite, be it that of an infant or an adult. In the baptism of an infant, for example, great stress is placed on the responsibility of the parents and godparents, as well as on the immediate community, to nurture the baby in the ways of Christ. Any sense of magic attached to the ritual, even though mistakenly, has been put to rest. At Mass, the sense of personalism and community has been greatly strengthened by the inclusion of all as participants, whether it be by all worshipers responding to the prayers of the celebrant, by the community joining in the hymns, by the reception of the Eucharist in one's hands (as a sign of inclusion in the priesthood of the faithful), by the exchange of the kiss of peace, or in various other ways. All of these changes are meant to help Catholics deepen their relationship with Christ.

In regard to the sacraments, perhaps the most dramatic occurrence was the change at Mass from Latin to the vernacular. This was done to help augment the participation of all in attendance and to strengthen the sense of Christian community. It is interesting to note that the first official decree of Vatican II, *The Constitution on the Sacred Liturgy* issued on September 29, 1963, was a broad plan for liturgical reform that was to be implemented during the following months and years. In fact, by 1970 the essential changes had been completed. The changes began in April of 1964 when, at communion, Catholics began answering "Amen" as the priest gave them the host and said, "Corpus Christi" ("The Body of Christ"). As insignificant as it may seem, this "Amen" was the beginning of a greater personal and community involvement. On the first Sunday of Advent that same year, American Catholics went to Mass and heard their first official half-English, half-Latin Mass. This was rather confusing since the congregation read their prayers and responses in English and then watched as the priest shifted back to Latin for the recital of orations, the canon, and all prayers recited only by himself. Laity were chosen to read the Epistle and Responsorial. In November of 1964, Pope Paul VI then reduced the eucharistic fast to one hour, rather than from midnight of the night before, and water was allowed to be taken at any time. These changes in the fasting laws were made to encourage greater numbers of Catholics to more fully participate in the Mass by receiving Holy Communion. The difficulty of the previous fasting laws made it rather burdensome for many to receive communion.

Altars were being turned around in 1964, and for some this resulted in self-consciousness at finding oneself being so directly addressed by the celebrant. It was equally difficult for many priests. The ingrained habits of years had to be broken. The priest had to learn new attitudes toward the rubrics of the Mass again when, in May of 1967, Rome eliminated numerous genuflections: altar kissing, signs of the cross over the offerings, and the custom of keeping thumbs and forefingers joined after the consecration of the bread and wine. During the same month, permission was given for the Latin canon to be read aloud and for the English (vernacular) translation of the canon to be prepared. Saturday evening Masses were officially approved, along with the practice of receiving communion while standing. In the spring of 1969 the new lectionary was completed and a new Order of Mass was published that gave a framework that would not need substantial alteration in the near future. The entire Mass was now in English. Further, the rubrics frequently called attention to the need for flexibility, adaptation, and imagination. Since 1970 Catholics have learned, though at times with great difficulty, that different styles of liturgy are needed for different people, since there are so many subjective differences among the faithful. They have also learned that not all the Sunday Masses need to be celebrated in exactly the same modality. Accepted differences in music and style for the good of the community were established.

Many Catholics were greatly troubled when the Latin Mass was changed. There are several reasons for this kind of reaction. Because the Latin Mass had symbolized the unity of Catholicism (the Mass was said exactly the same everywhere in the world) some felt the changes were the beginning of disunity. They failed to see the difference between unity and uniformity, which was understandable since the Catholic Mass had not changed since the introduction of the Tridentine (from the Council of Trent) Mass in 1570. The Latin Mass, especially when accompanied by Gregorian music, was aesthetically beautiful, far more so than the Mass as presently recited in English. Still, it is difficult to explain the survival of Latin in the liturgy during a four-hundred-year period (1570–1963) that saw the language die while being transformed into the Romance languages of Europe. One reason, undoubtedly, was that the liturgy in the vernacular had been regarded by Catholics since the sixteenth century as the mark of Protestantism. Since there was so much hostility between Catholics and Protestants, it seemed unreasonable to adapt to a liturgical style that would give credibility to what Protestantism had opted for at its very inception. Some also felt that the Latin Mass symbolized the timeless and changeless reality of Roman Catholicism. But this simply was not so. The Roman Catholic Church has never been timeless or changeless. As Vatican II clearly points out, Christians are the pilgrim people of God. Nonetheless, such was the perception of many Catholics, a perception that had been fostered by attitudes conveyed in the *Baltimore Catechism* as well as many other instructional manuals. Ultimately, the liturgical changes inaugurated by the Vatican Council, including the use of the vernacular, were brought about to allow the laity (few of whom knew Latin) to become active participants at the Mass. Such participation was fostered to underscore the idea that the Mass, by its very nature, is not a private devotion but a community action. In the judgment of most observers in the Church, the long-term effects of this change will surely strengthen the unity of Roman Catholicism.

For the sacraments to be meaningful they must stem from a vital Christian community, a Christ-centered discipleship. This means that stress must be placed on the local community, the parish. Roman Catholicism is composed of thousands upon thousands of such local parishes, and each parish must constantly strive to represent Christ. We should recall here that just as Jesus is the primary sacramental sign of the Father, so is the Church the primary sacramental sign of Jesus. But the Church does not exist in theory alone. The Church, the People of God, exists primarily in the concrete, in the local Christian community, in the parish.[5] No two parishes will ever be exactly alike since the lives of their parishioners are lived, at least to some extent, under different circumstances. Such differences are manifest when comparing Catholic parishes in different countries such as, for example, the United States and Nicaragua. There are often great differences in the operations of parishes within the same city. The Word of God must come alive in different situations and different contexts. The Gospel must be translated in terms of real-life situations and this process must be celebrated within a given situation, culture, and historical moment. Here we enter the broad domain of liturgy, which includes the seven sacraments, but much more besides. It includes the whole range of Christian life that encompasses social justice, ecumenism, and love of neighbor. If the parish is vibrant, the sense of Christian community will become clearer with each passing day. But in a vitalized Christian parish that is truly a sacramental sign of Christ, its members will continually rediscover and live the mystery of Christ found in the Scriptures and with ever greater appreciation will come to understand how they are encountered by Christ. They will also come to understand more fully how Christ is encountered not only in the sacraments but even in the most prosaic events of the day.

A question that is often raised by other Christians concerns the Catholic belief that there are seven sacraments. Protestant Christianity believes there are only two sacraments, baptism and the Lord's Supper. Both are acknowledged by Jesus and are clearly attested in Scripture: baptism in John 3:5, Matt. 28:18–19, and Mark 16:6, etc.; and the Eucharist in Matt. 26:26–28, Luke 22:14–20, and Mark 14:22–25, etc. But regarding the other five, Protestant Christianity believes their institution by Christ is nowhere to be found in the Bible. Catholicism, on the other hand, officially teaches that there are seven sacraments and that all seven were instituted by Christ. Scriptural references are, in fact, provided by the Bible for the other five. For example, concerning confirmation read Acts 8:15–17; for reconciliation, Matt. 16:19 and John 20:19–23; for marriage, Matt. 19:3–9 and Ephesians 5:13–33; for holy orders, 2 Tim. 1:6; and for the anointing of the sick, Luke 5:13–18 and James 5:14–15.

Nevertheless, Catholicism substantiates the sevenfold nature of the sacraments not by biblical prooftexting. As a matter of fact it allows that the biblical evidence is not necessarily sufficient to justify all seven sacraments. Rather, Catholicism begins with the notion that the Church itself, as the primordial sacrament of Christ, is the visible earthly representation of the grace of redemption. Catholicism also argues that Christ himself laid down the sevenfold direction of the visible sacramental acts of the Church.[6] Scriptural data exists for baptism, reconciliation, the Eucharist, holy orders, and to a certain extent, confirmation. As for matrimony and the sacrament of anointing of the sick, it is more difficult to produce data referring explicitly to Christ's will. But Catholicism does presuppose the implicit will of Christ in regard to these sacraments. Catholics experience the actuality of these sacraments and believe they are de facto acts that are fundamentally expressive of the life of the Church. The Church understands her own nature by experiencing it. The Church recognizes these acts that flow from her sacramental nature as fundamentally and unconditionally the fruits of that nature, and so they are recognized as truly sacramental actions. The Church could not deduce the sevenfold nature of the sacraments in the abstract but instead recognizes its essence in its concrete fulfillment.

As far as the sacraments that are not clearly found in Scripture are concerned, namely confirmation, matrimony, and the anointing of the sick, Catholicism presupposes that the implicit will of Christ is responsible for their existence. In regard to the anointing of the sick, the Church was led in its decision through the apostle's practice of this action in James 5:14–15. Such a conclusion is consistent with the messianic healing of the sick that was quite evidently intended by Christ to be carried out by the early Church. Concerning marriage, St. Paul gives a Christian appreciation of its role in God's plan and sees the conjugal relationship of husband and wife as an image of the relationship between Christ and the Church (Eph. 5:25–33). This bond, in turn, stresses the preexisting connection between the Church (the sacramental sign of salvation) and matrimony as a sacramental sign. Concerning confirmation, Christ did not say to the apostles at a given moment that he was instituting this sacrament. However, during his earthly life he did promise the Holy Spirit to them, and on Pentecost Sunday he sent the Holy Spirit in the form of tongues of fire (Acts 2:3). In order that all Christians might receive the same spirit, the apostles adopted the rite of laying their hands upon the heads of believers as the sign and seal of the gift of the Holy Spirit. In adopting the form of laying on of hands, they were following a gesture often used by Christ himself who laid his hands on people while healing, blessing children, and working miracles.

The sacraments are special moments in the life of a Christian. They can be prepared for and intensified in the everyday acts of life that are performed out of love for Christ. But they can also be weakened by not attempting to live one's day in a loving Christian fashion, but rather by giving in to selfishness and self-serving attitudes. Thus, the sacraments cannot be isolated from the organic unity of a full Christian life. They are culminating moments in one's Christian journey and should never be considered isolated actions.[7] It is very important to see the sacraments in relationship to the whole of Christian life. This can be done by comparing the Christian life to marriage. For example, when a married couple makes love, which is a sacramental act, it is not automatically fulfilling of that couple's relationship. Rather it is dependent on the manner in which the man and woman have related to each other in those actions preceding the act of intercourse. If they have been considerate, affectionate, and tender to each other in the everyday events preceding intercourse, the act itself will be truly representative of those moments and will indeed be symbolic of their love and, thus, a culminating event. But if they have been inconsiderate, harsh, and lacking in tenderness, the act of intercourse will not be as fulfilling as it should be. This does not negate the act, but it does describe the kind of preparatory qualities needed to allow the act to be as fulfilling as possible. The same preconditions apply to the Eucharist. Surely it is important that one receive communion at Mass, which itself is a table fellowship with Christ. But the sacrament will be a greater or lesser sign of one's relationship with Christ depending on the quality of one's love of Christ and love of neighbor as determined by one's daily actions and on the quality of one's habit of prayer and meditation.

A final statement about the meaning of the sacraments should be made. It can happen that one's experience of God may indeed be more intense outside the sacraments than during the moment one receives them. An encounter with a loved one by means of a letter, a tender smile or touch, the majesty of a sunset, and a variety of other possibilities—all these may bring one to feel God's presence with greater intensity than may ever occur in the reception of a sacrament. Such bestowals of grace may, in fact, raise a Christian to greater spiritual heights than the sacraments themselves. It should be understood that the sacraments determine the objective importance of certain moments in life. However, besides such moments that are objectively decisive, there surely can be others that subjectively are of vital importance. For those who love Christ their relationship to him is constant, and there are many moments in such a relationship that are not produced by the sacraments per se. Rather, the sacraments are necessary as important markers, as milestones along the way, so that by living the Christian life to its fullest an individual may become more and more one with Christ.

Summary

Roman Catholic teaching maintains that the seven sacraments of the Church are key moments in a believer's relationship with Christ. They help one to respond to Christ in a unique manner as well as allow one to be nourished and nurtured by him from the beginning of their Christian existence to the moment of death.

Catholic theologians today understand Christ himself, as the Word of God become human, as the primordial sacrament of one's encounter with God. In addition, the Christian church is understood as the basic sacrament of Jesus. This wider use of the term *sacrament* is an indication that the sacraments of the Church are being understood less as detached events of grace between God and humankind, and more especially as meaningful moments within God's plan of salvation. Catholic doctrine teaches that each of the seven sacraments responds to a deep personal need for Christ's redemptive presence at critical moments in each person's life-history.

The renewal of the sacramentality of the Church that began at Vatican II is aimed at helping Catholics to understand the symbolic significance of each sacrament in order to help them become better witnesses of Christ. Thus the changes in the Mass called for by Vatican II were adopted to help augment the participation of all in attendance and to strengthen the sense of community. Further, the sacrament of marriage was enhanced by allowing the couple greater input in the marriage ceremony. The couple may choose the Scriptures, ask family or friends to serve as lectors, or select the music. This adds greatly to the celebration of marriage and manifests in a unique way the couples' personal relationship with Christ as well as the community involvement of their fellow Christians. Among other things, the newly married couple pledge that they will be true signs of Christ.

Catholic doctrine maintains that there are seven sacraments. The Church does not rely on biblical evidence for its belief, but argues that Christ himself laid down the sevenfold direction of the visible sacraments and believes they are de facto acts that fundamentally express the Church's life. The Church understands her own nature by experiencing it. It recognizes these acts that flow from her sacramental nature as fundamentally and unconditionally the fruits of that nature and so they are understood as truly sacramental actions.

The sacraments are special moments in the life of a Christian. They can be prepared for and intensified in the everyday acts of life that are performed out of love for Christ. But they can also be weakened by not attempting to live one's day in a loving Christian fashion, but rather by giving in to selfishness and self-serving attitudes. Thus, the sacraments cannot be isolated from the organic unity of a full Christian life.

Study Questions

1. Give a brief history of the development of the sacraments beginning with the teaching of Tertullian and continuing to the close of the Council of Trent.

2. How have Karl Rahner and Edward Schillebeeckx broadened the meaning of the word *sacrament?*

3. Since Vatican II how has the Church helped Catholics to gain a better personal relationship with Christ and a better sense of community in its reform of the following sacraments: reconciliation, marriage, baptism, and the Eucharist (Mass)?

4. Describe the changes that took place in the celebration of the Mass between 1963 and 1970. Why were these changes made?

5. For the sacraments to be especially meaningful, what role must each local parish play?

6. Why does the Church teach that there are seven sacraments?

PART III

The Future:
Movements in the Church

7

The Ecumenical Movement

The ecumenical movement was officially accepted by the Catholic Church during the 1960s due to the influence of Pope John XXIII and the Second Vatican Council. The word *ecumenical* has a variety of meanings, but here it is used to refer to that movement that has as its goal the "fostering of unity among Christians." *The Decree on Ecumenism* states, "The 'ecumenical movement' means those activities and enterprises which, according to various needs of the Church and opportune occasions, are started and organized for the fostering of unity among Christians."[1] Because of limitations of space, we will examine primarily the relationship between Roman Catholic and Protestant Christians. A notable omission will be the relationship between Roman Catholicism and Eastern Orthodoxy, not because this is unimportant, but because it is so important that it deserves far greater treatment then space allows in this volume. And since we are primarily concerned with the Church in the United States, at the end of this chapter we will extend the ecumenical outreach and briefly examine the Roman Catholic–Jewish dialogue that, for Catholics, had its formal beginning at Vatican II in *The Declaration on the Relationship of the Church to Non-Christian Religions.* The selection of the dialogue between Roman Catholics on the one hand, and Protestant Christians and Jews on the other hand, is dictated by the basic socio-religious groupings in the United States, namely, Catholic, Protestant, and Jewish.

Roman Catholicism and Protestant Christianity

From the beginning of the Protestant Reformation in the early sixteenth century until the acceptance of *The Decree on Ecumenism* at Vatican II, the attitude of Roman Catholics toward Protestant Christianity was clearly negative and polemical, as was the disposition of Protestants toward Catholics. There was mutual distrust and suspicion. But in the twentieth century many ecumenical pioneers arose, both Protestant and Catholic, who felt scandalized by the division among Christians. They realized that Christians are called to be one and that the primary biblical basis of all ecumenical concern is Jesus' prayer in the upper room as recorded in the Gospel of John, 17:20–21, in which Jesus says, "I pray not only for these, but for those also who through their words will believe in me. May they all be one. Father, may they be one in us, as you are in me and I am in you, so that the world may believe it was you who sent me." Among the twentieth-century Catholic ecumenists one of the most important was Fr. Yves Congar, O.P. Several of Congar's early books on ecumenism were withdrawn from circulation by Rome, and for a time he was also removed from his teaching position. Fortunately, Congar lived to see his ecumenical seeds bear fruit at Vatican II.

Catholics and Protestants who were raised prior to Vatican II can recount many tales from their youth regarding Catholic and Protestant relationships that seem rather incredible to their children. Interfaith marriages were discouraged to such an extent that when they did occur, even under the best circumstances, they were almost always traumatic. Such marriages were witnessed in the priest's rectory or held at the communion rail in church, but never in the sanctuary of the church. These rules were made to show the Church's disapproval of such marriages. Many a sad story can be told regarding interfaith wedding ceremonies. Today the attitude is quite different and much more positive. Ecumenical weddings witnessed by both priests and ministers are rather common and are quite beautiful. The reason for the more positive attitude stems from *The Decree on Ecumenism* in which the Catholic Church, for the first time since the Protestant

Reformation, officially teaches that Protestants are not only truly Christians but also that the Holy Spirit works through Protestant churches and ecclesial communities. In other words, they are saved not despite but because they are Protestant. Protestants and Catholics are brothers and sisters under the same Lord. Many Protestant denominations that entered the ecumenical movement several decades before Catholicism officially did so, share the same positive appreciation of their Catholic counterparts. Nevertheless, many theological differences still remain that must be resolved before an even deeper unity can result; moreover, centuries of antipathy between Protestants and Catholics will not be easy to erase.

The sources of the antipathy between Catholics and Protestants for the past four-and-a-half centuries were many. Certainly the sixteenth-century theological arguments about the meaning of grace, the relationship between good works and faith, the role of the pope, and the significance of tradition vis-à-vis Scripture continued to serve as points of separation. Ecclesiology also was very prominent. Catholics and Protestants, practically speaking, defined one another out of the Christian church. As was seen in Part I, the Catholic definition included only things Catholic (the pope and the seven sacraments, for example) whereas the Protestant definitions included only things Protestant, which certainly excluded any idea of the pope or of seven sacraments. Of course, cultural differences played an important role. For example, in a lecture delivered at a national Newman convention in New York City in 1963, then bishop (later Cardinal) Wright, of Pittsburgh, facetiously said that the reason most of the Irish were Catholic was because they had discovered that most of the English were Protestant. He was opting for better relations among Christians, but was observing that a very real obstacle to be overcome was the hostility of various cultures toward one another. All of these factors militated against any real dialogue between Catholics and Protestants. As a result, hostilities increased through the years. It may be in certain instances that absence makes the heart grow fonder, but when the separation begins in negative fashion and includes bloodshed on both sides, as time passes and positions harden the end result is even more divisive and polemical.

Protestant ecumenism received its impulse from the vast expansion of the foreign missionary movement in the nineteenth century. The missionaries soon realized that although the Gospel was being preached, denominational divisiveness was proving to be an obstacle and even a scandal in foreign lands. A symbol of the attempt to come to terms with Protestant disunity was the Edinburgh Conference in 1910. It was not a formal meeting of churches as such but rather of many missionary societies. Conference members sought to arrive at a common missionary strategy in order to avoid a spirit of competition. Edinburgh had limited success, but it created a new spirit for many and spawned a number of important conferences that ultimately led to the formation of the World Council of Churches in 1948. To clarify the purpose of this organization W. A. Visser 't Hooft, its general secretary, wrote the following in 1948:

> The World Council of Churches is essentially an instrument at the service of the churches to assist them in their common task to manifest the true nature of the church. It is an instrument and must therefore never be considered as an end in itself. The important thing is not the World Council as an organization. It is therefore a sign of confused thinking to speak of the World Council itself as the World Church. And it is completely erroneous to suggest that the World Council is or has any ambition to become a Super Church, that is, a center of administrative power.[2]

Dr. Visser 't Hooft went on to say that the World Council of Churches "can and must work to create a situation in which there is so much in common between the churches, that there is no adequate reason for them to remain separate from each other."[3]

Because of the attitudes engendered by the World Council and other ecumenical groups, many Catholic thinkers entered into an ecumenical dialogue. The Instruction of the Holy Office in Rome entitled *Ecclesia Catholica,* issued on December 20, 1949, gave impetus to Catholic ecumenism. Although the instruction appears rigid and filled with many warnings in the light of present-day understanding, it nevertheless made clear that Catholics should become involved in the movement. However, it contains a warning against too much involvement by the laity and maintains that ecumenism should mainly be the work of priests and other religious figures. It was through Vatican II that the Catholic Church wholeheartedly entered the ecumenical movement, but it was Pope John XXIII who led the way.

John XXIII built upon the foundation of many Catholic ecumenists who preceded him. But in calling together the council he insured that the ecumenical movement would formally and structurally become a part of Roman Catholicism. Pope John himself created the Secretariat of the Promotion of Christian Unity to help prepare the council.

The secretariat provided (and continues to provide), for the first time in Roman Catholic history, a structure for ecumenical activity. Augustine Cardinal Bea, S.J., a German biblical scholar, was appointed the head of the Secretariat. It was run by Msgr. (now Cardinal) Jan Willebrands, a leading Dutch ecumenist. Most of the conciliar issues dealing with ecumenism were handled by the secretariat, which produced the preliminary text for the documents dealing with ecumenism, religious liberty, revelation, and the Church's relationship to Judaism. Pope John also enlarged the ecumenical spirit of the council by inviting Protestant and Orthodox observers to attend it. The contribution of these observers proved to be a great boon to the deliberations of the council, particularly regarding *The Decree on Ecumenism.*

A number of important themes run through this decree. There is a recognition of the mutual responsibility of both Catholics and Protestants for the sins of Christian division. There is also recognition of the consequent need for inner renewal as the basis for ecumenical relationships. And there is an emphasis that the Church is indeed the "pilgrim people of God" and so must always be aware of its need for ongoing reformation. But the major breakthrough of the document is the acknowledgment of the "ecclesial reality" of Christian churches other than the Roman Catholic Church. The decree uses the phrase *churches and ecclesial communities* to refer to all other Christian churches. This phrase is used in direct relationship to the decision made in *The Dogmatic Constitution on the Church,* which states that the Church "subsists in" the Catholic Church, thus suggesting that Eastern Orthodoxy and Protestant Christianity are members of Christ's mystical body. Such an attitude marks a basic change in Roman Catholic thinking, especially in regard to Protestant Christianity. Orthodox Christianity had always been considered a valid and fruitful church by Roman Catholicism, possessing true bishops, priests, and sacraments. But the Catholic attitude toward Protestantism was one that viewed Protestant churches purely as an individual religious phenomenon. In other words, Protestants were seen as religious individuals upon whom God had somehow bestowed his grace, but whose corporate life as members of a Protestant church per se was devoid of grace. They were saved despite their Protestant affiliation. Since Vatican II, Roman Catholicism now teaches that the Holy Spirit works through Protestant "churches and ecclesial communities" and not just in spite of them. God gives his gifts to Protestant Christians in their corporate ecclesial life and not merely in their individual encounters with God.[4] Also, liturgical actions are now understood in such a way that "these actions can truly engender a life of grace, and can rightly be described as capable of providing access to the community of salvation."[5] The council, then, makes very clear the Catholic acceptance of the fact that in regard to other Christian churches, "the Spirit of Christ has not refrained from using them as a *means of salvation* [emphasis mine]."[6]

The Decree on Ecumenism gives very specific direction for ecumenical activities. Three areas are encouraged in regard to ecumenical sharing: common dialogue, common action, and common worship. As for common dialogue, the decree states that from such interdenominational exchanges "there will emerge still more clearly what the position of the Catholic Church is. In this way, too, [the decree continues] we will better understand the attitude of our separated brethren."[7] Now that other Christians are fully appreciated as brothers and sisters under the same Lord, a true dialogue can result, rather than the monologue that usually resulted when Catholics and Protestants spoke to one another in the past. Such present-day communication can only lead to a fuller Christianity for everyone and a better understanding of the diverse Christian community. In regard to the second area of ecumenical sharing—common actions—Christian churches have cooperated often since Vatican II in the realm of social justice. In the United States this has been especially true in regard to civil rights, the peace movement, feeding and sheltering the poor, and the sanctuary movement. Such sharing breaks down many barriers and helps those involved to discover the depth of Christianity in the hearts of those with whom they share. The third area of ecumenical sharing suggested is common worship. The decree states:

> In certain special circumstances, such as prayer services "for unity" and during ecumenical gatherings, it is allowable, indeed desirable, that Catholics should join in prayer with their separated brethren.[8]

There have been many interdenominational prayer services in the years following Vatican II. Although the need for honest theological exchange is of utmost importance, it may well be that coming together in prayer in the name of Christ is the most critical activity of all. In such prayer services, the various Christian groups come together in the name of Christ and in Christ. Certainly as Jesus tells us: "For where two or three meet in my name, I shall be there with them" (Matt. 18:20). In the past there was such a stress on differences in mutual interpretations of the meaning of the Christian faith that Christians were not only inhibited, but frequently impeded from loving one another with a truly Christian love. Hopefully, by praying together and discovering Christ in their midst, this negative process will continue to be reversed. It is amazing how much understanding can be engendered when one approaches another individual or group with a loving attitude. On the other hand, to attempt to deal with another individual toward whom you are mistrustful or even hateful is a fruitless undertaking.

The Decree on Ecumenism makes clear that for a true dialogue with other Christian communities to be honest, the basic differences that continue to exist should be clearly understood and delineated. Differences that have endured for more than 450 years simply cannot be ignored. An attitude of ecumenical romanticism would be foolish and ultimately injurious to the promotion of a sound Christian unity. Since Vatican II, the many formal dialogues that have been undertaken between Roman Catholicism and Lutheran, Episcopal, Presbyterian, and other Christian communities have been very fruitful because the various differences have been honestly examined and discussed in a clear-minded fashion. The results have been startling and mutually enriching even though there is still much work to be done from a theological point of view. But there has been a good beginning.

The Church is presently living "between the times" in the sense that the style of church life that existed from the sixteenth century until Vatican II is now being replaced by the style of church life inaugurated at the council. Many areas of church life are undergoing modification, and this is clearly the case in the area of Christian relationships. Christian reunion cannot simply be left to the "experts." Parishes must continue to promote mutual dialogue, common action, and common prayer services if Christian ecumenism is to be successful. It was Christ himself who prayed that his followers might all be one. As long as Christian communities remain divided, the division itself will remain a counter-sign to the world-at-large, especially when various denominations attack other Christian groups in an unloving manner.

Summary

Protestant ecumenism received its impetus from the vast expansion of the foreign missionary movement in the nineteenth century.

Denominational divisiveness proved to be an obstacle and even a scandal in foreign lands. A symbol of the attempt to come to terms with Protestant disunity was the Edinburgh Conference in 1910. Edinburgh had limited success, but it created a new spirit for many and spawned a number of important conferences that ultimately led to the formation of the World Council of Churches in 1948.

It was through Vatican II that the Catholic Church wholeheartedly entered the ecumenical movement. *The Decree on Ecumenism* recognizes the "ecclesical reality" of Eastern Orthodox and of Protestant Christianity, and it gives very specific direction for ecumenical activities. Three areas are encouraged in regard to ecumenical sharing: common dialogue, common action, and common worship. In the years since Vatican II, considerable progress has been made in all three areas. But there is still much work to be done.

The Catholic-Jewish Dialogue

In recent years much has happened positively in Jewish-Catholic relations. Historic antagonism between the faith communities has been diminished. Again, using Vatican II as a paradigm, we can trace the development of the dialogue now taking place.

The Declaration on the Relationship of the Church to Non-Christian Religions, issued at Vatican II on October 28, 1965, contains a statement on Jewish-Christian relations entitled *Nostra Aetate.*[9] This statement is quite brief, and yet it contains several very important principles. It maintains, for example, that the covenant God made with the people of Israel, as recorded in their scriptures, is irrevocable. The statement also affirms that the Christian church is a partner in the covenant with the God of Israel, although the exact relationship between what Christians refer to as the Old Israel and the New Israel, the Old Testament and the New Testament, remains a problem and an apt subject of the dialogue that has begun between the Jewish and Catholic communities. Finally, in this document, the Catholic Church explicitly rejects any thought of Jewish collective guilt for the death of Jesus and all theories that might suggest the contemporary Jewish people as anything less than the chosen people of a divine covenant.

Approximately nine years later, the Commission for Religious Relations with the Jewish People, which is located at the Vatican and headed by Cardinal Jan Willebrands, issued on January 2, 1975, a new and very interesting document entitled "Guidelines and Suggestions for Implementing the Conciliar Declaration *Nostra Aetate.*"[10] This document advises Christians that they must strive to acquire a better knowledge of the basic components of the religious traditions of Judaism and that they must learn how Jews define themselves in the light of their own religious experience.[11] In turn, for the dialogue to be fruitful, Jews must learn how Christians define themselves.

In "Guidelines and Suggestions," stress is laid on the need to study the existing links between the Christian liturgy and the Jewish liturgy. It is also stated that, when commenting on biblical texts, emphasis should be laid on the continuity of the Christian faith with that of earlier covenants without minimizing those elements of Christianity that are original. Regarding liturgical readings, Christians are advised that care must be taken to see that homilies based on these readings do not distort their meaning, especially when referring to passages that seem to show the Jewish people in an unfavorable light. For example, it is observed that the phrase *the Jews,* as used in the Fourth Gospel, sometimes means, according to the context, "the leaders of the Jews" or "the adversaries of Jesus," but surely not the Jewish people in general. "Guidelines and Suggestions" also encouraged joint social action "in the spirit of the prophets," seeking social justice at every level: local, national, and international.

Generally speaking, "Guidelines and Suggestions" was favorably received by the Jewish community. But there is one area of controversy, a very important one, that eventually must be resolved. The document in question makes no mention of the State of Israel.[12] The Israeli press offered serious objection to this omission. And it is probably fair to admit that this is a valid complaint since it seems to violate the document's call to understand the Jewish people in terms of their own self-definition. The problem here centers on the fate of the Palestinian Arabs. Perhaps this highlights the necessity and the importance of the need for further dialogue as well as the need for the great openness of spirit and diffidence with respect to one's own prejudices that is necessary if the dialogue is to be successful.

Presently, the major obstacle to dialogue between Jews and Christians lies in the fact that for all practical purposes there simply has been no communication between them for almost two thousand years. This gap in communication was occasioned, to a great degree, by Christian theological prejudices against the Jewish people that were later highlighted to a shameful extent by persecutions of the Jews, both bloody and unbloody. As a result, there still exists much mutual ignorance of one another's religious convictions.

From the Christian standpoint, in order to prepare for open dialogue with Judaism, it can be of great benefit to study and appreciate the history of Jewish-Christian relations as well as the theological prejudices that have motivated Christian anti-Semitism through the centuries. There must be a corrective to centuries of Christian misrepresentation and neglect of Jewish history. Christianity's persecution of the Jews in past centuries is an area not generally known, at least in any detail, by the Christian populace, even though most Jews are painfully aware of this history.[13]

The roots of anti-Semitism in the Greco-Roman world, in the New Testament, among the Church Fathers, and, finally, in the social structures of Christendom must also be studied. It seems clear that at its root anti-Semitism springs directly from theological anti-Judaism.[14] It was Christian theology that developed the thesis of the eternal reprobate status of the Jew in history as a punishment for rejecting and killing Christ. This laid the foundation for the demonic view of the Jewish people that, in turn, fanned the flames of popular hatred. This hatred was not only inculcated by Christian preaching and biblical exegesis, but it became incorporated into the structure of both Christian canon law and the civil law formed under the Christian emperors, as expressed in the Codes of Theodosius (A.D. 428) and Justinian (sixth century).[15] The anti-Judaic laws of the Church and the Christian state laid the basis for the inferiorization of the civic and personal status of the Jews in the nineteenth century. Anti-Semitism arose once again in the twentieth century with incredible fury under Adolf Hitler.[16]

In June of 1985, the Vatican's Commission for Religious Relations with the Jews issued a document entitled "The Jews and Judaism in Preaching and Catechesis" in order to promote a greater and more informed awareness of Judaism in the religious education of Roman Catholics. This document adds greater light to the teaching of *Nostra Aetate* and to the 1975 "Guidelines and Suggestions." The text of this latest document can be found in *Ecumenical Trends,* published by the Greymoor Ecumenical Institute.[17] Many areas treated in the earlier church statements are enlarged upon. The document consists of six sections that discuss the following religious topics: teaching and Judaism, relations between the Old and New Testaments, the Jewish roots of Christianity, the Jews in the New Testament, the liturgy, and Judaism and Christianity in history.

The document reminds us of the dialogue begun at Vatican II and adds important nuances of historical and biblical awareness that can greatly enhance the Jewish-Christian relationship. Nevertheless, it remains true that the dialogue between Jews and Christians that began with the publication of *Nostra Aetate* in 1965 is still in an embryonic stage. If the dialogue is pursued in earnest much can be accomplished. Jews and Christians have a vital stake in seeking to overcome the widespread religious illiteracy in the United States and in the counterculture of paganism and hedonism that threatens all religiously based values. If the dialogue is indeed effective it will clarify, for both Christian and Jew, their understanding of one another's religious traditions and, in so doing, open new insights into the nature of the Godhead that each community professes.

If Christians and Jews can replace vague notions and stereotyped images about what it is that genuinely concerns their respective communities and work out joint approaches to their common religious and societal problems, they will have taken a positive step in the direction suggested at Vatican II in *Nostra Aetate* that called for "mutual knowledge and reciprocal respect."

Summary

In recent years much has happened positively in Jewish-Catholic relations. Historic antagonism between the faith communities has been broken through. At Vatican II the statement *Nostra Aetate* contained several important principles that helped to open up a deeper and more realistic Christian understanding of Judaism. Christians are understood as partners in the covenant with the God of Israel, and any thought of Jewish collective guilt for the death of Jesus is repudiated. Further, the Jewish people are understood to be the chosen people of a divine covenant.

Since Vatican II the Church has issued two formal statements concerning Jewish-Christian relations. In 1975, the document "Guidelines and Suggestions for Implementing the Conciliar Declaration *Nostra Aetate*" was issued. In 1985, the Vatican's Commission for Religious Relations with the Jews issued a document entitled "The Jews and Judaism in Preaching and Catechesis." Both statements have furthered the dialogue with Judaism and have helped enrich mutual understanding. Presently, the major obstacle to dialogue between Jews and Christians continues to lie in the fact that, for all practical purposes, there simply has been no dialogue between the two faith communities for almost two thousand years.

Study Questions

1. What is the meaning of *ecumenical* as used in this chapter?
2. Describe the sources of antipathy between Catholics and Protestants in the past four-and-a-half centuries.
3. What is the primary role of the World Council of Churches?
4. Describe four major themes that are found in *The Decree on Ecumenism*.
5. In regard to ecumenical sharing three areas are singled out in *The Decree on Ecumenism*. Briefly discuss each of these areas.
6. What important principles are found in the statement *Nostra Aetate* concerning Jewish-Christian relations?
7. In the 1975 statement "Guidelines and Suggestions for Implementing the Conciliar Declaration *Nostra Aetate*," what additional principles concerning Jewish-Christian relations are given?

8

The Charismatic Movement (Renewal)

The **charismatic** movement has reminded Catholics of the role of the Holy Spirit in the life of the Church. Previous to the inception of the charismatic renewal in the 1960s, the Holy Spirit was not stressed in Catholic thinking in the same manner as it is today. And yet the Holy Spirit is the Paraclete (helper) promised by Jesus who will be with the Church until the Second Coming (see John 14:26). In the New Testament we learn how vital the Holy Spirit is to the life of the Christian community. We read of the transformation of the disciples by the reception of the Spirit at Pentecost, which marks the birth of the Church (Acts 2:3ff.). The presence of the Spirit manifests itself externally in such phenomena as the gifts of tongues and prophecy (I Cor. 12–15) and directs the officers of the Church in important decisions (Acts 13:2, 15:28, and 20:28). The list of the power of the Holy Spirit goes on and on as we read the pages of the New Testament.

Perhaps most important for the Church of today as well as for the Church of the future is the reminder the entire community receives from charismatic Catholics of the dynamic role of the Holy Spirit in the life of the Church. Those participating in the charismatic renewal lift up the teaching that the Holy Spirit is not restricted to those who belong to the charismatic renewal but rather is given to the entire Christian community. If there is to be an overall renewal of the Church, it will only be accomplished—all else not withstanding—through prayer and the power of the Holy Spirit. Surely it was by the power of the Holy Spirit that Vatican II was convened and brought to such a successful conclusion. The council explicitly teaches that it is the Holy Spirit who renews the Church. In *The Dogmatic Constitution on the Church* we read, "By the power of the Gospel He [the Holy Spirit] makes the Church grow, *perfectly renews her*, and leads her to perfect union with her Spouse [emphasis mine]."[1] And yet the charismatic renewal, despite its contributions, has confused and, at times, angered those who are not involved in this seemingly new episode in the history of the Church.

It is obvious that many American Catholics are, in fact, greatly disturbed by the charismatic renewal that has been occurring in the Church since the conclusion of Vatican II. Even though many of those same Catholics have no significant firsthand experience of either Catholic charismatics or Protestant pentecostals, they associate the two groups with one another and feel that the "holy rollers" they heard so much about in their youth really have no place within Catholicism. After all, such people seem to be fanatics, and their religion is fundamentalist, anti-intellectual, and anti-institutional. Their fundamentalism makes them intellectually inflexible and dogmatic in all their attitudes to the point where they confuse piety and theology. Such a pattern makes them morally rigoristic. Further, they "speak in tongues," which to an outsider appears to be nothing more than irrational babbling. They stress **Spirit-baptism** and the experience of the Holy Spirit. If religion is based primarily on experience, aren't they on a collision course with their membership in a structured church? And the objections go on. Yet the Catholic charismatic renewal has not clashed with the hierarchy. As a matter of fact, the charismatic movement operates within the Church and with the blessing of the American bishops. We will analyze the renewal to see why this is so, and we will also try to clarify some of the misconceptions those outside the movement still hold. But at the outset it should be made clear that there are many forms of piety within the Church that Catholics are free to accept or reject depending upon their own dispositions. The charismatic renewal is one example.

In the United States the charismatic renewal began at Duquesne University, Pittsburgh, in 1963. It was not accidental that this occurred during the early months of Vatican II. The council itself in *The Decree on the Ministry and Life of Priests* put "renewal of the Church" in first place among the "three pastoral goals of the Council," which it lists as "inner renewal of the Church, the spread of the Gospel throughout the world, and dialogue with the modern world."[2] And, as we have seen, the council teaches that it is the Holy Spirit who renews the Church. The council also teaches that the role of the Holy Spirit is to act as the giver of those gifts of the Spirit that lead to the renewal of the Church. *The Dogmatic Constitution on the Church* states, "By these gifts he [the Holy Spirit] makes them fit and ready to undertake the various tasks or offices advantageous for the renewal and upbuilding of the Church."[3] Many believe that this statement, among others, provided the theological foundation of a "charismatic renewal of the Church."[4]

There was debate at the council concerning the gifts or charisms of the Holy Spirit. Cardinal Ruffini argued that charisms have no important part to play in the life of the modern Church even though they were greatly in evidence in the apostolic era. He went on to say that such gifts (e.g., speaking in tongues and healing) subsequently became so rare as to have practically ceased. Cardinal Suenens's reply to Ruffini, which prevailed at the council, maintained that the charisms are not "peripheral or accidental phenomenon in the life of the Church, but rather are of vital importance for the building up of the mystical body."[5]

A logical question would then be, "How would such charisma manifest themselves in the concrete?" To answer this question it is first necessary to define what is meant by a **charism**. A charism is a manifestation of the Holy Spirit (1 Cor. 12:7), a coming to visibility of the Spirit who operates in each person for the common good (1 Cor. 12:6), that is, in the service of the Church and the world. Such charisms or gifts are many and are given by the Spirit at will. All Christians have such gifts, but they must be utilized if reform is to be effective. Indeed St. Paul taught that the Holy Spirit "distributes different gifts to different people just as he chooses" (1 Cor. 12:11). *The Dogmatic Constitution on the Church* states, "These charismatic gifts whether they be the most outstanding or the more simple and widely diffused, are to be received with thanksgiving and consolation, for they are exceedingly suitable and useful for the needs of the Church."[6] Such charisms manifest themselves in the concrete in every Catholic parish throughout the world. Parishioners would have a role and a ministry according to the gifts they had received from the spirit for the upbuilding of the community. And at the parish level each person would have the opportunity to use the gifts he or she had received under the leadership of their pastor. In a real sense, then, all Catholics are charismatic, and all are called to share their gifts with the entire Christian community.

But what of those who belong to the charismatic renewal in the narrower sense, namely, those who attend prayer meetings and are involved with Spirit-baptism, speaking in tongues, healing, and prophecy? These people tend to pray with their hands upraised and their eyes closed! Aren't they rather elitist in their attitude and perhaps even pharisaical? There is no easy answer to this question because some charismatics may well fit this description. But this would refer only to a small fringe of the renewal. Charismatics know that to concentrate only on the more extraordinary gifts of the Holy Spirit, or to claim to be superior Christians, is unacceptable.

Though the term *movement* is being used in reference to the charismatic renewal, it should be pointed out that the adherents of the renewal try to avoid this word since it carries some negative connotations. The term is borrowed from cultural anthropology and in many ways can be correctly applied to the renewal.[7] At the popular level, however, a kind of distortion often takes place by putting the term into a theological context. From this perspective, charismatic movement is used to refer to a kind of capturing of the Holy Spirit and his gifts by the members of the movement. Often those using the term in this narrower sense restrict the meaning of charism to the "word gifts" such as tongues, prophecy, interpretation, wisdom, and knowledge. Lest any such limiting connotation be placed on them, large numbers of Catholic charismatics no longer use the term *Catholic charismatic movement* and have instead adopted the term *Catholic charismatic renewal.* They have done so because those within the renewal do not claim to be the only ones who possess the Holy Spirit and the charisms. They know that these gifts belong to the entire Christian community. What they desire and pray will happen is that all members of the Church will open themselves up to the full spectrum of gifts that are offered by the Holy Spirit.

The Catholic charismatic renewal, as indicated earlier, began at Duquesne University in Pittsburgh in 1963 and soon took root at the University of Notre Dame and the University of Michigan as well. The renewal quickly spread, and by 1970 there were many prayer groups scattered throughout the United States. Spontaneous prayer meetings had been going on for several years before 1966 at both Duquesne and Notre Dame but now became infused with charismatic elements.

Though certain parallels can be found in the Wesleyan-Holiness tradition, the Catholic renewal drew heavily from contemporary Catholic spirituality. For example, many of the earliest members had belonged to the Cursillo movement that long had practiced small group spontaneous prayers as well as group reunions where participants spoke freely to one another of their experiences of Christ. So when the first group of Catholics from Duquesne, who were curious about and very interested in the phenomenon referred to as "baptism in the Holy Spirit," attended a neo-Pentecostal prayer meeting conducted by Methodists, Episcopalians, Presbyterians, and some members of denominational Pentecostal churches, they felt fairly comfortable. The meeting took place while sitting in a circle in a living room. The Catholics found the structure and many of the elements of the service rather similar to their own practice of group prayer. They soon started their own prayer meetings and structured it in a similar manner.

Most Catholic prayer groups have as few as ten and as many as one hundred participants. Prayer meetings, which form the core of the renewal, are usually held once a week, though this varies. They are often structured so that all sit in a circle facing one another. As groups become larger, seating is arranged in concentric circles. This arrangement encourages each member to share his or her particular gifts with the whole community. The emphasis is on the presence of Christ in the midst of his people. Stress is also placed on the priesthood of all the faithful and on the diversity of ministries to be found within the Church.

Generally a prayer meeting begins with the singing of hymns, although music is interspersed throughout the service. Handclapping and rhythmic bodily swaying often accompany the congregational singing. The leader of the meeting then welcomes everyone and encourages them to participate in faith and to focus their hearts on the Lord's presence in their midst. He or she also encourages all to use their spiritual gifts properly. The use of gifts occurs throughout the meeting. Spontaneous prayer regularly includes the use of tongues, prophecy, and testimony. Many groups choose a speaker to give testimony, teach, or preach. Following this, a few minutes of common silence is observed. Toward the end of the meeting members often express their personal intentions, needs, and requests for prayer.

In contrast to the Pentecostal order of service, Catholic prayer meetings usually do not end with an "altar call" or an invitation for those who do not belong to the group to ask for baptism in the Spirit at their initial meeting. Rather the meeting is directed toward worship in praise and thanksgiving to God the Almighty Father through Jesus as Lord and Savior that is carried out through the power of the Holy Spirit. Preparation for initiation into a Catholic charismatic prayer group occurs for the most part by means of a program that is called the "Life in the Spirit Seminar,"[8] which was developed by the Word of God, a charismatic community in Ann Arbor, Michigan. The seminar removes the event of Spirit-baptism from the realm of an isolated religious experience and places it in the context of a basic explanation of the Gospel, of conversion to Jesus, and of the need for the power of the Holy Spirit to live a full Christian life. The event of Spirit-baptism is placed at the center of the ongoing need of a mature Christian life of prayer, study, service, and involvement in the Christian community. The "Life in the Spirit Seminar" is made up of seven instructions that are given by the leader of the seminar team. He or she is aided by several men and women from the prayer group who serve as team members. Small discussion groups are formed, and all pray that the newcomers may commit or recommit their lives to Christ and accept the workings of the Holy Spirit in their lives.

Praying for baptism in the Spirit takes place during the fifth session of the seminars. The session opens with some preliminary remarks from the leader who explains that the group will make a commitment to Christ and that there will be prayers of exorcism and the laying on of hands. Then, after an opening hymn and a period of prayer, those who are praying over the candidates exorcise each of them and lay hands on them, praying for them to be baptized in the Spirit. Exorcism here refers to casting out evil spirits or telling evil spirits to leave a person or place. It does not imply that a person is possessed by evil spirits. When everyone is finished praying, the leader calls the whole group together. By this time some of the newcomers have usually received the gift of tongues, and those who have not are asked to pray for this gift. Everyone who has completed the seminar is asked to remain in the prayer group and to continue the process that has begun by joining one of the growth courses or Bible studies offered by the group.

Spirit-baptism, which is such an important concept in the renewal, refers to a group of Christians praying over one of its members so that he or she will receive the Holy Spirit in its fullness, as did the apostles on Pentecost Sunday. The term also refers to the divine response to this prayer, especially as it affects the life of the person who is being "baptized." Some Pentecostal churches identify Spirit-baptism with the reception of the gift of tongues, no doubt because tongues (**glossolalia**) is a very fundamental charism. But this is not so in Catholicism. To make such an identification is seen to be presumptuous since it is up to the will of the Holy Spirit to deal with each person according to that individual's specific spiritual needs. Catholic charismatics simply disagree with those who demand the gift of tongues as the only certain proof of the presence of the Spirit or who regard the gift as an absolute precondition for authentic possession of the other charismatic gifts.

Some Catholics are afraid that those in the charismatic renewal may be practicing a fraudulent version of the sacrament of confirmation. But this is not the case. Spirit-baptism is not understood to be a sacrament. The group that prays with an individual gathers around that person not to administer a sacrament but because they wish to express, by an external sign—namely, the laying on of hands—that they are joining their prayers to those of the person who is seeking a fuller share in the gifts of the Holy Spirit. Baptism and confirmation are sacraments of initiation into the living of the Christian life and can be received only once, although it is believed that the special graces of each sacrament are present throughout one's life. And so it is deemed appropriate that a confirmed Christian turn to God to beg for greater docility to the grace of confirmation, and that his or her prayer should be supported by other members of the Christian community. Those who thus join their prayers with those of the person in question are expressing their solidarity not only with the individual but also with the bishop who confirmed him or her. In Spirit-baptism individuals, in effect, are asking the Holy Spirit to take them in their present state of spiritual development and to transform them. Spirit-baptism is basically a prayer to the Father in the name of Jesus that the Holy Spirit will come upon a person who has decided to break with sin and seek the light of Christ. It is a form of prayer that seeks the individual to be fully docile to the inspirations of the Holy Spirit and completely open to whatever charismatic gifts the Holy Spirit may offer. In terms of its effects it is commonly observable that those who receive Spirit-baptism have an experience with the triune God that produces a new or greater desire for prayer and a stronger desire to know the Scriptures. There is also a deeper awareness of God's presence as well as an increase of love together with a greater ability to express that love.

What most intrigues many people about the charismatic renewal is the gift of speaking in tongues. Most charismatics deplore the excessive emphasis on glossolalia in discussions about their movement. Yet this phenomenon inevitably attracts attention because it is so unusual and spectacular in nature. Many outsiders consider it bizarre and irritating and, most of all, unnecessary for the practice of Christian living, although it is very commonly practiced among Pentecostal and charismatic Christians. Why is this done and what does it mean? Before proceeding further it might prove helpful to note that many great movements of spiritual renewal through the years have often emphasized notions that seemed to be unusual and even bizarre such as the gift of tears, fasting, the breathing techniques of **hesychasm**, and the **yoga** and **zen** postures of meditation. These practices, however, serve as catalysts for opening spiritual paths that have been blocked by inhibitions and barriers that are often erected by various peoples and that stand in the way of a vital relationship with God.

The word *glossolalia* comes from two Greek words: *glossa,* which means "tongues" and *lalein,* which means "to speak." The verb *lalein* can signify any utterance of sound whether it be intelligent or intelligible. *Glossa* can mean "language" in the broadest sense such as that used by whales or elephants, for example. It can also refer to a specific language in the narrower sense, such as English or French, in which specific words and grammar are used. In reference to the gift of glossolalia, it can be used collectively by a whole group or by an individual. When an individual speaks in tongues it is not mumbling or gibberish. Rather as René Laurentin observes, the speaker "utters a rhythmic sequence of distinct, articulated, structured sounds (or syllables) that possess a degree of coherence and phonetic clarity."9

When a person speaks in tongues he or she is not delirious or in a trance. The speaker remains in full possession of his or her senses, but what is said is usually not understood by the person speaking or the people who are present. The speaker is aware of what he or she is doing and of what is happening outside the experience and can cease speaking in tongues at any point. Someone in the group inevitably is given the gift of interpretation of tongues, which refers to an intuitive understanding of the meaning. Interpretation does not refer to a translation of what has been articulated.

But why speak in tongues at all? Why not simply speak in a rational and, even, spontaneous manner when addressing God? Does not the use of glossolalia put religion in a bad light and hold it up to the ridicule and disdain of many believers and nonbelievers alike? To answer these questions it is necessary to point out that glossolalia is a very specific mode of prayer. Those who speak in tongues agree that to do so has a liberating effect. It removes many inhibitions and diminishes the fear of approaching the ineffable God. It aids one to pray more frequently and to become more aware both of one's own sinfulness and of God's greatness. It strengthens intercessory prayer, which is often inhibited, as St. Paul tells us in Rom. 8:26 by the fact that "we cannot choose words in order to pray properly." Glossolalia is a kind of sacred language. To speak in tongues is also to use a kind of sacred language for prayer. Until recently this role was played by the use of Latin during Catholic Mass, which was a kind of sacred language set over ordinary language. The fact that so many Catholics greatly miss the use of Latin helps explain that it is not by chance that the use of glossolalia appeared within Catholicism at about the same time that Latin disappeared. Glossolalia, then, is a preconceptual, nonrational language by which one speaks to God as the Wholly Other.

Glossolalia, like the other gifts of the Holy Spirit, is given to render Christians more docile to the spirit of Christ so that the recipients might become more like Christ, the Spirit-filled Messiah. It is a gift of prayer and, in its use, as is true of all the gifts, it must be regulated by the law of Christ-like love as St. Paul reminds us in 1 Cor. 12–14.

Some would still agree with St. Augustine who wrote that certain charismatic gifts, among them the gift of tongues, were given by the Holy Spirit to the apostolic community to help enable the establishment of the Church. Augustine went on to argue that once the Church was formed into a cohesive whole, these gifts were withdrawn and replaced by other gifts. This is a defensible thesis, but it cannot conclusively be proven or disproven.[10] What is certain, however, is that this theory is but one hypothesis among many in reference to the purpose of the charismatic gifts. It is surely not a dogma of the Church. And since the Holy Spirit is free to grant his gifts any time and any place, it is presumptuous to think that he is limited by the theological utterances of even one as great as St. Augustine, or by any other theologian.

There are several dangers inherent in the Catholic charismatic renewal.

1. There is the danger of *separation,* that is, of leaving communion with Rome and establishing an independent

community, as has been evidenced at times. Yet the charismatic movement generally has been marked by a firm attachment to the Church and its leadership. There simply has been no confrontation of any significance against church hierarchy. To avoid such problems, prayer groups within the United States rarely celebrate Mass at their meetings in order not to entice members away from their parish Masses. To avoid competition with the Sunday services in their parishes, charismatics normally avoid having their weekly meetings on a Saturday or Sunday.

2. There is the danger of *fundamentalism,* that is, the naively literal and "obvious" interpretation of Scripture. Such an attitude ties the spirit to the letter of the Bible. Surely some Catholic charismatics are fundamentalist in this sense. But they are a distinct minority, and when they do dominate it usually indicates a manifestation of poor leadership in the group. On the whole, the movement is quite open to contemporary exegesis. At the same time, Catholic charismatics do practice a straightforward reading of the Bible that emphasizes the spiritual nourishment that can be gained by so doing. But, generally speaking, they are no more fundamentalists than other Catholics, and usually are far more devoted to reading and listening to the Word of God.

3. A third danger is that of *emotionalism,* meaning that charismatics tend to focus on feeling at the expense of reason. It is certainly true that the movement values the emotive level and encourages the expression of feelings. In doing so, there can be an overemphasis on the emotions. Basically, however, this movement recognizes that we must love God with our whole person, which includes not only the intellect and will, but the emotions as well. Everyone is different, and some people are very unemotional. But obviously many people join this movement, at least in part, because they do feel a need to express their emotions as they worship Christ, who is the "Lord of the Dance." This aspect of the charismatic movement should not be seen as a liability, but as an achievement.

4. A fourth danger, and one that brings the most frequent and serious criticism of the charismatic movement, is that it is *too introverted* and, thus, turns its membership away from

involvement in areas of social justice. The complaint is that charismatics focus on individual relationships but not on their responsibilities to society. This complaint was far more common in the late 1960s and early 1970s during the era of the Vietnam War. And it had a basis in circumstance. But as the charismatic movement has matured, so has the involvement of many prayer groups in areas of social concern. Today it would be fair to say that those in the charismatic movement are involved in areas of social justice in at least as great a measure as is true of the Christian population in general. This, however, is not to discount the fact that there seems to be an overall lack of participation at the political level and the level of social justice by Christians in the United States.

Much remains to be discussed concerning the Catholic charismatic renewal such as detailed explanations of the meaning of *healing, prophecy,* and other gifts. Books that treat these subjects will be listed in the "Further Readings" section. As for now, it can be said that the charismatic renewal is serving as a remedy for many who had been suffering from spiritual aridity. Charismatic communities are not only dynamic vehicles for prayer, but they also provide an outlet for like-minded Christians who are attempting to develop deeper relationships with Christ. This emphasis on community is an important element in the charismatic renewal and is necessary for the reinvigorating of the Church as a whole. The charismatic renewal is also rediscovering the Gospel as the "good news" and as a source of rejuvenation for true Christian living. The movement continues to profit from the enthusiasm that characterizes all beginnings. The scope and historical importance of the movement will be determined by the test of time. It already seems evident that in the coming years only a relatively small percentage of American Catholics will be members of the charismatic renewal. But the importance of the movement, both now and in the future, will remain essentially constant. Charismatic Catholics will continue to serve as an important reminder to the Catholic population as a whole that the continual renewal of the Church is the work of the Holy Spirit, and that the gifts of the Holy Spirit, in some fashion, are given to all Christians. Since all are called to the perfection of holiness, all will be expected to share their gifts with the Christian community for the continual upbuilding of the Body of Christ.

Summary

The charismatic renewal began in the United States in the mid-1960s. Perhaps most important for the Church of today as well as for the Church of the future is the reminder the entire Christian community receives from charismatic Catholics of the dynamic role of the Holy Spirit in the life of the Church, and that the Holy Spirit is not restricted to those who belong to the charismatic renewal, but is given to the entire Christian community. A further reminder is provided by charismatic Catholics that all Christians are called to a life of prayer and devotion to the sacred Scriptures. If there is to be an overall renewal of the Church, it will only be accomplished, all else not withstanding, by Christians who continually open themselves to the power of the Holy Spirit.

Many Catholics are disturbed by the charismatic renewal and feel that those who belong to the movement are "holy rollers." Yet the renewal operates within the Church and with the blessing of the American bishops. There are safeguards in relation to the gifts of the Spirit, such as speaking in tongues and healing, that must be observed. To this end "Life in the Spirit Seminars" are conducted to provide proper theological and spiritual direction.

When noncharismatics hear the term *Spirit-baptism* they are often afraid that those in the charismatic renewal may be practicing a fraudulent version of the sacrament of confirmation. But this is not the case. Spirit-baptism is not understood to be a sacrament. The group that prays with an individual for Spirit-baptism gathers around that person not to administer a sacrament but to express, by an external sign, namely, the laying on of hands, that they are joining their prayers to those of the person who is seeking a fuller share in the gifts of the Holy Spirit. In terms of its effect, it is commonly observable that those who receive Spirit-baptism have an experience of the triune God that produces a new or greater desire for prayer and a stronger desire to know the Scriptures.

The gift of speaking in tongues (glossolalia) offends many noncharismatics. But to speak in tongues is to use a kind of sacred language for prayer. Glossolalia, like the other gifts of the Holy Spirit, is given to render Christians more docile to the Spirit of Christ so that the recipients might become more like Christ, the Spirit-filled Messiah. It is a gift of prayer and its use, as is true of all the gifts, must be regulated by the law of Christ-like love as St. Paul reminds us in

1 Cor. 12–14. Yet there are dangers inherent in the use of these gifts that must be controlled through solid theological teaching, as St. Paul admonishes.

Study Questions

1. Give a brief history of the Catholic charismatic renewal in the United States. Where did it begin? Why did it occur?
2. Describe a charismatic prayer meeting.
3. Describe a "Life in the Spirit Seminar."
4. What is meant by the term *Spirit-baptism?*
5. Explain the meaning of the word *glossolalia.*
6. Why do charismatics feel the need to speak in tongues?
7. Discuss four dangers that are inherent in the Catholic charismatic renewal.

9

Women and Ministry

The Role of Women in the Ministry of the Church

Many serious questions concerning the role of Catholic women in the official ministry of the Church have been raised in recent years. Often the particular response to such questions produces great emotion. Some consider the idea of women serving the Church as deacons or priests to be a ludicrous betrayal of the Bible and of Catholic tradition and see such a notion as just another aspect of the kind of stridency they associate with the women's movement in general. After all, does not St. Paul say that women must maintain absolute silence in church (1 Tim. 2:9–15), wear head coverings (1 Cor. 11:10), and perform no official functions in the church except to teach younger women? Another and quite different response comes from those who maintain that the time is long past due for Catholic women to be given the same opportunities as men in serving the Church. Women by baptism are members of Christ's "royal priesthood" and we read in Gal. 3:28 that in Christ there is "neither male nor female but all are one in him." Those who respond this way believe that quotations given about silence, head coverings, and the like are simply cultural phenomena of St. Paul's day and, therefore, should be seen as historically conditioned statements that are not to be applied literally. In order to arrive at a deeper insight into the reasons for the present controversy, we will have to consider the scriptural references already given in relationship to St. Paul's attitude toward women in public ministry, together with what we read in the Gospels concerning Jesus' attitude and his statements about women. Though space will not allow a complete treatment of these biblical passages, insights into relevant scriptural statements will be given that should shed more light on the issues under discussion. The praxis of the early Church must also be considered as must the official teaching of today's Vatican.

The questions concerning the rights of Catholic women to participate in the fullness of church life are certainly a part of the consciousness-raising in regard to women that is taking place at so many levels throughout society. This phenomenon began about two hundred years ago as the result of the eighteenth-century Enlightenment that advocated the natural rights of every individual, including women. It is also the product of several larger movements since that time including, among others, the Industrial Revolution, the educational revolution, the suffragist movement, and finally World War I and World War II. Although the Industrial Revolution produced some very negative results such as inhumane working conditions and acute social dislocation, it spawned many positive breakthroughs as well. For the first time in Western society jobs were open to women outside the home on a large scale. Their world had widened. Also in the nineteenth century, the educational revolution made elementary education available to females as well as males, while higher education was also made available to some women. The suffragist movement gained the general right for women to vote in public elections in the United States immediately after World War I. Full citizenship raised their self-esteem and gave women an important tool to promote further reforms. World War I and World War II, which gave women greater opportunities in the job market while many men served in the military, also helped buttress women's self-esteem. A natural concomitant of all these changes was the stimulus to challenge many of the traditional ideas and regulations that the male-dominated society of the West inherited from the Greco-Roman tradition. And since the Church is a vital part of society, it is not surprising that important questions are being raised concerning the role of women in the life of the Church.

As a matter of fact, Vatican II asserted in *The Decree on the Apostolate of the Laity* that "since in our times women have an ever more active share in the whole life of society, it is very important that they participate more widely also in the various fields of the Church's apostolate."[1] This attitude was reaffirmed at the third Synod of Bishops that met in Rome in 1971: "We also urge that women should have their own share of responsibility and participation in the community life of society and likewise of the Church."[2] And yet women are, in fact and by law, excluded from the official ordained ministry of the Church. Both Pope Paul VI and now Pope John Paul II have made it very clear that the Church has no intention of changing the status of women vis-à-vis ordination into the official ministry of the Church. Both based their positions on the constant tradition of the Church. The same argument was used by the Sacred Congregation for the Doctrine of the Faith in 1976, which wrote that this constant tradition was rooted in the practice of Jesus and the apostles. It summarized the present position of the hierarchy with the statement that "the Church, in fidelity to the example of the Lord, does not consider herself authorized to admit women to priestly ordination." The text can be found in *Women Priests: A Catholic Commentary on the Vatican Declaration,* edited by Leonard Swidler and Arlene Swidler.[3]

It is clear that the crux of the problem with the ordination of women is rooted in the biblical interpretation of the practice of Jesus and the apostles as found in the New Testament. It is also evident that on the subject of women and ministry, many have read the Scriptures from the point of view of a theological presupposition that women are inferior to men, as based on the teachings of the Church Fathers, including both St. Augustine and St. Thomas Aquinas. The question facing biblical studies today is whether, such negative presuppositions not withstanding, the New Testament church allowed or disallowed women to serve in the ordained ministry of the Church. Even such a profound scripture scholar as Fr. Raymond Brown in his book *Biblical Reflections on Crises Facing the Church* disclaims his ability to determine the answer to this question in any absolute sense.[4] He simply attempts to make a contribution that, though partial, will help those seeking a solution to this problem.

Likewise, we are presenting a synopsis of some of the more important elements of the problem, not a full treatment of the issues. Therefore, we can only hope that what is said will provide readers with salient information and will encourage them to study the Scriptures with a fresher understanding of what the Bible may or may not be saying concerning ordained female ministers. In treating this issue, it will be necessary to ask if Jesus called women to the ministry and whether or not women participated in the ministry of the New Testament church. Finally, it will be important to determine whether or not there is anything inherent in the character of Christian ministry as found in the New Testament that would mandate the inclusion or exclusion of women.

Much of the received tradition regarding women's roles in the Church was established by the writings of the Church Fathers from the second through sixth centuries. These early theologians discussed women in a contemptuous manner, equating them with Eve, who is herself seen as the archetypal seductress. They recognize that women are baptized and redeemed by Christ; yet they seem to question whether women are fully redeemed. They wonder often whether women are not still cursed by God. Indeed, a dark note of doubt and denigration runs through all of patristic literature. Tertullian, a clergyman of the North African church writing early in the third century, summarizes this attitude when discussing the manner in which women should dress. He writes that a woman should dress "as Eve, mourning and repentant, that by every garb of penitence she might the more fully expiate that which she derives from Eve—the ignoring of the first sin, and the odium of human perdition . . . and do you not know that you are an Eve? The sentence of God on this sex of yours lives in this age: the guilt must of necessity live, too."[5]

Another African clergyman, St. Cyril of Alexandria, wrote that ever since Eve every woman is "death's deaconess" and her sex is "especially dishonored" by God and by men (*In Mattheum,* Matt. 28:9). But, on the other hand, "the male sex is ever elect of God, because it is a warrior breed, because it is capable of coming to spiritual vigor, *capable of sowing seed,* of teaching the rest, of tracing its steps to the mature measure of the fullness of Christ [emphasis mine]" (*In Mattheum,* Matt. 14:21).

St. Augustine (d. A.D. 430) regarded sexuality as residing within the animal domain and not properly human at all. He felt that since venereal pleasure is very intense, the sex act is alien to and overwhelms the spirit. Marital intercourse is, therefore, materially evil and is a venial sin. But since woman attracts and arouses man sexually, she is the more guilty party. Again, woman is cast in the role of a temptress, another Eve.

St. Thomas Aquinas, who died in 1274, dominated theology for centuries following his death just as St. Augustine had prevailed in Christianity during the centuries after he died. Their influence on present-day Catholic thinking is still enormous. St. Thomas, following the Greek philosopher Aristotle as well as the thinking of St. Paul and St. Augustine, believed man to be the true human being and woman a misbegotten male. Even though woman is the indispensable partner to man in the work of procreation, she is ontologically inferior and subject to him as to her head.[6] St. Thomas also believed that man's superiority is demonstrated in the act of intercourse since he bears the more active and therefore nobler role, while woman is passive and submissive.[7] Such misunderstandings about embryonic development further strengthened the male sense of superiority. While past ignorance of biology and consequent attitudes are understandable, the continuation of the sexual stereotype of the inferior female, and of woman as "another Eve," with all the implied negative connotations, cannot be easily tolerated. The Church needs a new anthropology that can no longer be the result of the male experience alone, but must well represent both male and female.[8]

Several nontheological factors impinge on the question of women serving in the active ministry. One factor is economic, namely, the availability of jobs. This has been a serious problem among various Protestant denominations—Episcopal, Lutheran, and Presbyterian, in particular—where there is an ample number of male ministers. Thus, some clergy fear that the ordination of women will create job shortages in some areas. But in Roman Catholicism a serious lack of priests is becoming more obvious with each passing year, and lack of available positions upon ordination does not seem to be a problem for some time to come. In some parishes Catholic nuns are serving virtually as assistant pastors in that they distribute communion, teach courses in Scripture, counsel, and perform other tasks that traditionally have been the duties of the ordained clergy. Such activities promote consciousness-raising, and for many the question inevitably will arise concerning the priesthood of women. If women are capable and accepted in all these pastoral areas, then why are they denied the fullness of the priesthood?

Another factor is sexual. If women are ordained to the priesthood and are celibate and working with male celibate priests, won't this be very tempting? Won't they fall in love and leave the priesthood to get married? Think of the scandal this would cause! But this is to beg the question since a male-dominated Church has already had many defections and scandals. A third factor, and one that cannot easily be ignored, comes from the fact that the Church is international. In the

United States there is a strong movement advocating female priests. American women are well-educated and are now accepted in many areas where they were once not permitted, be it in business, politics, or whatever. But this is not the case in Italy, Poland, and many other nations. Their cultures are not so open to women. The question here devolves on whether or not the ordination of female priests would be granted for the universal Church or for particular nations. If granted for the Church in its entirety, then the problems for women in many countries would be insurpassable for some time to come. If granted for particular countries, the results would be more positive. But would the Church ever act in this way? Many think not. A fourth factor is ecumenical. If Rome allows women to be ordained to the priesthood it may jeopardize reunion with the Orthodox, Anglican, and other Christian communions who do not accept the ordination of women into the priesthood. Yet all branches of the Church must be led by the Scripture and trust in the Holy Spirit for guidance. Reunion can only be valid if it is established on solid foundations. The question of women's ordination cannot be ruled out other than on biblical grounds.

Other objections have been raised, but it seems clear that women must first be given more public roles in the life of the Church so that a fair judgment can be made and prejudices broken down concerning the ordination of women. Women are now lectors and eucharistic ministers at Mass. If girls were allowed to serve the priest at Mass it would be another step toward greater visibility. Finally, as more and more female theologians produce scholarly and popular works, we will eventually be in a much better position to discuss the ordination of women as priests in an intelligent fashion.

Perhaps the most difficult objection to women's ordination— because it is most deeply rooted—is the supposition that in the Bible God has given a blueprint of the Church in which all the basic structures are worked out. Fr. Raymond Brown describes such an understanding in *Biblical Reflection on Crises Facing the Church*. As he notes, such blueprint thinking is not dead, but it has "little scholarly popularity."[9] For those who hold such a view there can be no ordination of women since this is simply not found in the blueprint. But there is another viewpoint that Brown refers to, for want of a better term, as "in-between ecclesiology."[10] This ecclesiology is somewhere between a blueprint model and an erector-set model. The latter is at the opposite pole from blueprint ecclesiology in that it maintains that Christians are free to go ahead and build the Church as utility directs. Brown sees such erector-set ecclesiology as paying too little heed to the will of Christ, the tradition of the Church, and the guidance of the Holy Spirit. He opts for in-between ecclesiology because it recognizes that history and sociology almost certainly played a role in the development of church structure, especially the pattern of the single bishop and the college of priests surrounding Jesus that had emerged by the end of the first century. The earliest statements about this structure see it as symbolically representing the model of Jesus surrounded by his disciples. Thus the will of Christ has meaning in such ecclesiology, even if the working out of that will is conceived in a more subtle way than is proposed in blueprint ecclesiology.

But precisely because there is no blueprint per se, it is not inconceivable, in view of new historical circumstances, that the Church through in-between ecclesiology can continue its discovery of Christ's will. Such a discovery may imply change and may eventually even lead to the ordination of women as priests.

Summary

In the past two centuries, beginning with the Enlightenment of the eighteenth century, consciousness-raising with regard to women has been taking place. This phenomenon is the product of several larger movements such as the Industrial Revolution, the educational revolution, the suffragist movement, and, finally, World War I and World War II. As a matter of fact, Vatican II, in *The Decree on the Apostolate of the Laity,* stresses that women should participate in the various fields of the church's apostolate. Yet women are still excluded from the official ordained ministry of the Church.

Much of the received tradition regarding women's roles in the Church was established by the writings of the Church Fathers during the second through sixth centuries. These early theologians discussed women in a contemptuous manner. A dark note of denigration runs through all of patristic literature, and is found in the writings of St. Augustine and of St. Thomas Aquinas as well. They saw woman as "another Eve," with all the implied negative connotations in such a symbol. The Church clearly needs a new anthropology that represents both male and female.

There are several nontheological factors that impinge on the question of women serving in the active ministry. One factor is economic, the availability of jobs, but this would not be a problem in Catholicism for the foreseeable future. Another factor is sexual. Male and female celibates working together could cause unnecessary temptation, although this objection begs the question since the Church with only male celebates has had many defections. Of the remaining factors, perhaps the most telling is the ecumenical. If Rome allows women to be ordained to the priesthood, it may jeopardize reunion with the Orthodox, Anglican, and other Christian communities. No doubt. But all these branches of the Church must be led by the Scriptures and trust in the Holy Spirit for guidance. It is not inconceivable that in view of new historical circumstances the Church will continue its discovery of Christ's will. Such a discovery may imply change, even regarding the ordination of women as priests.

Jesus and Women

In order to understand Jesus' attitude toward women and ministry one must recall the manner in which women were treated in first-century Judaism. Women were described in rabbinic literature as temptresses, vain and frivolous. Though not common, polygamy was still permitted during Jesus' lifetime. Male children were viewed as preferable to female children. Every morning Jewish men prayed in thanksgiving to God that they had been created male and not female. Wives were generally confined to the home and in the presence of others they had to cover their heads and wear veils. Women were not permitted to receive any education. Their testimony was not accepted as evidence at court. Legally, women were considered the property of men. In the Jewish religion they were subordinate and silent and were not counted among the *minyan,* the quorum of ten men who had to be present for worship to take place. And the list goes on. In short, it was a man's world.

Despite the strictures of his society, Jesus showed a high regard for women. His preaching revealed a remarkable balance for the concerns of men and women. For example we read:

> The kingdom of heaven is like a mustard seed which a man took and sowed in his field.

Matt. 13:31

The kingdom of heaven is like the yeast a woman took and mixed in with three measures of flour till it was leavened all through.

Matt. 13:33

Then of two men in the fields one is taken, one left; of two women at the millstone grinding one is taken, one left.

Matt. 24:40–41

There are many other examples where Jesus addressed women with the same respect and concern he displayed toward men. Women are spiritually akin to Jesus as are men: "Here are my mother and my brothers. Anyone who does the will of my Father in heaven, he is my brother and sister and mother" (Matt. 12:50). Christ performs miracles for women as well as men (see Matt. 8:14–15, 9:24–26, 9:20–22, and 15:22–28). As a matter of fact, in none of Jesus's words and deeds does he give any suggestion that the spiritual potentialities of women are inferior to those of men. And in regard to marriage Jesus boldly stated, "The man who divorces his wife and marries another is guilty of adultery against her" (Mark 10:11). Previously, no one had taught that adultery could be committed against a wife. Adultery was always understood as a crime against the property right of a husband. Jesus' meeting with the Samaritan woman at the well has only recently been understood in all its revolutionary significance. That Jesus spoke to a woman—and a Samaritan at that—in a public place was scandalous. It broke all conventions. Hearing Jesus' message of good news, she hurries to tell it to her fellow townspeople. And Jesus does not prevent her from doing so because she is a woman. It is also clear that certain women were disciples of Jesus, another unusual fact of his ministry. All four evangelists agree that women were the first witnesses to, and first preachers of, the resurrection of Jesus. In other words, Jesus elevated the role of women to an incredibly high degree among his followers.

But did he ordain women to the priesthood? The answer is no. Nor did he ordain men. He called his disciples to follow him and to preach his word. Yet he did not establish structural offices, much less a hierarchy of offices, during his lifetime. As a matter of fact, the Christian priesthood, as we know it today, did not develop until the end of the first century. Scripture scholars and church historians are in general agreement about this fact. There is only one title used in the New Testament to describe the ministry of Jesus' followers before his Resurrection: discipleship. Among his disciples we know there were many women: Mary, his mother; Mary Magdalene; Johanna, the wife of Chuza; Susanna; and others.

In the early years of the Church, observes Elizabeth Tetlow in *Women and Ministry in the New Testament*, "Christians continued to recognize the Jewish priesthood and to participate in temple worship" (see Acts 2:46 and 21:26).[11] Raymond Brown suggests that a Christian priesthood could not develop until the Church had broken off from Judaism and acquired a self-identity as a distinct religion, and until it had developed its own sacrificial cult for which the presence of priests was needed.[12] The first condition occurred after the Temple was destroyed in A.D. 70 and Christianity was banished from the synagogue in A.D. 85. The second condition was met when the Eucharist began to be understood as a cultic sacrifice toward the end of the first century.

The Eucharist had, of course, been instituted by Christ and had been celebrated since early in Christian history by various ministers, especially by those who were disciples, apostles, presbyter-bishops, and presiders at the Eucharist. It was from these offices or ministries that the priesthood eventually emerged. As we have seen women were disciples, and some were most probably "presiders at the Eucharist." Some women were also prophets (1 Cor. 11:5 and Acts 21:9), and prophecy was a liturgical ministry. Prophets presided at eucharistic worship (Acts 13:1–2 and Didache 15:1–2). It is also possible that women were present at the Last Supper, since all four Gospels mention the presence of not only the Twelve but of disciples as well. Disciples was a broader term than just the Twelve and, as we have seen, included some women. Thus, though the early history of eucharistic worship in the Church has remained clouded in obscurity, it is quite possible that women were among the first Christian ministers of the eucharist. This possibility is increased when we realize that there were women missionary apostles, at least in the Pauline churches, and one woman, Junia, is explicitly called an apostle by St. Paul in Rom. 16:7.

We can conclude then that in keeping with Jesus' own example of relating to women as persons with the same need of salvation as men and who were equally to be loved and listened to, the early Church gave to women a status unusual for the times. However, two serious questions remain. Why were there only men among the twelve apostles? How can women be priests, "other Christs," since they are obviously female and Jesus was male?

As to why there were only men among the twelve apostles, it seems clear that they had a very specific theological function in the early Church, even though the historical role of the individual members of the Twelve was not very different from that of other apostles. And there were other apostles, including James, Paul, and Barnabas. The Twelve played a special role immediately after the Resurrection. For this reason it was theologically necessary that Matthias be elected to replace Judas. The apostles symbolically represented the twelve tribes of Israel and thus symbolized the completeness of the new people of God at two important moments: at Pentecost, which was the beginning of the Church, and at the eschaton, the Second Coming of Christ, which marked the end of the Church as a historical institution. Once this symbolism had been portrayed at Pentecost, it was no longer necessary that there be twelve historical persons, and so the individual apostles were not replaced after their death. But it was due to this symbolism, the representation of the completeness of Israel, that the members of the Twelve were all men. In Judaism, as we have noted, Israel was legally constituted only by men. The fact that all were male, though important symbolically, had nothing to do with the ministry of the Church. As we have seen, in the earliest Church the roles and functions that later came to be associated with the priestly ministry were never limited to the Twelve. For that matter some functions, such as being administrator of a local church or a leader of public worship, are not explicitly attributed to the Twelve in the New Testament, even though it can be presumed readily that they did, in fact, preside at the Eucharist.

The next question pertains to the fact that Jesus was a male. In Roman Catholic symbolism, the priest is referred to as "another Christ." Even though every Christian is called to be another Christ, a priest is believed to represent Christ in a special way as one through whom God communicates grace, particularly sacramental grace, to his people. In Jesus the Word became flesh as a male and so, some will argue, that to truly represent him as "another Christ" one must be male. This was the argument used in the 1976 Vatican declaration that stated that priests must be male because only males can be the natural signs of Christ. Certainly, since the beginning of the second century, when Christianity adopted the model of the Levitical priesthood from Judaism, this has been the case and has become the tradition in Roman Catholicism. It is well known that the Levitical priesthood was open only to men. But must this be so? And is it not also true that women can be "natural signs of Christ?" Many maintain that the religion of the time and place made it expedient that God become man, not woman. How else could he have been heard? But they go on to add that the symbolism of "another Christ" need not be attached to maleness, but to humanity. As Raymond Brown writes, "If the theology of the priest as another Christ is meant to draw attention to the continued mediatorship of *humanity* in God's giving of grace, one might argue that a priesthood involving both males and females is a better symbol of humanity and overcomes the biological limitation of the incarnation."[13] Were one to accept Fr. Brown's statement, no obstacle would stand in the way of ordaining females from the point of view of sexuality. Nevertheless, it is also not difficult to discern why there is disagreement on the matter, especially from the point of view of tradition. Be that as it may, the executive board of the Catholic Biblical Association of America in a statement entitled *Women and Priestly Ministry: The New Testament Evidence* concludes the section "The Praxis of Jesus and the Apostles" by stating, "Thus, the claim that the intention and example of Jesus and the example of the apostles provide a norm excluding women from priestly ministry cannot be sustained on either logical or historical grounds."[14] And the debate continues.

Summary

Despite the strictures of his society, Jesus showed a high regard for women. There are many examples of Jesus addressing women with the same respect and concern he showed men. His followers were called disciples, and among his disciples there were many women. The priesthood, as we know it today, was not established until toward the end of the first century. The Eucharist had, of course, been instituted by Jesus and had been celebrated since early in Christian history, yet it is possible that women were among the first Christian ministers of the Eucharist.

The reason there were only men among the Twelve is that they had a very special function to perform. The Twelve symbolized the completeness of the new people of God at Pentecost, as they will at the Second Coming. In Judaism, Israel was legally constituted only by men. Thus, the fact that all twelve were male, though important symbolically, had nothing per se to do with the ministry of the Church being of necessity male.

In Jesus the Word became flesh as a male and so, some will argue, that to truly represent him as "another Christ" one must be male. The Vatican declaration of 1976 argued that priests must be male because only males can be natural signs of Christ. Many maintain that the religion of Jesus' time made it expedient that God became male, not female. But they go on to add that the symbolism of "another Christ" need not be attached to maleness but should be broadened to include all humanity. Fr. Raymond Brown writes that one might argue that a priesthood involving both males and females is a better symbol of humanity and overcomes the biological limitations of the Incarnation.

St. Paul: Women and Ministry

The picture of the ministry of women that emerges both from the Acts of the Apostles and from most of the Pauline epistles is of women fully accepted by the Christian community, laboring side by side on an equal footing with men in the work of spreading the Gospel. Men certainly predominated, as would be expected in the culture of the day, but women were given a status in the Church quite unusual for the times. In the New Testament there were not ministries of men or ministries of women but rather only ministries of Jesus in which both men and women served. Generally speaking, Christian ministry in the New Testament is ministry of service. There were apostles, prophets, teachers, evangelists, and deacons, and all served the Church, each with his or her own gifts, for the building up of the Christian community. As we have seen, the exclusion of women came only toward the end of the first century when the office of priesthood formally was instituted and was modeled on the Levitical priesthood of the Old Testament. This was clearly a postbiblical development.

When reading the epistles of St. Paul, one is struck by the role women played. Their names are well known: Phoebe, Lydia, Synteche, Evodia, Priscilla, and Eunice, among others. But the same Paul who praises these women placed restrictions on the women of Corinth because of their exuberance in their new-found freedom in the Lord. Paul felt that they were departing too much from the cultural norm. The restrictions in 1 Cor. and 1 Tim. have burdened women to the present time and have barred women from any effective participation in the decision-making processes in the Church. And yet it is important to note that in the New Testament there are no texts that address the specific question of women and Church office. Only three epistolary passages deal with women in the assembly (1 Cor. 11:36, 14:33a–35; 1 Tim. 2:11–15), and these are simply disciplinary regulations pertaining to proper conduct. The exclusion of women from Church office cannot be deduced from these texts.

In 1 Cor. 11:36, Paul instructs women to wear a headdress, which was the customary attire when praying or prophesying, so that they would not appear eccentric or cause scandal. Even though Paul attempts to ground this regulation in the order of creation, the Church has acknowledged the cultural contingency of the regulation by no longer imposing the rule. Paul's motivation in laying down this code is understood as disciplinary, not dogmatic. He is speaking to a particular situation in a particular time and place. In 1 Cor. 14:33a–35, women are forbidden to speak in the assembly. The verb used is *lalein*, which means "to speak." It is incorrect to translate *lalein* as meaning "to teach" and to use this verse as though it means women are forbidden from the official function of teaching. Such an interpretation is unwarranted by the text and the context. Rather the context indicates the prohibition is against asking questions (v. 35) or in some way disturbing the assembly (vs. 28, 30). It is in the First Letter to Timothy, a pastoral epistle that is generally assumed to have been written in a later period, where women are admonished not "to teach" (*didaskein*) but to be submissive and silent (1 Tim. 2:11–15). That this is not a universal principle is clear since women in Paul's churches not only prayed and prophesied at worship (1 Cor. 11:5) but also exercised the ministry of teaching (Acts 18:26). If the command for silence were to be taken literally here, then should we not also accept as literal the stern orders given by Paul that women are not to wear braided hair, gold, pearls, or expensive clothes (1 Tim. 2:9)? It seems clear, then, that these three passages, which limit women's role to what is decent and customary, are pastoral regulations motivated by the social and cultural factors of Paul's day and cannot be taken as universal theological laws relating to ministry in the Church.

Summary

The picture of the ministry of women that emerges both from the Acts of the Apostles and from most of the Pauline epistles is of women fully accepted by the Christian community and laboring side by side with men in the work of spreading the Gospel. Men certainly predominated, as would be expected in the culture of the day, but women were given a status in the Church quite unusual for the times.

When reading the epistles of St. Paul one is struck by the role women played. Paul also placed restrictions on the women of Corinth because of their exuberance in their new found freedom in the Lord. Yet the epistles contain no texts that address the specific question of women and the Church office. Only three epistolary passages deal with women in the assembly (1 Cor. 11:36, 14:33a–35; 1 Tim. 2:11–15), and these are simply disciplinary regulations pertaining to proper conduct. The exclusion of women from Church office cannot be deduced from these texts. Current biblical scholarship is in the process of rediscovering the prominent role of women in ministry in the New Testament. The Church has changed direction in the past under the guidance of the Holy Spirit and may do so in the future regarding the ordination of women into the priesthood.

Conclusion

An examination of the biblical evidence in the New Testament indicates that women exercised roles and functions that later were associated with priestly ministry. The arguments against the ordination of women to the priesthood based on the practice of Jesus and the Apostles, St. Paul, and the early Church do not seem to be absolute. The evidence, even though not decisive by itself, does seem to many to point toward the ordination of women. The crux of the problem, as indicated earlier, lies in the interpretation of Scripture. The study of Scripture is a developing science, and current biblical scholarship is in the process of rediscovering the prominent role of women in ministry in the New Testament. New discoveries in this area, as have occurred in other areas of biblical scholarship in the past, may eventually bring about a change in the Church's position. But for the immediate future there seems to be little realistic hope for the ordination of women to the priesthood. The Church has evolved in new directions many times in the past under the guidance of the Holy Spirit. As women continue to serve the Church so positively in a variety of new ministries, the stimulus for change may well be provided.

Study Questions

1. In the past two hundred years what societal changes have occurred that helped promote consciousness-raising with regard to women?
2. How did the Church Fathers understand women's roles in the Church? Explain and give examples.
3. Describe some of the nontheological factors that impinge on the question of women serving in the active ministry.
4. How were women described in the rabbinic literature of Jesus' day?
5. What was Jesus' attitude toward women? Give five examples.
6. Why were the Twelve all males?
7. Are there examples in Scripture of Jesus using women in ministerial roles?
8. Give arguments for and against regarding the necessity that all priests be male.
9. What was the role of women in the Pauline churches?
10. Are there passages in St. Paul's letters that forbid women from serving in Church offices? Explain.

10

Roman Catholicism and Social Justice

Social Justice in the Church Universal

Catholic **social doctrine** concerning the rights of human beings has its roots in the New Testament and in the writings of the Church Fathers, as well as in the works of the great medieval theologians such as St. Thomas Aquinas. However, only when Pope Leo XIII wrote his encyclical *Rerum Novarum* (On the Condition of the Worker) in 1891 did Catholicism begin to enunciate in a conscious and systematic fashion a theology of social justice for the modern world. Beginning with *Rerum Novarum,* a body of official Catholic teachings with regard to modern social and economic questions has come into existence. Pope Leo XIII's encyclical gave Catholicism's answer to problems created by the Industrial Revolution. The economic situation of the late nineteenth century, which included the spread of laissez-faire capitalism and the Marxist response, demanded such an answer. Official Catholic social teaching has been developed by subsequent popes throughout the twentieth century.

There are two distinct stages in the development of modern Catholic social doctrine. The first stage began with *Rerum Novarum* and includes the teachings of Pius XI's *Quadragesimo Anno* (Reconstructing the Social Order) in 1931, together with the social teachings of Pope Pius XII, who was pope from 1938 to 1958. During stage one the popes based their thinking on the principles of natural law. Such an approach tends to deal with moral issues in the abstract, that is, according to universal norms rather than in the light of particular historical circumstances and situations. This classicist approach emphasizes the *purpose* of human existence in such a way as to imply that one can find in the nature of humanity a blueprint for growth and development. The second stage in the development of Catholic social doctrine begins with Pope John XXIII and Vatican II. Pope John XXIII opened a new era in Catholic social thought in his encyclical letters *Mater et Magistra* (Mother and Teacher) in 1961 and *Pacem in Terris* (Peace on Earth) in 1963. In these letters and in the writings of Vatican II as well as in the teachings of Popes Paul VI and John Paul II, there is a fundamental shift in methodology from classicism to historical consciousness.

Historical consciousness considers moral problems from a concrete perspective and in terms of the circumstances of a particular action. A moral theology based on a historically conscious methodology stresses personal responsibility—to God, to oneself, to the Church, and to the entire human community. Such a theology does not assume a predetermined plan that is knowable in light of reason (natural law). A historically conscious approach to moral questions does not reject natural law and the place of norms and obligations, but it does insist that such norms and obligations never fully embody the values that they seek to express. As Richard McBrien observes: "The values (e.g., the dignity of human life) may be absolute, but the norms to realize them (e.g., no killing) are relative to the historical situations."[1]

Stage One: Pope Leo XIII to Pope Pius XII

Rerum Novarum, written by Pope Leo XIII in 1891, was the first in a series of important social teachings by the Catholic Church. The central issue in these teachings is the dignity of the human person. In *Rerum Novarum,* Pope Leo XIII defends the human person against the encroachments of the modern state. Since humankind precedes the state, political, economic, and legal structures are only as good as what they can do for human beings. The state exists for the good of its citizens. Pope Leo writes that social morality is not purely the product of human choice, but rather it is the result of the natural law that is understood as an objective order written into creation that balances freedom and restraint. The natural law theory is understood as a middle ground between the tyrannies of the left and the tyrannies of the right. *Rerum Novarum* criticizes the economic abuses of the day. Brought to task are systems that strip workers of their dignity by refusing to pay them decent wages. This theme of human dignity is again stressed by Pope Pius XI in *Quadragesimo Anno* in 1931. The principal problems discussed by Pius XI are those found in *Rerum Novarum;* namely, the role of government in society and in regard to the economy, the principle of a just wage, the right of workers to organize, and a critique of both capitalism and socialism. For example, Pope Pius XI rejects the Marxist-Leninist philosophy outright, but he also condemns capitalism's tendency to reduce human beings to their economic functions as workers.

Pope Pius XII never produced a social encyclical equal in importance to *Rerum Novarum* or *Quadragesimo Anno,* but he was fully committed to the social justice mission of the Church. He opposed nazism and communism and promoted the rights of all human beings. Totalitarian states swallow up individuals. Human beings are simply objects to be used and, if necessary, discarded by those who rule totalitarian governments. Pius XII's teaching amounted in practice to acceptance of the capitalist system as the only feasible alternative to fascism and communism.

Stage Two: Pope John XXIII and Vatican II

Pope John XXIII begins a new era in Catholic social thought with his encyclicals *Mater et Magistra* and *Pacem in Terris.* In these documents, the pope places human rights in the more international context of the 1960s. These encyclicals have impressed many theologians and world leaders with their comprehensive view of the world community as seen in terms of an updated, more flexible, and historical theory of natural law. In *Mater et Magistra,* Pope John recognizes that the international community is undergoing so much change that a more dynamic view of human rights is necessary. The encyclical refers to the growing material interdependence of the nations of the world and seeks to provide a moral framework for the political, economic, and strategic issues facing the human community. *Mater et Magistra* also recognizes the need for additional state intervention to bring about greater justice both in industry and in agriculture. This elevated role of the state marks a change from the teaching of earlier popes. In *Quadragesimo Anno,* Pope Pius XI taught that the state should let subordinate groups deal with issues of public concern whenever possible. *Mater et Magistra* teaches that the state now has a greater role to play because recent development and greater complexities make it necessary for public authorities to attempt to overcome injustices within society and among nations. *Mater et Magistra* occasioned a strong reaction, both positive and negative, and marked the first public dissent in contemporary American Catholic history from a papal encyclical. As William F. Buckley wrote in the *National Review,* "Mater, si; magistra, no" ("Mother, yes; teacher, no").[2]

Pope John XXIII continued with this same basic approach in *Pacem in Terris,* again focusing on the rights and duties of the human person. Pope John takes a comprehensive view of the worldwide struggle for human dignity and supports movements that are attempting to gain a greater share in the political process. He encourages women who refuse to accept discrimination; people who oppose colonialism; and oppressed races who opt for emancipation. The pope also calls for a ban on all nuclear weapons and condemns the arms race.

At Vatican II, *The Pastoral Constitution on the Church in the Modern World* incorporated many of the ideas found in Pope John XXIII's social encyclicals. This document teaches that since the world seems to be at a critical point in history as it experiences incredible cultural and social changes, the Church cannot stand by in an indifferent posture. Rather, the Church wishes to lend its support and encouragement to every effort to promote human freedom and dignity. Pope Paul VI wrote the encyclical *Populorum Progressio* (The Progress of Peoples) in 1967. In this letter he deals with a topic that *The Pastoral Constitution on the Church in the Modern World* touches on only briefly, namely, the question of economic development and the duty of advanced nations to come to the aid of underdeveloped nations. Pope Paul encourages urgent reforms and bold transformations. He also makes clear that the Church does not have the competence to propose concrete solutions to social problems but has the role of moral critic and prophet, and must win from its members a commitment to participate actively in working for a more humane world.

In 1971, Pope Paul VI wrote another encyclical entitled *Octagesima Adveniens* (The Eightieth Year) that analyzes the problems faced by postindustrial societies that have been greatly transformed by technology and its effects. The letter returns to the idea of how advanced and underdeveloped nations are related internationally. In emphasizing the responsibility of the political sector in the task of assuring justice for people in society, Pope Paul VI takes Catholic social teaching a step beyond Pope John XXIII and states that the ultimate decision in the social and economic field, both national and international, rests with political power. In sum, if other means fail to provide minimum justice for citizens, state intervention may be not only legitimate, but absolutely necessary.

The Third International Synod of Bishops wrote *Justice in the World* in 1971 and affirmed the social teachings of Pope Paul VI's encyclicals. The bishops say that when a society marginalizes a significant number of its people by placing them on the sidelines economically, politically, or culturally, then that society is in need of reform. Any reform can be judged as successful or not by the degree to which it increases the participation of the marginalized. If the poor, women, children, the aged, racial minorities and the handicapped—all those who have tended to become marginalized—are not justly treated, then the society in question cannot be considered either progressive or Christian. The bishops add that the Church itself must first strive to be just in its own community if it is to speak about justice to others. They present what might be called a bill of rights for Church members. Within the Church, rights must be maintained: rights of women to a share of responsibility and participation, the right to a decent wage, the right to suitable freedom of expression, the rights of the accused, and the right of citizens to some share in determining and deciding what is done.[3] Finally, the bishops say that the Gospel must penetrate every aspect of human existence. Concerning the mission of the Church, they write, "Action on behalf of justice and participation in the transformation of the world fully appear to us as a constitutive dimension of the preaching of the gospel, or, in other words, of the Church's mission for the redemption of the human race and its liberation from every oppressive situation."[4] In light of this statement, the mission of the Church is a mission of evangelization that includes as a constitutive dimension action on behalf of justice and the transformation of the world. Without a social justice mission one does not have Church or the Gospel.

It is clear that since the completion of Vatican II official Catholic social teaching has continued and extended the effort to relate the Gospel and faith directly to the daily life of Christians in this world. The first encyclical of Pope John Paul II *Redemptor Hominis*

(Redeemer of Humankind), written in 1979, continues the Church's effort to develop a sense of social justice among Roman Catholics. Pope John Paul II focuses on the ethical implications of Christology and anthropology since his encyclical is primarily concerned with human dignity and social justice as rooted in the saving work of Christ. The Christian community must constantly work on behalf of human dignity, consistent with the teachings of Vatican II and especially of *The Declaration on Religious Freedom.* In his second encyclical *Dives in Misericordia* (Rich in Mercy), written in 1980, Pope John Paul II deepens the themes found in *Redemptor Hominis* and makes clear that God's full plan for the human race necessitates that we go beyond a legalistic sense of justice to an attitude of heartfelt mercy.

Pope John Paul II wrote another encyclical *Laborem exercens* (On Human Work) in 1981, which is a critique of Marxism and of rigid capitalism. "Rigid" capitalism must be reformed if the rights of the worker are to be respected. There are grave deficiencies in the communist system that make workers feel they are only cogs in a huge machine. The truth that must be emphasized in opposition to both systems is the priority of the individual person over means of production. In this letter, the pope stresses the need for labor unions, which are seen as vehicles in the struggle for social justice. Another important aspect of the encyclical is what the pope writes concerning the differing roles laity and clergy should play in working for justice. The laity's competence in secular affairs enable them to make wise decisions in implementing the Church's vision of social justice. The clergy should not become directly involved in politics but should offer a vision of a just social order. One of the noteworthy aspects of the encyclical is the pope's recognition of the need of the poor to take responsibility for their own advancement. Great stress is laid on the solidarity of the poor and the oppressed, and both groups are encouraged to struggle to overcome the disadvantages imposed on them. The pope's concept of solidarity allows for confrontation of the oppressed with the oppressed. The notion of confrontation is a significant contribution to the social thought of the Church that, in the past, was played down in describing the struggle for social justice.

Pope John Paul's latest encylical on social justice is *Centesimus Annus* (The Centenary), which commemorates the centenary of Pope Leo XIII's encyclical *Rerum Novarum. Centesimus Annus* is dated May 1, 1991, International Workers Day, and it is historically important for a variety of reasons. The encyclical updates the teaching of *Rerum Novarum* regarding socialism and includes the following: an endorsement of democracy and the market economy, a diagnosis of the collapse of socialism, a rather surprising critique of the welfare state, and an emphasis on the dangers and limitations of state power. The encyclical is revolutionary because it places Roman Catholicism firmly within the free market camp. It marks a new point of departure for Catholic social teaching since Pope John Paul II never implies that socialism and capitalism are morally equal, an attitude some felt could be detected in his 1987 encyclical *Sollicitudo Rei Socialis.*

In *Centesimus Annus* the pope rejects a market system that is purely materialistic and not limited by laws and spiritual values that place the economic system at the service of human freedom in its totality—the core of which is ethical and religious. The letter also has a considerably different tone from that of the U.S. bishops in their 1986 statement on the American economy that repeatedly called for increasing the role of government to remedy social problems. The pope questions the legitimacy of extensive intervention by the state, which he refers to as the "social assistance state." He believes that such intervention leads to a loss of human energies and an "inordinate increase of public agencies which are dominated by bureaucratic ways of thinking rather than by concern for serving their clients." He further adds such agencies are accompanied by an enormous increase in spending.

Centesimus Annus represents an authentic development in Catholic social justice teaching. It also represents a retrieval of the private property theory of medieval scholastic theology. The impact of this encyclical will be both social and theological, and it will also be pastoral. It supports the role of private individuals in their business activities and challenges them to use their wealth wisely to satisfy the needs of the poor. The encyclical also suggests that the most effective way to fight poverty in the Third World is to permit free economies to take root and grow in order to create jobs, augment exports, attract foreign investments, and build infrastructure. *Centesimus Annus* is an important event for the Catholic Church and demands careful study.

Summary

There are two stages in the development of modern Catholic social doctrine. Stage one begins with Pope Leo XIII's encyclical *Rerum Novarum* in 1891 and continues through the papacy of Pope Pius XII, who died in 1958. During this period, the popes base their thought on the principles of natural law and on the dignity of the human person. The popes describe the role of government as it pertains to the following areas: the economy, the principle of a just wage, and the right of workers to organize. They also give critiques of capitalism and communism. Stage two in the development of modern Catholic social doctrine begins with Pope John XXIII and Vatican II. Pope John's encyclicals *Mater et Magistra* (1961) and *Pacem in Terris* (1963) have impressed theologians and world leaders alike with their comprehensive view of the world community as seen in terms of an updated, more flexible, and historical theory of natural law. The encyclicals present a clear shift in methodology from the ahistorical classicism of previous documents to a mode of historical consciousness stressing personal responsibility and the values underlying norms and obligations. Pope John understood the role of the state as more necessary than in the past in seeking social justice. This is due to the greater complexities in the modern world and because of the closer interrelationship among nations.

The mission of the Church is to evangelize, and this demands positive action by church leaders and church members on behalf of the Gospel and, therefore, on behalf of justice. Without a social justice mission, one does not have the Church or the Gospel. All Christians have an active role to play in the mission of the Church. Pope Paul VI and Pope John Paul II have written encyclicals that stress the dignity of all human beings and the need for all Christians, both clergy and laity, to work for social justice.

Social Justice and the American Catholic Church

Most Catholics in the United States know very little about the history of social ethics in this country. There are several reasons for this lack of knowledge.[5] First of all, textbooks used in moral theology before Vatican II were either written by Europeans or derived from European texts and few, if any, references to the United States are found in these works. Second, until Vatican II emphasis was placed on the official teaching of the popes in their encyclicals and addresses so that little or no mention was given to specifically American contributions.

Third, until around the time of Vatican II, there were few intellectual contributions to the American scene or to the universal Church made by Catholics in the United States.[6] But as a result of Vatican II, there has been a renewal of moral theology in the Church as a whole and in the life of the local church as well, including the Church in the United States. This involvement of the American[7] church is seen especially in the recent letters of American bishops on social issues, especially their statements on peace and the economy. In analyzing social justice in American Catholicism, two stages will be considered: American social ethics from the time of Msgr. John A. Ryan until Vatican II and from Vatican II until the present.

Stage One: Msgr. John A. Ryan to Vatican II

Msgr. John A. Ryan (1869–1945) was the best known Roman Catholic social ethicist in the United States during the first half of the twentieth century. His significance was enhanced by his positions as professor of moral theology at the Catholic University of America in Washington, D.C., from 1915 to 1939, and as director of the Social Action Department of the National Catholic Welfare Council, the national organization of the American Catholic bishops from 1920 to 1945. Social Catholicism became a major force in the United States only after World War I with the founding of the Social Action Department of the National Catholic Welfare Council (N.C.W.C.), which was headed by Msgr. Ryan. Its first major statement was *The Bishops' Program of Social Reconstruction,* issued in 1919. Popularly known as the *Bishops' Program,* it became more widely known than any of the other sixty or more postwar proposals for social reconstruction issued by the Social Action Department of N.C.W.C. The *Bishops' Program* did not seek revolutionary reforms in the American economic system, but it did propose legislation for the following: guarantee of the rights of workers to bargain collectively, social security, a legal minimum wage, laws against child labor, adequate housing for the working classes, and health and unemployment insurance. Some critics denounced the *Bishops' Program* as socialistic, yet most of its proposals were incorporated into the New Deal legislation of the 1930s. Pope Pius XI's encyclical *Quadragesimo Anno* of 1931, which called for changes in the economic system, fortified Ryan's position since there seemed to be close agreement between the *Bishops' Program,* Roosevelt's New Deal, and the pope's program of reconstruction.

In the 1930s, a significant development in social Catholicism emerged in the form of the Catholic Worker movement, founded by Dorothy Day and Peter Maurin in 1933. Both in theory and in practice the movement espoused a radical type of social ethics based on the Gospel. Day and Maurin were firm believers in the kind of personalist ethic that has now become the basis of Catholic social teaching. They believed in the value of the individual and the need to identify with the poor. The Catholic Worker program is threefold. First, the clarification of the ideology of the membership is presented in *The Catholic Worker,* which was inaugurated in May of 1933. The paper strongly opposes the present economic order with its emphasis on profit, wealth, and materialism and insists on a personalism stressing the basic equality of all. The emphasis on personalism takes concrete form in the proposal of a Christian utopian community where there would be no coercive government.

Second, the Catholic Worker program calls for houses of hospitality in Catholic parishes. In fact, such houses came into exir . . ice only in the worker homes where the poor and the derelict were ied, clothed, and sheltered. The first house of hospitality was opened in the Bowery in New York City, in 1933. Many other such houses were opened throughout the United States by members of the movement. There are more than twenty of these houses in the United States today.

The third part of the program promoted the formation of communes where members could work and study together in self-contained Christian communities. Such communes have never worked and have been a real problem within the Catholic Worker movement.

The Catholic Worker movement continues to play a prophetic role in American Catholicism. It challenges a Catholic mentality that often has equated morality with church attendance on Sunday, abstinence from meat on Fridays, and opposition to indecent movies. The movement has helped many Catholics to adopt a more gospel-like view of morality and to see the need for social reconstruction.

Dorothy Day died on November 19, 1980. She was buried in a grave provided by the archdiocese of New York. Her biographer recalls an incident at her funeral that, in many ways, is symbolic of her life. He writes:

> At the church door, Cardinal Terrence Cooke met the body to bless it. As the procession stopped for this rite, a demented person pushed his way through the crowd and bending low over the coffin peered at it intently. No one interfered, because, as even the funeral director understood, it was in such a man that Dorothy had seen the face of God.[8]

After World War II and with the beginning of the Cold War, American Catholicism spent much of its energy crusading against communism. This attitude was dominant throughout the 1950s. The social and economic goals of the 1930s were set aside by many Catholics since to criticize capitalism in any way was seen as lacking loyalty to the United States.

In the 1960s, social activism came out of its period of dormancy as many Catholics joined Dr. Martin Luther King, Jr., in the civil rights movement. Priests, nuns, and Catholic laity were involved in peace marches led by Dr. King and the Southern Christian Leadership Conference. Many Catholics, including a number of bishops, supported César Chavez in his efforts to organize migrant farm workers. Daniel and Philip Berrigan, together with other Catholics, faced the wrath of conservative Catholics in their nonviolent demonstrations against the Vietnam War and other social evils. The shock of Watergate in the 1970s and Irangate in the 1980s only increased the importance of ethical reflection and action for American Catholics.

Vatican II and the papal encyclicals of Pope John XXIII, Paul VI, and John Paul II have had a great influence on Catholic social teaching in the United States. The Council Fathers recognized that both faith and the Scriptures have to be related ever more intimately to daily life in the world. Stimulated by this challenge, the American bishops have become very active in social justice issues. The bishops have presented a program of social action that includes the spectrum of pro-life issues linking abortion to a variety of other social evils such as hunger, poverty, unemployment, capital punishment, and nuclear war. The bishops have taken strong positions on other important problems as well. Since 1971 they have spoken in favor of arms reduction, selective conscientious objection, national health insurance, decent housing, human rights in Chile and the nations of Central America, racial justice, the family farm, and a variety of other issues. Their stance on these issues is progressive, and prophetic as well, since they are often speaking against public opinion and governmental policy.

The most daring initiatives of the American Catholic bishops are their pastoral letters on peace, written in 1983, and on the U.S. economy, written in 1985. The bishops recognize in these letters that they are addressing two different audiences—their fellow believers who are members of the Church and the broader public that does not necessarily share their beliefs. In those instances where they address the public at large, the letters refrain from appealing to specifically

Christian sources. The letters have opened a new chapter in American Catholicism's effort to bring about social justice. At the same time, the letters startled the average American, including many Catholics, who were not cognizant of the great range of social issues addressed by the bishops since the close of Vatican II.

The bishops' pastoral letter on war and peace in the nuclear age, *The Challenge of Peace: God's Promise and Our Response,* originated in November of 1980 at the annual meeting of the National Conference of Catholic Bishops in Washington, D.C.[9] The document was prepared by a committee of bishops chaired by Archbishop (now Cardinal) Joseph Bernardin. The pastoral letter is a model of how religion and politics can interact in a pluralistic society. The decision to engage in dialogue not only with the Catholic community but with the entire American public, including the government, had precedent in two recent Church teachings. In *Pacem in Terris* Pope John XXIII addressed not only Catholics but "all Men of Good Will." Pope Paul VI used the same approach in his 1964 encyclical *Ecclesiam Suam.* Further, *The Pastoral Constitution on the Church in the Modern World* of Vatican II was addressed "to the whole of humanity." When the bishops speak to Catholics in their letter on peace, they appeal to Scripture, papal teachings, and councils. This approach is found in Part I ("Peace in the Modern World: Religious Perspectives and Principles") and in Part IV ("The Pastoral Challenge and Response").[10] In addressing the wider civic community, the bishops appeal to human reason and experience—to what Catholics refer to as the natural law. This approach is found in Part II ("War and Peace in the Modern World: Problems and Principles") and in Part III ("The Promotion of Peace: Proposals and Policies").[11]

In producing the letter on peace, the bishops went through a long process of consultation with a variety of groups: biblical scholars, moralists, arms control experts, top officials in the Reagan administration, including two former secretaries of defense, military leaders, peace activists, and others. The hearing process ended with a full day of discussion with representatives of the Reagan administration. As Richard P. McBrien points out in *Caesar's Coin,* the bishops were trying to be faithful to a principle enunciated by Vatican II: "namely, that the Church must interpret the gospel only after 'scrutinizing the signs of the times,' that is, it must make a concrete examination of the moral questions to be addressed before moving to a theological reflection on them."[12]

In the letter on peace, the bishops observe that Jesus himself is the supreme example of a peacemaker. They point out that although the Church has sanctioned war as a last resort throughout most of its history on the basis of the "just war" theory, times have changed. We now live in a nuclear age. Because of the threat of nuclear annihilation, we are forced to make a fresh appraisal of war. The data shows that nuclear war is an immediate threat to civilization as we know it and to the lives of all human beings. As a result, the bishops arrive at several conclusions. First, they oppose use of all nuclear weapons directed at population centers, including retaliatory action that would "strike enemy cities after our own have already been struck." They also rule out a first strike as morally unjustifiable, and they base their decision on their "extreme skepticism about the prospects for controlling a nuclear exchange." The bishops do feel it is morally justified to maintain nuclear weapons as a deterrent until alternative methods of defense can be found. However, they argue that to possess nuclear weapons is permissible only if limited to a "sufficiency" to deter; thus, the quest for nuclear superiority is not legitimate. Finally, deterrence must be considered as only a step in the path to nuclear disarmament. The bishops recognize that sincere Catholics may disagree with their conclusion and make clear that such disagreement is acceptable.

The other landmark pastoral letter of the American bishops, *On Catholic Social Teaching and the U.S. Economy,* is likewise a challenge to all American citizens.[13] The bishops wished to add their voice to the public policy debate about the direction that the U.S. economy should take. They again consulted with experts who could contribute to the writing of the letter. Symposia and conferences were held at various Catholic and non-Catholic institutions of learning throughout the United States. Among those consulted were businesspersons, labor leaders, economists, politicians, social scientists, government officials, theologians, scripture scholars, and others. The drafts of the pastoral letter were circulated publicly, and criticism was welcomed from all quarters. The process of writing this letter, as was true of the letter on peace, is instructive. As Fr. Charles Curran writes:

> The very process itself has been a great teaching tool in terms of awakening consciousness both within the Church and society in general to the moral issues involved in the United States economy. The dialogical and collegial style of writing this document contrasts with the approach still used in most

Catholic documents, especially those emanating from Rome. An increasing difficulty will be experienced in the future for Church authorities to propose documents that have not been prepared with this same wide-ranging and public dialogue.[14]

The pastoral letter considers four specific areas: employment, poverty, food, and agriculture, and the relationship between the United States and the world economy. Among other items, the bishops call the current level of poverty and unemployment in the United States "a social and moral scandal." They ask for a renewal of the war on poverty and call for a reduction of unemployment to 3–4 percent. To lower the unemployment rate certain means are suggested such as the use of public service jobs and a reform of the welfare system that would provide a national minimum benefit for welfare recipients. The bishops also suggest a restructuring of the tax system to eliminate taxation of the poor. The most striking aspect of the entire letter is its strong critique of current American cultural and economic values.

The letter on the economy represents a progressive approach. A strong conservative reaction to the ideas of the bishops was issued by many writers. One of the conservative critics is Michael Novak, who is the most prominent and prolific author in this area. In *Freedom with Justice: Catholic Social Thought and Liberal Institutions,* Novak proposes a realism that accepts human limitations and sinfulness, rejects utopian solutions, and criticizes the Catholic tradition for its insistence on distribution rather than on the call to creatively produce more wealth.[15] Other conservative writers argue that the Church should not be so specific in its teaching on social issues and should not take such a generally liberal approach.[16]

Both the pastoral letter on peace and the letter on the U.S. economy recognize that sincere Catholics may disagree with the conclusions reached in these documents. The bishops point out that when they present concrete moral judgments, they do not intend these norms to be binding in conscience since it is impossible to attain the same degree of certitude about specific moral judgments as is possible in the case of universal moral principles. The bishops also state that the Church's teaching authority simply does not have the same binding power when it deals with technical solutions involving particular means as it does when it speaks of principles or ends. What the bishops are trying to do is to awaken American Catholics to the problems of social justice. They are encouraging Catholics and others to become involved in the struggle for peace and human rights. The bishops have made great efforts to present the issues to the public. It is hoped that out of this process the Church will emerge as a force for peace and justice in a manner that respects and heightens the true dignity of all human beings.

Summary

Social justice issues first became noteworthy in American Catholicism in 1919 with the publication of *The Bishops' Program of Social Reconstruction* that sought legislation to guarantee a legal minimum age, social security, and laws against child labor. Msgr. John A. Ryan, who was the director of the Social Action Department of N.C.W.C., provided leadership to American Catholicism on social justice issues until his death in 1945. In the 1930s, the Catholic Worker movement was founded and headed by Dorothy Day and Peter Maurin. They espoused a radical type of social ethics based on the Gospel that continues to play a prophetic role for Catholics in the United States today. After World War II and through the 1950s, American Catholicism spent much of its energy crusading against communism. As a result the social and economic goals of the 1930s were set aside.

In the 1960s, social activism came out of its period of dormancy as many Catholics became involved in the civil rights and the migrant workers' movements and joined coalitions that opposed the Vietnam War. Vatican II and the social encyclicals of Pope John XXIII, Pope Paul VI, and Pope John Paul II influenced American bishops to become very active in social justice issues. The bishops have presented a program of social action since 1965 that includes the spectrum of pro-life issues linking abortion to a variety of other social problems such as hunger, poverty, unemployment, capital punishment, and nuclear war. Since 1971 they have spoken in favor of arms reduction, selective conscientious objection, decent housing, and a variety of other issues. The most daring initiatives of the American Catholic bishops are their pastoral letters on war and peace in the nuclear age and on the U.S. economy. Their stance on the issues presented in these pastoral letters is both progressive and prophetic since they often speak against public opinion and governmental policy. The letters have opened a new chapter in American Catholicism's effort to bring about social justice.

Liberation Theology in Latin America

The term *liberation theology* is familiar to many people in the United States, but its meaning is often not well understood. In North America the average reader knows that liberation theology is associated with Latin America and with the Catholic Church and that this theological orientation deals with the plight of the poor and the need for societal change. It is also generally known that liberation theology opposes capitalism especially as practiced in the United States by multinational corporations. What causes confusion is that liberation theology, on the one hand, has been criticized by Pope John Paul II for its use of Marxist thinking and, on the other hand, wins approval from many Latin American bishops and theologians. Because of the proximity of the United States to Latin America, U.S. citizens, particularly U.S. Catholics, need to make an effort to understand what liberation theology is attempting to accomplish and to be aware of its meaning and importance in the present development of Latin American Catholicism.

Gustavo Gutiérrez, who is one of the most prominent of the liberation theologians, points to the conference held by the bishops of Latin America in Medellín, Colombia, in 1968, as the birthdate of liberation theology.[17] The theme of the conference was "The Church in the Present-Day Transformation of Latin America in the Light of the Council."[18] It is clear that the 145 cardinals, bishops, and priests who attended the conference had been deeply influenced by Vatican II. Many of them had been participants in the ecumenical council. Those attending the Medellín conference had also been influenced by Pope Paul VI's encyclical *Populorum Professio* of 1967 that had directly addressed the Latin American situation. These leaders of the Latin American church met at Medellín determined to define the role of the Church in confronting the social and political problems of their people. Sixteen documents were produced at Medellín that treated subjects such as the poverty of the Church, justice, the mass media, peace movements, and lay movements. The essence of the Medellín documents is epitomized in two of its passages:

> By its own vocation Latin America will undertake its liberation at the cost of whatever sacrifice.[19]

> The Lord's distant commandment to "evangelize the poor" ought to bring us to a distribution of resources and apostolic personnel that effectively gives preference to the poorest and most needy sectors.[20]

The Medellín conference presented an unambiguous statement that the Church should exercise a "preferential option for the poor." This ideal has become the basis of liberation theology. However, the documents produced at Medellín do contain enough ambiguity that they can be favorably quoted by both proponents and opponents of liberation theology. Not surprisingly, the documents do a better job of analyzing present conditions in the Church and in society than in proposing solutions. Nevertheless, what Medellín did accomplish, as Philip Berryman writes, was "to give a green light to creative minorities all over the continent whose participation in the liberation struggle has led to a radicalization of the themes presented at Medellín."[21]

Base (Basic) Christian Communities

Liberation theology did not emerge from Vatican II or from Medellín, although both served as catalysts, but rather had its origin in the lives of the poor and the oppressed in Latin America, especially in the small basic Christian communities that appeared in the 1960s. These communities, found mostly in rural areas and on the outer edges of the cities, are formed by simple Christians who come together to worship God, study the Bible, and attempt to live in such a way as to make Christ real in their lives. There are several hundred thousand basic Christian communities in Latin America today. Such communities are local, small-scale (twenty or so members), grass roots, and are rooted in the realities of the daily lives of the people.

Liberation theology begins with these small Christian communities. It is the daily prayerful action and reflection of these communities, their response to their own oppressive situation, that produces liberation theology. In fact, as Fr. Leonardo Boff points out, the theology of liberation does not have a "founder."[22] Such theology is simply the language of a church involved with the poor and committed to their spiritual and material liberation. Those theologians who deal with the faith experience of the poor simply develop and interpret the reflections of these Christians. Such theologians are the representatives of this type of Church in the realm of theory "somewhat as the Evangelists are looked on today as the 'redactors' of the memory and living faith of the primitive Christian community.[23]

One of the problems for a North American or any non-Latin in attempting to understand liberation theology, according to Boff, is that liberation theology "cannot be understood merely by reading books and articles. The books and articles absolutely must be connected with the soil of the Church and of society, from which these writings have sprung, inasmuch as they seek to interpret and illuminate that Church and that society."[24] Boff also cautions that liberation theology is "not understood, nor can it be understood, by the satiated and satisfied—by those comfortable with the status quo."[25] Though Boff's warnings are well taken, it remains useful and even necessary for Christians from other backgrounds to attempt to analyze and understand liberation theology since it represents such a powerful and creative force in Latin America, an area that contains nearly half of the worldwide Roman Catholic population.

Most observers consider Fr. Gustavo Gutiérrez of Peru to be the preeminent Latin American liberation theologian. His *Teología de la liberación,* published in 1971 (the English translation, *A Theology of Liberation,* was published in 1973) is still seen as the cornerstone of liberation theology. Gutiérrez and the other liberation theologians believe that the primary task of theology is not to convince the nonbeliever of the "truths" of the Christian faith, but rather it is to help free the oppressed from their inhuman living conditions.[26] In this way the "truth" of theology becomes the "liberation" of the oppressed. Gutiérrez uses the term *liberation* in three senses. First, *liberation* refers to freedom from oppressive economic, social, and political systems. Second, *liberation* means that human beings should take control of their own destiny. Third, *liberation* means being emancipated from sin and accepting a new life in Christ. Liberation includes all three meanings and not only the first meaning as some critics indicate. Nevertheless, liberation theology primarily develops the social dimension of faith. Still, it must be emphasized that the basis and point of departure of the theology of liberation is the theological virtue of faith. In fact, it is in virtue of the transcendent dimension of faith that a liberation theology is possible at all.[27]

In *A Theology of Liberation,* Gutiérrez speaks for many liberation theologians when he says that the inherent weakness of any capitalist system is its inability to liberate the oppressed, because its profit orientation impels it to discourage Third World countries from taking the initiative to develop their own industrial capabilities. Liberation theology is convinced that one of the major causes of poverty and oppression in Latin America has been and remains the economic policies of the United States government and of multinational corporations—policies that aid repressive governments in Latin America. Thus, the Third World nations, according to Gutiérrez, remain pawns "useful only for high production through the exploitation of the labor force."[28]

Although Gutiérrez is critical of capitalism, he is careful not to insist that socialism is the only answer to the problems of the Latin American nations. He understands that socialism, like capitalism, is subject to many possible interpretations. Gutiérrez insists that liberation must never be equated with any social system. But he goes on to say that in order to achieve liberation from foreign capitalist domination, socialism "represents the most fruitful and far-reaching approach."[29] He does not recommend a socialism imported from the First World, such as might be found in Sweden or some other European nation, but rather a socialism that would be indigenous to Latin America.

One of the most common accusations leveled at liberation theology is that it is "based" on or "inspired" by Marxism. Liberation theologians consider such thinking to be mythological and argue forcefully that the basis or inspiration of their theology is the Christian faith. As Leonardo Boff writes, "Marxism is a secondary, peripheral issue. When Marxism is used at all, it is used only *partially* and *instrumentally*." In the same paragraph Boff goes on to say:

> It is the faith that assimilates or subsumes elements of Marxism, then, and not the other way about. And the assimilation is effected from a point of departure in the community of the poor, so that the elements assimilated are profoundly transformed in the very assimilation, in such a way that the result is no longer Marxism, but simply a critical understanding of reality.[30]

Boff admits that when Marxist elements have been subsumed by liberation theologians they have not always done so with "adequate lucidity, perspicacity, and maturity. But we are improving along the way."[31]

It is very difficult to find a liberation theologian who would completely accept Marxism. Deane William Ferm, who has done extensive study of the writings of liberation theologians, expresses surprise in discovering how few references there are to Karl Marx in the writings of liberation theologians. He also observes that references to Marx are laced with a "heavy dose of emendation."[32]

Liberation theologians often distinguish Marx's social analysis from his atheism. Marx's analysis of class conflict, ideology, and the effects of capitalism are accepted as basically correct. How then is the Marxist analysis assimilated so that it is no longer "Marxism" but simply "a critical understanding of reality?" The notion of class conflict as used by liberation theologians helps to provide an answer to this question. Most of the liberation theologians attempt to distinguish their idea of class conflict from that of the militant Marxists by setting it in a context of love, not hatred, a love that reaches out even to one's enemies. They have their own version of a classless society in mind, their own utopian model. It is a model in which the hunger of one member of society castigates the abundance of another brother or sister.

Latin American liberation theology remains a troubling problem in the mind of Pope John Paul II and Vatican authorities. In September of 1984, Cardinal Joseph Ratzinger, prefect of the Congregation for the Doctrine of the Faith, published a thirty-five page document entitled *Instruction on Certain Aspects of the Theology of Liberation.*[33] *Instruction* officially condemns some of Leonardo Boff's views as found in his book *Church, Charism and Power: Liberation Theology and the Institutional Church,* which was originally published in Brazil in 1981.[34] In this volume, Boff presents the Church not primarily as the sacrament of salvation but as a church of the poor, a church that insists that without the preaching of justice there is no Gospel of Jesus Christ. The book also critiques the hierarchical structure of the Church. Cardinal Ratzinger's *Instruction,* which was approved by Pope John Paul II, said that his congregation felt that some of Boff's statements imperiled the sound doctrine of the Church. *Instruction* does not impugn the theology of liberation at its root, but it does show extreme severity concerning its present performance. The most critical point of *Instruction* is an expression of fear that Marxism will cause Christians to deviate from the faith and betray the poor. Shortly after the publication of *Instruction,* Cardinal Ratzinger met with Boff— who was accompanied by two Brazilian cardinals—to discuss Boff's views. It was agreed that further and continuing dialogue was necessary since both sides felt this had been lacking. As a matter of fact, *Instruction* calls for such dialogue in the hope of enriching the Church. It is important to note that neither Boff himself nor liberation theology in toto was condemned by *Instruction.*

Nevertheless, Boff was silenced by Rome for about one year in 1985 because Cardinal Ratzinger felt some of the ideas he expressed in *Church, Charism and Power* were not in accord with church doctrine. During that period, Boff ceased to preach or to publish his opinions. Again, in 1991, he was silenced by Rome. He was ousted as editor of the magazine *Vozes* and ordered not to publish his theological views for one year. Boff's brother Waldeman has stated that two editions of *Vozes* dealing with married priests and church social action were the immediate causes of Leonardo's dismissal from the theological magazine.

Pope John Paul II's attitude toward liberation theology is influenced partly by the events of 1979, when he attended the Third Conference of Latin American bishops in Puebla, Mexico. This conference convened in January of 1979 to discuss the problem of evangelization. In the decade between the second conference at Medellín and the meeting at Puebla, conservatives had gained power in the Latin American hierarchy and had voiced their opposition to liberation theology. The conservatives felt that liberation theology had shored up the Marxist revolution and reduced Christianity to radical politics. Such accusations were seen as caricatures and vehemently denied by the liberationists. Pope John Paul II attended this conference and made every effort to steer a middle course between the conservatives and the liberals. He condemned social injustice and oppression, but he also objected to priests who became too involved in the political process. The Puebla documents cover a great many topics, and both proponents and opponents of liberation theology can find sections that support their views, as was true at Medellín. Gary MacEoin claims that the Puebla conference did not condemn liberation theology, but rather ignored it.[35] Most commentators would agree, however, that the spirit of the Medellín conference—which spawned liberation theology—survived at Puebla. They would also agree that liberation theology was not condemned.

Those who attempt to understand liberation theology need to realize that although the method of practicing theology is the same for all liberation theologians, the results are not monolithic in any sense of the term. Liberation theologians represent a plurality of theological, social, and political views. There is a vitality and creativity in their writings. As the European theologian Edward Schillebeeckx remarks:

> The most competent theologians of the West today, including both Europe and the Americas, are the liberation theologians. We learn a great deal from them. We're too academic. The liberation theologians make us reflect out of the life of the Christian community.[36]

What Schillebeeckx says in this passage is important. He is observing that liberation theology emerges from the life of the Christian community in Latin America. The vitality of this theology is nourished by the vitality of the Church and vice versa. Schillebeeckx is also referring to the different methods of practicing theology as found in Europe and the United States, on the one hand, and in Latin America, on the other hand. The classical approach to theology of the former starts with an analysis of nature and attempts to show God's presence in the physical world, whereas liberation theology begins with the Christian experience of the marginalized poor in order to obtain social justice. The word *marginalized*, according to Brazilian archbishop Dom Helder Camara, refers to anyone who is left by the wayside in the economic, social, political, and cultural life of his or her country.[37]

The goals of the two methods are quite different. The classical method seeks, above all, to understand reality through human reason and tends to be abstract and unchanging, whereas liberation theology seeks primarily to transform reality through social action. The two approaches are quite different, but not necessarily incompatible. For example, Gustavo Gutiérrez does not deprecate the importance of classical theology. He contends that the first act in liberation theology is action, but when it comes to the second act, reflection, he believes he can be as erudite and analytical as any theologian of his time.[38] Gutiérrez would be the first to admit that liberation theology is not the only theological model, but he insists that it is an authentic model and deserves a fair hearing. Clodovis Boff, among others, also sees the value of the classical method. He writes, "Well, if a 'liberation theologian' wishes to produce a real theology, I don't know of a better place to look for the rules for its production than in Thomas Aquinas."[39] Boff also makes clear that liberation theology must not be opposed to scholastic theology as if it were a new kind of science, since it certainly is not.

The methodology of liberation theology has been discovered and is being developed. However, it has not yet produced a new synthesis of faith. To do so remains one of its concrete tasks. Liberation theology is still in its infancy and has a great deal of growing up to do. It must improve its theoretical status and learn to articulate itself in a more consistent fashion so that it corresponds more adequately with the practice of the church community throughout the world. Liberation theology clearly is a "Church theology" based on the experience of the People of God, and for this reason it needs to be in closer contact with the authorities of the universal Church. And, as Fr. Leonardo Boff writes, it is of the greatest importance for the theology of liberation "always to maintain a spirit of self-criticism, eschewing all false security and triumphalism."[40] In other words, to remain healthy, liberation theology must remain humble and resist the temptation of thinking it has all the answers.

Summary

Liberation theology began in 1979 with the meeting of the Latin American bishops at Medellín, Columbia. This theology reflects the thinking of members of basic Christian communities, which were organized for the first time in the 1960s. Generally speaking, liberation theology seeks to free human beings from oppressive economic, social, and political systems, to emancipate them from sin, and to encourage them to accept a new life in Christ. Although liberation theology primarily develops the social dimension of Christianity, its basis and point of departure is the theological virtue of faith. It is because of the transcendent dimension of faith that a liberation theology is possible at all.

Liberation theology is opposed to capitalism as it is practiced in the United States and in multinational corporations because it believes such a system is one of the primary causes of poverty in Latin America. Some form of socialism is seen to be the answer when it comes to a restructuring of the socioeconomic systems in Latin America. Because of this kind of thinking, liberation theology is often thought of as being Marxist inspired. Liberationists consider such accusations as mythological and argue forcefully that the basis of their theology is the Christian faith. When Marxist theory is used at all, it is applied sparingly and is assimilated into the Christian faith in such a fashion that it is profoundly transformed. At least this is the goal of most liberation theologians. Though liberation theology borrows elements of Marxist socioeconomic analysis, most of its writers completely disassociate themselves from Marx's atheism. Such usage troubles some Catholic leaders, including Pope John Paul II and Cardinal Joseph Ratzinger, prefect of the Congregation for the Doctrine of the Faith. In September of 1984, Cardinal Ratzinger published a thirty-five page document, *Instruction on Certain Aspects of the Theology of Liberation,* that condemned some of Fr. Leonardo Boff's views.

Instruction was issued under the signature of Pope John Paul II, and although it does not impugn liberation theology at its root, it shows extreme displeasure concerning liberation theology's present performance. The need for continuing dialogue between Rome and liberation theologians is needed and called for in *Instruction.*

A real problem in understanding liberation theology is its theological method. Whereas classical theology's starting point is an analysis of nature, which tends to be theoretical and abstract, liberation theology begins with the experience of the poor. The goal of classical theology is to understand reality, whereas the goal of liberation theology is to transform reality through social action. The two approaches are quite different but not necessarily incompatible. In order to develop a real compatibility, liberation theology must remain in dialogue and in tension with classical theology. In the meantime, it continues to work for the advancement of the people of Latin America.

Study Questions

1. What are the two stages in the development of modern Catholic social doctrine?
2. Why is the encyclical letter *Rerum Novarum* so important in the development of Catholic social justice?
3. Discuss the importance of Pope John XXIII's encyclicals *Mater et Magistra* and *Pacem in Terris.*
4. Did Vatican II add new dimensions to Catholic social justice? Explain.
5. How did Pope Paul VI deepen the sense of Catholic social responsibility?
6. What "rights" of church members were presented in 1971 by the Third International Synod of Bishops?
7. Discuss the basic content of Pope John Paul II's encyclical *Laborem exercem.*
8. Why are many American Catholics unaware of the history of Catholic social ethics?
9. What was the *Bishops' Program?* Who was Msgr. John A. Ryan?

10. Is it correct to say that the Catholic Worker movement played a prophetic role in American Catholicism? Why?

11. List some of the issues that the American Catholic bishops have supported since the end of Vatican II.

12. Is it fair to say that the most daring initiatives of the American Catholic bishops have been their pastoral letters on peace and on the U.S. economy? Explain.

13. Do many sincere Catholics disagree with the solutions proposed in their bishops' pastoral letters? If so, what is the value of writing such letters?

14. When and why did liberation theology originate?

15. What is a base (basic) community?

16. According to Fr. Leonardo Boff, why is it so difficult for North Americans to understand liberation theology?

17. Discuss the content of Fr. Gustavo Gutierrez's book *A Theology of Liberation.*

18. Why is liberation theology opposed to capitalism as it is found in the United States and in multinational corporations?

19. Is liberation theology based on or inspired by Marxism?

20. Does Pope John Paul II approve liberation theology?

21. What is the difference of starting points between classical and liberation theology?

Epilogue

The Church in the Year 2000

We are presently at the close of a period of history. Since the time of St. Paul, Christianity has been concentrated in the West. When we study church history it is not surprising that over 90 percent of the material concerns the Western Church. The age of European supremacy reached its peak and also the beginning of its descendancy during World War II. Asia and Africa were still controlled in great measure by Europe. But, following the war, colonialism began to topple. In 1945 there were fifty-seven nations throughout the world. By 1985 the number had reached 159. It is only now that we can truly begin to speak of a world history. Until recently world history was divided into three stages of European history: antiquity, the Middle Ages, and the modern period. But, in fact, the first stage of real *world* history has just begun. We can now also speak of Christianity as a World Church. The center of gravity has shifted from Europe and North America to the southern hemisphere. In 1970, 51 percent of all Catholics were living in the southern continents of Latin America, Africa, and Asia-Oceania. By 1980 the proportion had risen to nearly 58 percent and by the year 2000, 70 percent of all Catholics will be living in the southern hemisphere; generally speaking, in the Third World.

It was during the reign of Pope Paul VI (1963–78) that the Church of the West became the Church of the world since during that period the shift of the statistical center of gravity took place. Indigenous bishops came to predominate. Today in Africa approximately 75 percent of the bishops and nearly 95 percent of the episcopacy in Asia are natives of those continents. During his pontificate, Pope Paul VI became the first pope to leave Europe. He visited all six continents, a sure sign that the Church has indeed become a world church. Pope John Paul II has continued this practice.

With the coming of the third millennium much of the leadership in Roman Catholicism will originate in the Church of the southern hemisphere. Pope Paul VI in his encyclical letter *Evangelii Nuntiandi* twice referred to the special contribution already being made by the bishops of the Third World. With the rise of the Church in the southern hemisphere new challenges will be forthcoming. Until Vatican II, complete uniformity was found in the Catholic Church. Everywhere basically the same catechism was used, the same Latin liturgy was celebrated, together with the same centrally controlled Church discipline. As long as the Church lived in a European cultural setting, such uniformity was more or less acceptable. But since the Church now exists on six continents, each with its own cultures, politics, and ecclesial consciousness, adaptation of purely external details such as church music, mode of dress, etc., will not be enough. The Church must become radically incarnated into those cultures. Vatican II cautiously acknowledged such a goal in *The Dogmatic Constitution on the Church* (Nos. 13 and 23), but Pope Paul VI did so even more specifically in *Evangelii Nuntiandi* when he spoke of the need for the incarnation of the Church in diverse cultures. Pope Paul speaks in this encyclical letter of the need for legitimate pluriformity (No. 63), not as a threat to unity, but as an enrichment, as a God-given expression of unity in diversity. The passage from uniformity to pluriformity will continue to produce tensions between local churches and Rome. The transition from a Jewish to a gentile Christian church took place under tension as is evidenced in the life of St. Paul. So too will the transition from a Western Church to a World Church.

New questions will arise in theology as is already evident in the development of liberation theology; so, too, in ethics, as is clear from the problems being experienced in Africa concerning marriage customs and polygamy. At the same time, contributions to the World Church will be made by the Third World communities. New insights in the field of liturgy may come from the African continent and, in the area of mysticism, from Asia. Much give and take will be involved. There will be mutual exchanges in theology, both dogmatic and pastoral, and in the mode of Christian living. But hopefully, under the direction of the Holy Spirit, Catholicism and Christianity in its fullest dimension will increasingly become one Church and one humanity. The Church in the year 2100 will undoubtedly look very different in its outward appearance than it does today, although the substance of the faith will be the same. The next one hundred years will be challenging and exciting, and filled with difficult and tense moments, which is nothing less than a sign of life and a confirmation that the Holy Spirit will be with the Church always.

Notes

Part I

Chapter 1

[1] Heiko Oberman, *Forerunners of the Reformation,* trans. Paul L. Nyhus (New York: Holt, Rinehart and Winston, 1966).

[2] St. Robert Bellarmine, *De Controversiis Christianae Fidei Adversus Nostri Temporis Haereticos,* vol. 2 of *Opera Omnia* (Frankfurt a-M., 1965), 111).

[3] Ibid., 74.

[4] George Lindbeck, *The Future of Roman Catholic Theology* (Philadelphia: Fortress Press, 1970), 20.

[5] Georges de Santillana, *The Crime of Galileo* (Chicago: University of Chicago Press, 1955).

[6] Paul Johnson, *A History of Christianity* (New York: Atheneum, 1985), 384–95.

[7] Raymond Brown, *The Critical Meaning of the Bible* (New York: Paulist Press, 1981); see also James L. Price, *Interpreting the New Testament* (New York: Holt, Rinehart and Winston, 1971).

[8] For further study of American Catholicism see Andrew M. Greeley, *The Catholic Experience* (New York: Doubleday, 1967); see also John Cogley, *Catholic America* (New York: Doubleday, 1974). Also important in this regard is John Tracy Ellis, *American Catholicism* (Chicago: University of Chicago Press, 1956).

9   Romano Guardini, *The Church of the Lord,* trans. Stella Lange (Chicago: H. Regnery, 1966).

10 Jacques Maritain, *An Essay on Christian Philosophy,* trans. Edward H. Flannery (New York: Philosophical Library, 1955).

11 For an excellent survey of modern Roman Catholic theology, see T. M. Schoof, *A Survey of Catholic Theology: 1800–1970* (New York: Paulist Press, 1970).

12 Henri de Lubac, *The Drama of Atheist Humanism,* trans. Edith M. Riley (New York: World Publishing, 1963).

13 Yves Congar, *Lay People in the Church* (Westminster, Md.: Christian Classics, 1985).

14 Karl Rahner, *Theological Investigations,* vols. 1–20 (Baltimore: Helicon Press, 1961–1981).

15 Pope Pius XII, *Humani Generis,* encyclical letter of Pope Pius XII (New York: Paulist Press, 1950).

Chapter 2

1   Edward Schillebeeckx, *The Real Achievement of Vatican II,* trans. H. J. Vaughn (New York: Herder and Herder, 1967), 9.

2   Walter M. Abbott, ed., "The Dogmatic Constitution on the Church" in *The Documents of Vatican II* (New York: America Press, 1966), 17–18.

3   Karl Rahner, *The Church After the Council,* trans. Davis C. Herron and Rodelinde Albrecht (New York: Herder and Herder, 1966), 19–29.

4   George Lindbeck, *The Future of Roman Catholic Theology* (Philadelphia: Fortress Press, 1970), 20.

5   Abbott, 23.

6   Ibid., 205.

7   Ibid., 232.

8   Ibid., 233.

9   Ibid., 241.

10 Jerald C. Brauer, "Religious Freedom as a Human Right," in *Religious Liberty: An End and a Beginning,* ed. John Courtney Murray, S.J. (New York: Macmillan, 1966), 46.

11 Donald J. Wolf, S.J., *Toward Consensus: Catholic-Protestant Interpretations of Church and State* (Garden City, N.Y.: Doubleday, 1968).

12 John Courtney Murray, S.J., "De Libertate Religiosa: An Interpretative Analysis," in *A Journal of Church and State* VIII (Winter 1966): 33. See also I. E. Love, *John Courtney Murray: Contemporary Church-State Theory* (Garden City, N.Y.: Doubleday, 1965).

13 John Courtney Murray, S.J., "The Problem of Religious Freedom," *Theological Studies,* 25 (December 1964): 503–75.

14 Carillo de Albornoz, as quoted in Donald J. Wolf, S.J., "American Catholic Theories of Church-State Relations," in *Current Trends in Theology,* ed. Donald J. Wolf, S.J. and James V. Schall, S.J. (Garden City, N.Y.: Image Books, 1966), 192–95.

15 Abbott, 675.

16 Ibid., 677.

17 Ibid., 679–80.

18 Ibid., 686–87.

19 Ibid., 685.

20 Murray, "The Problem of Religious Freedom," 530.

21 Abbott, 679.

22 J. P. Migne, *Theologiae cursus completus: Series Graeca,* Vol. 46 (Paris: Typographi Brepols), 524.

23 Albornoz in Wolf, 71.

24 Abbott, 683–84.

25 Ibid., 683.

26 Ibid.

27 Ibid., 673.

28 Ibid., 674.

29 Gabriel Moran, *Theology of Revelation* (New York: Herder and Herder, 1966).

30 Abbott, 661–63.

31 Monika Hellwig, *What Are the Theologians Saying?* (Dayton, Ohio: Pflaum Press, 1970), 1–21.

Chapter 3

1   Walter M. Abbott, ed., "The Declaration on the Relationship of the Church to Non-Christian Religions," in *The Documents of Vatican II* (New York: America Press, 1966), 662–63.

2   Ibid.

3   Karl Rahner, "Christianity and the Non-Christian Religions," *Theological Investigations,* trans. Cornelius Ernst (Baltimore: Helicon Press, 1961), I, 165.

4   Abbott, 26.

5   Ibid.

6   Eugene Hillman, *The Church as Mission* (New York: Herder and Herder, 1965), 131.

7   Ibid., 100–28.

8   Paul Tillich, "Missions and World History," *The Theology of the Christian Mission,* ed. Gerald H. Anderson (Nashville: Abingdon Press, 1961), 283, 286.

9   Paul Tillich, *My Search for Absolutes* (New York: Simon and Schuster, 1967), 140–41.

10 Karl Rahner, *The Christian of the Future,* trans. W. J. O'Hara (New York: Herder and Herder, 1963), 83.

11 Ibid.

Part II

Chapter 4

1   Henry Denziger, *Enchiridion Symbolorum, Definitionum, et Declarationum de Rebus Fidei et Morum,* ed. Adolf Schonmetzer, S.J., 36th ed., no. 301 (New York: Herder and Herder, 1976), 108.

2   Ibid., no. 3434, 672.

3   Raymond Brown, *Jesus, God and Man: Modern Biblical Reflections* (New York: Macmillan, 1967), 82–86.

4 Walter Kasper, *Jesus the Christ* (New York: Paulist Press, 1976), 104–11. In this section, Kasper analyzes two other titles attributed to Jesus: Son of man and Son of God.

Chapter 5

1 *Origins,* 14 (November 15, 1984), no. 22 and 23.

2 Walter M. Abbott, ed., "Dogmatic Constitution on the Church," in *The Documents of Vatican II* (New York: America Press, 1966), 67.

3 Ibid., 243.

4 Ibid., 639–40.

5 Dietrich Bonhoeffer, *The Cost of Discipleship* (New York: Macmillan, 1963), 45–60.

6 Hans Urs von Balthasar, "Eschatology," in *Theology Today,* ed. F. Boechle, (Milwaukee: Bruce, 1965), 53.

7 Lindbeck, *The Future of Roman Catholic Theology* (Philadelphia: Fortress Press, 1970), 53

8 Karl Barth, *The Humanity of God,* trans. John Newton Thomas (Richmond, Va.: John Knox Press, 1960), 61.

9 Karl Rahner, "The Christian Among Unbelieving Relations," in *Theological Investigations,* trans. Karl H. and Boniface Kruger (Baltimore: Helicon Press, 1967), III, 371.

10 Ibid., 371–72.

11 Ibid.

12 C. S. Lewis, *Letters to Malcolm: Chiefly on Prayer* (New York: Harcourt, Brace, Jovanovich, 1966), 108–9.

13 Sean Fagan, *Has Sin Changed?* (Garden City, N.Y.: Image Books, 1979), 164–68.

14 Abbott, 253.

15 Ibid., 255.

16 Ibid., 250.

17 Ibid., 255.

18 Charles E. Curran, Robert E. Hunt, et al., *Dissent in and for the Church* (New York: Sheed and Ward, 1970), 112–13.

19 James P. Hannigan, *What Are They Saying About Sexual Morality?* (Ramsey, N. J.: Paulist Press, 1982), 48–61.

20 Charles E. Curran, "Sexual Ethics: A Critique," in *Issues in Sexual and Medical Ethics* (Notre Dame, Ind.: University of Notre Dame Press, 1978), 38.

Chapter 6

1 For an excellent history of the development of the sacraments, together with a pastoral analysis of the role of each sacrament in the life of Catholics today, see William J. Bausch, *A New Look at the Sacraments*, revised ed. (Mystic, Conn.: Twenty-Third Publications, 1983). Another excellent book is Bernard Cooke's *Sacraments and Sacramentality* (Mystic, Conn.: Twenty-Third Publications, 1983).

2 Edward Schillebeeckx, *Christ: The Sacrament of the Encounter with God* (New York: Sheed and Ward, 1963), 3–89; see also Karl Rahner, *The Church and the Sacraments* (New York: Herder and Herder, 1966), 11–75.

3 George J. Dyer, ed., *An American Catholic Catechism* (New York: Seabury Press, 1975), 107–10.

4 Ibid., 106–7.

5 Schillebeeckx, 200–16.

6 Rahner, *The Church and the Sacraments,* 41–75.

7 Karl Rahner, "Personal and Sacramental Piety," in *Theological Investigations,* trans. Karl H. Kruger (Baltimore: Helicon Press, 1963), II, 109–33.

Part III

Chapter 7

1 Walter M. Abbott, ed., "Decree on Ecumenism," in *The Documents of Vatican II* (New York: America Press, 1966), 347.

[2] W. A. Visser 't Hooft, ed., *The Evanston Report* (London: SCM Press, 1955), 25.

[3] Ibid., 26.

[4] Abbott, 342.

[5] Ibid., 346.

[6] Ibid.

[7] Ibid., 353.

[8] Ibid., 352.

[9] Ibid., 660–68.

[10] For the complete text of "Guidelines and Suggestions for Implementing the Conciliar Declaration *Nostra Aetate*," together with a Catholic and Jewish reaction, see *Face to Face,* vol. 1 (Summer 1975). *Face to Face* is published by the Anti-Defamation League of B'nai B'rith, 315 Lexington Avenue, New York, N.Y.

[11] See John T. Pawlikowski, *What are They Saying about Christian-Jewish Relations?* (New York: Paulist Press, 1980), especially 33–67.

[12] Ibid., 109–28.

[13] See Leon Poliakov, *The History of Anti-Semitism,* trans. Richard Howard (New York: Schocken Books, 1974).

[14] Rosemary Ruether, *Faith and Fratricide: The Theological Roots of Anti-Semitism* (New York: Seabury Press, 1974).

[15] Thomas A. Idinopulus and Roy Brown Ward, "Is Christianity Inherently Anti-Semitic," *Journal of the American Academy of Religion* 45 (June 1977): 193–214.

[16] Pawlikowski, 129–41.

[17] *Ecumenical Trends* 14 (October 1985): 138–44.

Chapter 8

[1] Walter M. Abbott, ed., "Dogmatic Constitution on the Church," in *The Documents of Vatican II* (New York: America Press, 1966), 24.

[2] Ibid., 559.

3 Ibid., 30.

4 Francis A. Sullivan, S.J., "The Ecclesiological Context of the Charismatic Renewal," in *The Holy Spirit and Power,* ed. Kilian McDonell, O.S.B. (Garden City, N.Y.: Doubleday, 1975), 122.

5 Léon-Joseph Cardinal Suenens, "The Charismatic Dimension of the Church," *Council Speeches of Vatican II,* ed. Yves Congar, Hans Küng, and Daniel O'Hanlon (London: Paulist Press, 1964), 18–21.

6 Abbott, 30.

7 Kilian McDonell, O.S.B., "Holy Spirit and Christian Initiation" in *The Holy Spirit and Power,* ed. Kilian McDonnell, O.S.B. (Garden City, N.Y.: Doubleday, 1975), 66–67.

8 Kevin M. Ranaghan, "Liturgy and Chrisms" in *The Holy Spirit and Power,* ed. Kilian McDonell, O.S.B., 161–66; see also Richard Quebedeaux, *The New Charismatics,* II (San Francisco: Harper and Row, 1983), 72–80.

9 René Laurentin, *Catholic Pentacostalism,* trans. Matthew J. O'Connell (Garden City, N.Y.: Image Books, 1978), 73.

10 See Donald J. Gelpi, S.J., *Pentacostalism: A Theological Viewpoint* (New York: Paulist Press, 1971), 136–38.

Chapter 9

1 Walter M. Abbott, "Decree on the Apostolate of the Laity," in *The Documents of Vatican II* (New York: America Press, 1966), 500.

2 "Justice in the World," (Washington, D.C.: United States Catholic Conference, 1971), 44.

3 Leonard Swidler and Arlene Swidler, eds., *Women Priests: A Catholic Commentary on the Vatican Declaration* (New York: Paulist Press, 1977). The text of *The Declaration on the Question of the Admission of Women to the Ministerial Priesthood,* which was published in Rome on October 15, 1976, is found in *Women Priests,* 38ff.

4 Raymond E. Brown, *Biblical Reflections on Crises Facing the Church* (New York: Paulist Press, 1975), 50, 51.

5 Tertullian, *De Cultu Feminarum* 1:1.

6 St. Thomas Aquinas, *Summa Theologica,* I, 92, 1 and 2.

7 Ibid., III, Suppl. 65:5.

8 Brown, 57–60.

9 Ibid., 55.

10 Ibid., 57–60.

11 Elizabeth M. Tetlow, *Women and Ministry in the New Testament* (New York: Paulist Press, 1980), 67.

12 Raymond Brown, *Priest and Bishop* (New York: Paulist Press, 1970), 17–19.

13 Ibid., 60.

14 Quoted in Tetlow, 117.

Chapter 10

1 Richard P. McBrien, *Catholicism* (Minneapolis: Winston Press, 1980), 942.

2 William F. Buckley, "This Week," *National Review* 11 (August 12, 1961): 88.

3 David J. O'Brien and Thomas A. Shannon, eds., *Renewing the Earth: Catholic Documents on Peace, Justice and Liberation* (Garden City, N.Y: Doubleday Image Books, 1977), 400.

4 Excerpt from "Justice in the World," in O'Brien and Shannon, 391.

5 For an overview of the development of social ethics in the United States, see Charles E. Curran, *American Catholic Social Ethics: Twentieth Century Approaches* (Notre Dame, Ind.: University of Notre Dame Press, 1982); see also Charles E. Curran, *Toward an American Catholic Moral Theology* (Notre Dame, Ind.: University of Notre Dame Press, 1987).

6 Curran, *American Catholic Social Ethics,* 1–2.

7 *American* is used here only in regard to the Church in the United States.

8 William D. Miller, *Dorothy Day: A Biography* (San Francisco: Harper and Row, 1982), 517, as quoted by Lawrence S. Cunningham, *The Catholic Heritage* (New York: Crossroad, 1985), 175; see also 170–75 for a brief analysis of Dorothy Day; also Charles E. Curran, *American Catholic Social Ethics,* 130–71 for a deeper analysis of the Catholic Worker movement.

9 The final draft of the letter appears in *Origins* 13 (May 19, 1983): 1–32. The document was also published in booklet form by the United States Catholic Conference, Washington, D.C.

10 See Richard P. McBrien, *Caesar's Coin* (New York: Macmillan, 1987), 197.

11 Ibid.

12 Ibid., 198, 195–202. See also "Pastoral Constitution on the Church in the Modern World," n. 4. in *The Documents of Vatican II,* ed. Walter M. Abbott (New York: America Press, 1966).

13 The final draft of this letter appears in *Origins* 16 (November 27, 1986): 411–55.

14 Curran, *Toward an American Catholic Moral Theology,* 183. See also chapter 8, "An Analysis of the United States Bishops' Pastoral Letter on the Economy," 174–93.

15 Michael Novak, *Freedom with Justice: Catholic Social Thought and Liberal Institutions* (San Francisco: Harper and Row, 1984).

16 J. Brian Benested, *The Pursuit of a Just Social Order: Policy Statements of the U.S. Bishops, 1966–1980* (Washington, D.C.: Ethics and Public Policy Center, 1982).

17 Deane William Ferm, *Third World Liberation Theologies: An Introductory Survey* (Maryknoll, N.Y.: Orbis, 1983), 17.

18 *The Church in the Present-Day Transformation of Latin America in the Light of the Council: Second General Council of Latin American Bishops,* 3rd ed. (Washington, D.C.: National Council of Catholic Bishops, 1979).

19 Ibid., 23.

20 Ibid., 175.

21 Philip Berryman, *Basic Ecclesial Communities: The Evangelization of the Poor* (Maryknoll, N.Y.: Orbis, 1976), 26.

22 Leonardo Boff and Clodovis Boff, *Liberation Theology* (San Francisco: Harper and Row, 1986), 19.

23 Ibid., 10.

24 Ibid.

25 Ibid.

26 For an excellent introduction to the writings of the most important liberation theologians see Ferm, *Third World Liberation Theologies,* especially 1–60.

27 Boff and Boff, 17.

28 Gustavo Gutiérrez, *The Power of the Poor in History* (Maryknoll, N.Y.: Orbis, 1983), 84.

29 Gustavo Gutiérrez, *A Theology of Liberation,* (Maryknoll, N.Y.: Orbis, 1973), 90.

30 Boff and Boff, 22.

31 Ibid., 23.

32 Ferm, 112–13.

33 The entire document was published in the *National Catholic Reporter* (September 21, 1984), 11–14.

34 Leonardo Boff, "Church, Charism and Power" in *Liberation Theology and the Institutional Church* (New York: Crossroad, 1985).

35 Gary MacEoin and Nivita Riley, *Puebla: A Church Being Born* (New York: Paulist Press, 1980), 101.

36 Edward Schillebeeckx, *Il Regno Attrealita,* no. 18 (October 15, 1984): 446–47.

37 As quoted by Robert McAfee Brown, *Theology in a New Key* (Philadelphia: Westminster, 1978), 60.

38 Gutiérrez, *The Power of the Poor in History,* 84.

39 Clodovis Boff, "Saint Thomas Aquinas and the Theology of Liberation," *Dominican Ashram* 5 (September 1986): 132.

40 Boff and Boff, 37.

Glossary

In the text, words that can be found in the glossary are printed in boldface (first appearance only). Glossary entries that did not appear in the text are not in boldface here.

Assimilationists: American Catholic bishops of the nineteenth century such as John Ireland of St. Paul, Minnesota, and James Cardinal Gibbons of Baltimore, Maryland, who believed that immigrant Catholics should become Americanized in every way as soon as possible. They believed American culture to be a positive force.

Assumption: The dogma, defined by Pope Pius XII in 1950, stating that the body of the Blessed Virgin Mary was taken directly to heaven after her death.

Beatific vision: By definition of Pope Benedict XII, the act whereby the blessed in heaven see God face to face; that is, it is the clear, intuitive, immediate sight of God.

Biblical criticism: The scientific study and analysis of the human elements that have entered into the composition and preservation of the Scriptures. Such study has been encouraged and fostered by the Church, most notably by Pope Leo XIII in *Providentisimus Deus* (1893) and by Pope Pius XII in *Divino Afflante Spiritu* (1943). In all biblical criticism, the Catholic Church insists that its scholars recognize the Bible as the inspired word of God that is not to be treated as merely a secular piece of writing.

Casti Connubii: An encyclical letter written by Pope Pius XI in 1930 forbidding the use of artificial contraception.

Catechesis: The oral instruction that can be accompanied with visual or printed aids whereby the faithful are taught the Scriptures and the teachings of the Church.

Catechism: Among early Christian writers this meant both the subject matter and the method of instruction. Today the word *catechism* usually refers to the text or manual that summarizes Catholic doctrine.

Charism: This word comes from the Greek and means any gift or favor. As used by St. Paul and applied to Christians, charism refers to extraordinary gifts granted to Christians by the Holy Spirit—e.g., wisdom.

Charismatic: One who manifests and is open to the gifts of the Holy Spirit.

Church Fathers: This title is given to the great Christian writers and bishops of the early Christian centuries beginning with St. Clement of Rome (d. A.D 97) and ending with St. Gregory the Great (d. A.D. 604).

Clericalism: The domination of the life of the Church by the clergy.

Conciliarism: A theory emanating in a variety of forms from canonists of the twelfth and thirteenth centuries, according to which an ecumenical council was held to be superior to the authority of the pope.

Counter-Reformation: A movement of Catholic reform that began in reaction to the Protestant Reformation and led to the convening of the Council of Trent (1545–63).

Cosmology: The study of nature or the physical world, especially regarding its ultimate causes.

Covenant: A contract or compact made between God and his people. In the Old Testament, the term refers to God's agreements with the people of Israel.

Deism: The theory that accepts the existence of God on purely rational grounds but denies, doubts, or rejects as incredible

Christianity as a supernatural religion. Thus, revelation, miracles, grace, and mysteries are excluded from acceptance by what is called the "rational man." Deism differs from rationalism in that it accepts a personal God and adheres to what is called "natural religion," even though it does not accept a supernatural order.

Development of doctrine: This term refers to growth in the Church's understanding of the truths of divine revelation; that is, the gradual unfolding of the meaning of what God has revealed. The Church presumes that the substantial truth of a revealed mystery remains unchanged. What changes is the subjective understanding of the revealed truth.

Diaspora: Refers to Jewish communities that settled outside of Palestine.

Doctrine: An official teaching of the Church.

Dogma: A doctrine that is promulgated with the highest Church authority and solemnity. If denied, it is a heresy. Every dogma is a doctrine, but not every doctrine is a dogma.

Ecclesial: That which pertains to the Church as a mystery, as distinguished from that which pertains to the Church as an institution.

Ecclesiology: The theological study of the nature of the Church.

Ecumenical: Literally "universal." Commonly used to identify the general councils of the Church. The term also refers to the movement toward reunification of the separated churches of Christendom.

Ecumenism: The modern movement toward Christian unity whose Protestant origins stem from the Edinburgh World Missionary Conference in 1910 and whose formal Catholic beginnings stem from Vatican II.

Encyclical: A papal document treating matters related to the general welfare of the Church and "circulated" to Catholics throughout the world.

Eschatology: Literally "the study of the last things." Such a study includes the following: the kingdom of God, judgment, heaven, hell, purgatory, the resurrection of the body, and the Second Coming of Christ.

Eucharist: Literally a "thanksgiving." The word is commonly used to denote the Mass or the Lord's Supper.

Fortress mentality: A reaction taken by the Catholic Church beginning with the Protestant Reformation and intensifying following the French Revolution. It was basically a defensive posture against the world-at-large.

Fundamental option: The radical orientation of one's whole life toward or away from God. Our destiny is determined by this fundamental choice, not by individual actions, unless those actions are such that our basic relationship with God is fully engaged.

Gallicanism: A form of national conciliarism [see above] peculiar to France (Gaul), and implicitly rejected by the First Vatican Council (1869–70).

Grace: The condescension and benevolence shown by God to the human race; that is, the unmerited gift of God bestowed on human kind for its eternal salvation.

Glossolalia: This term comes from the Greek words *glossa,* which means "tongues," and *lalein,* which means "to speak." Speaking in tongues is one of the gifts of the Holy Spirit.

Heaven: Theologically, heaven is a metaphor for the fullness of salvation enjoyed by those who are ultimately saved by God. They enjoy the beatific vision [see above].

Hell: The term derives from the North Germanic *hel,* "realm of the dead." It represents failure to reach heaven and implies the state of final personal alienation from God. The magisterium of the Church teaches that hell exists, that punishment begins immediately after death (without awaiting the Last Judgment), and that it lasts forever.

Hesychasm: A system of mysticism first practiced by Orthodox monks of Mt. Athos in the fourteenth century. Drawn from Platonist philosophy and borrowing from yoga practices, hesychasm was a form of quietism, i.e., it stressed inner silence and accepted the spiritual ideal that perfection was the complete passivity of the soul.

Hierarchy: Etymologically the Latin *hierarchia* means "holy authority." It is the body of ordained ministers in the Church. The hierarchy of the Church contains two distinctions. By reason of holy orders (ordination), the hierarchy is composed of the pope, bishops, priests, and deacons. By reason of jurisdiction, the hierarchy is made up of the pope and the bishops under his authority. This jurisdiction, in turn, can be shared with priests and deacons.

Historical-critical method: A theological and philosophical mentality that is attentive to the impact of history on human thought and action and that, therefore, takes into account the concrete and the changeable. The historical-critical method attempts to discover the original formulation of a belief and the motives and forces, whether personal or social, underlying that belief, which played their part in the development of a particular dogma.

Historicism: A theory that says that the course of human history is determined by a series of laws, not by the actions of people. These laws cannot be altered and no human decisions or actions can prevent them from working.

***Humanae vitae*:** The encyclical written by Pope Paul VI in 1968 condemning as immoral all artificial means of birth control.

Hypostatic union: The mysterious union of Jesus' divine and human natures in the person (*hypostasis*) of the Logos, i.e., in the second person of the Trinity.

Imprimatur: The Latin word means "let it be printed," and it is used by Church authorities to grant permission for the printing of writings, prayers, pictures, and other materials. Authors are free to obtain the imprimatur either from the bishop where they reside or where it is printed. Generally, the imprimatur, together with the bishop's name and date of approval, is to appear in the publication.

Jansenism: A movement in seventeenth and eighteenth century Europe that had its origin in the book *Augustinus*, published in 1640, two years after the death of the author, Cornelius Jansen, bishop of Ypres. Jansenism was especially strong in France. It stressed moral austerity, the evil of the human body and of human desires, and an elitist notion of salvation (Jesus died for a few). Jansenism was carried from France to Ireland and then to the United States in the nineteenth and early twentieth centuries.

Kingdom of God: The reign, or rule, of God. It is the presence of God in one's heart, among various communities, and in the world-at-large, renewing and reconciling all things. It is both a process (reign of God) and the reality towards which the process is moving (kingdom of God).

Legalism: Overemphasis on the letter of the law to the detriment of the value or values contained in the law; or observance of a law to such a degree that the spirit of the law suffers or is lost completely.

Liberation theology: A type of theology that emphasizes the theme of liberation found in both the Old and the New Testaments and reinterprets all doctrines in terms of that theme. Forms of liberation theology include Latin American, Asian, African, African-American, and feminist.

Limbo: The abode of souls excluded from heaven, but who do not suffer any other punishment. Limbo is the place or state for those who have deserved neither beatitude nor damnation.

***Limbus infantium*:** The limbo of infants. The permanent state of infants who die in original sin but who are innocent of any personal guilt.

***Limbus patrum*:** The limbo of the fathers refers to the place where the saints of the Old Testament remained until Christ's coming and redemption of the world.

Liturgy: A public service, duty, or work. Today, liturgy refers to the official public worship of the Church and is thus distinguished from private devotion.

Magisterium: The teaching authority of the Church vested in the pope as the successor of St. Peter, in the bishops as successors of the apostles, and to others by reason of scholarly competence (theologians and biblical scholars).

Manichaeism: A dualistic religion begun in the third century A.D. by a Persian named Mani, Manes, or Manichaeus (A.D. 215–75). In Manichaean teaching, there are two ultimate sources of creation, good and evil.

Mass: The sacrifice of the Eucharist that is the central act of worship in the Catholic Church. Mass is a late form of *missio* (sending) and refers to the custom whereby the faithful are sent to put into practice what they have received from Christ by attending the service.

Messiah: Hebrew for the "anointed one" who was to usher in a golden age for Israel. Christians believe Jesus is the *Christ* ("anointed one" in Greek) and interpreted the arrival of the kingdom in spiritual terms.

Modern mentality: A frame of mind induced by technology and especially by the innovations brought about by advances in communication and transportation. The term implies the problem of choosing from a fairly large number of choices.

Modernism: A collective term for certain false or distorted theological views that arose about the year 1900 from the legitimate desire to proclaim the Christian faith to the people of that time in an understandable manner. According to modernism, religion is essentially a matter of experience, personal and collective. There is no objective revelation from God to the human race. Pope Pius X condemned modernism in 1907 in two formal documents, *Lamentabili* and *Pascendi*.

Moralism: The attempt to live a morally good life independent of the practice of religion.

Moral theology: A branch of theology that analyzes the individual and social moral implications of the Gospel and that attempts to reach normative inferences for the conduct of the Church and its members.

Mortal sin: A fundamental rejection of the Gospel and/or of God, meriting eternal punishment.

Natural law: A philosophy that teaches the objective structures of human nature precede and make possible the freedom of humanity because they are implicitly affirmed even in their denial. Since these structures objectify the will of God, their creator, the law of obligation flowing from them is also called the natural law but in a quite different sense from that which the term has in the natural sciences.

Original Sin: The sin committed by Adam as the head of the human race and passed on to his posterity. In Catholic teaching the only two exceptions are Jesus and his mother Mary.

Orthodoxy: Refers to those Eastern churches that have not been united with Rome since A.D. 1054 but accept the ancient councils of the Church. These churches have their own liturgies and are comparatively autonomous. The Orthodox recognize the pope only as the patriarch of the West.

Parousia: The Second Coming of Christ at the end of history.

Pelagianism: The teaching of the monk Pelagius (early fifth century), which was combatted by St. Augustine. Pelagianism rejects the doctrine of Original Sin and denies the need of grace to observe the moral law. It was condemned as a heresy by the Church in the fifth century and again at the Council of Trent.

Pope: The word is derived from the old ecclesiastic Latin *papa*, meaning "father." The pope is seen by Roman Catholics as the "father" of Christendom since he is as the head of the Church believed to be the successor of St. Peter. He is also the bishop of Rome.

Purgatory: A process of purification for the souls of those who have died without being completely cleansed of the guilt of their venial sins and of the temporal punishment due because of their sins. Such souls must undergo purgatory before entering heaven.

Reformation: A complex series of religious, social, and political changes occurring in Christianity from the fourteenth to the seventeenth centuries that resulted in a break with Roman Catholicism by a variety of Protestant churches.

Reign of God: A dynamic expression for the Kingdom of God. The term refers to the kingdom as it is now in process.

Revelation: God's self-disclosure (literally "unveiling") to human kind through creation, persons, events, and, especially, through Jesus Christ.

Ritual: A formal religious ceremony or set of ceremonies, such as the Mass, that is celebrated according to a fixed pattern and is accompanied by fixed words.

Roman Curia: The entire organization of administrative and judicial offices through which the pope directs the operations of the Catholic Church.

Rubrics: The liturgical provisions or directives that guide bishops, priests, or deacons while celebrating the Mass, administering the sacraments and sacramentals, and preaching.

Sacrament: Generally speaking, any visible sign of God's invisible presence. Specifically, sacraments of the Church are signs through which the Church manifests its faith and communicates the grace of God that is present in the Church and in the signs themselves. The Catholic Church teaches there are seven sacraments: baptism, confirmation, Eucharist, penance, marriage, holy orders, and the anointing of the sick.

Sacramentals: Grace-bearing signs that do not fully express the nature of the Church and that, according to Catholic teaching, do not guarantee the grace associated with the seven sacraments—for example, the rosary, holy water, or religious medals.

Salvation: In biblical language, the deliverance from difficult circumstances or oppression from some evil to a state of freedom. Since sin is perceived as the greatest evil, salvation is understood primarily as liberation from sin and its consequences. Salvation is the end product of redemption. To be saved is to be fully and permanently united with God and with one another in God.

Serious venial sin: This refers to an action of a serious or grave nature, that in itself does not necessarily indicate that the fundamental relationship with God has been broken. The circumstances of the action, together with the questions of full knowledge of its gravity and full consent of the will, must be considered.

Social doctrine: The official teachings of the Church developed since the publication of Pope Leo XIII's encyclical *Rerum Novarum* (On the Condition of the Worker) in 1891 that point out the implications of the Gospel message in such areas as human rights, peace, and social justice.

Spirit-baptism: Not a sacrament but a prayer to the Father offered by an individual in community with Christian friends asking the Father, in the name of Jesus, to send the Holy Spirit upon a person who has decided to break with sin. The individual must be fully docile to the inspiration of the Holy Spirit and completely open to whatever charismatic gifts the Holy Spirit may offer. In terms of its effects, it is commonly observable that those who receive Spirit-baptism have an experience with the triune God that produces a new or greater desire for prayer and a stronger desire to know the Scriptures.

Summa Theologica: The principal doctrinal synthesis of medieval Catholic theology, written by St. Thomas Aquinas (1225–74).

Synod: An official assembly of church leaders gathered together to discuss and decide on matters pertaining to doctrine, discipline, or liturgy. Such meetings can occur at the international, national, regional, provincial, or diocesan level.

Theism: Belief in a personal and provident God. Theists can take on various forms such as monotheism (one God), polytheism (many Gods), or henotheism (one chief God among several).

Thomism: An approach to theology derived from the writings of St. Thomas Aquinas.

Transubstantiation: The Catholic teaching, accepted officially at the Council of Trent, that states that in the Eucharist the substance of the bread and wine are changed into the substance of the body and blood of Christ so that only the appearance of bread and wine remain, i.e., shape, size, color, etc.

Trent: City in northern Italy where the nineteenth ecumenical council was held between 1545 and 1563. The council was Catholicism's official response to the Protestant Reformation.

Triumphalism: A term of reproach against the Catholic church for its claim that it has the fullness of truth and, thus, the right to pass judgment on the personal and social obligations of humankind. This accusation was especially strong previous to Vatican II.

Ultramontanism: Literally "beyond the mountains" (the Alps). A form of rigid traditionalism developed in France following the

French Revolution. Its adherents were greatly loyal to the Holy See, which geographically was located across the Alps.

Vatican II: Council called by the Catholic Church in order to respond to the liturgical and pastoral needs of Catholics in the twentieth century. Significant changes were made in Catholic practice and attitude as well as in theological understanding.

Venial sin: A sin that involves less serious actions against God and neighbor, or where there is neither full consent nor full knowledge, if the matter is serious.

Vulgate: Latin version of the Bible compiled and translated by St. Jerome in the fourth century to provide one authorized version of the Bible to Christians rather than the many versions that were in circulation at the time. It was adopted at the Council of Trent as the only official Catholic version.

Yoga: Literally the word in Sanskrit means "to yoke." Today it is used in two senses: (1) to denote a technique or system by means of which a *yogin* attains to *moksha* or salvation, (2) to denote a system of philosophy—one of the six major schools that have developed in India.

Zen: Name of a Buddhist sect in Japan that makes the practice of meditation its central tenet. Many of its meditative techniques have been adopted by Christians to enhance their own meditation.

Further Reading

The following books are recommended for further reading. Adventurous readers may read the other, often more specialized resources given in the chapter notes.

Part I

Modern Catholicism: Background, History, and Development

Brown, Raymond. *The Critical Meaning of the Bible*. New York: Paulist Press, 1981. An excellent presentation of the meaning and value of biblical criticism and its assimilation into Catholic doctrine, theology, and practice.

Bokenkotter, Thomas. *Essential Catholicism*. Garden City, N.Y.: Image Books, 1986. A comprehensive and well-researched compendium of Catholic faith, belief, and practice that provides a useful and thorough examination of Catholicism today, in light of developments since Vatican II.

Cogley, John. *Catholic America*. New York: Doubleday, 1974. A thoughtful panorama of the history and character of Roman Catholicism in American culture.

Dolan, John P. *Catholicism*. Woodbury, N.Y.: Barron's Educational Series, 1968. A readable introduction to the history of Catholicism from its origins up to the conclusion of Vatican II.

Ellis, John Tracy. *American Catholicism*. Chicago: University of Chicago Press, 1956. Still considered a standard history of Catholicism in America.

Greeley, Andrew M. *The Catholic Experience.* New York: Doubleday, 1974. A very interesting sociological analysis of the Catholic Church in the United States, beginning with the first American Catholic bishop, John Carroll, through the presidency of John F. Kennedy.

Hellwig, Monika. *What Are the Theologians Saying?* Dayton, Ohio: Pflaum Press, 1970. A short, well-written presentation of the changing focus in Catholic theology written for those who have no specialized training in theology. Excellent for adult education courses and discussion groups.

Hillman, Eugene. *The Church as Mission.* New York: Herder and Herder, 1965. One of the finest explanations of the mission of the Church in terms of the theology of Vatican II.

Johnson, Paul. *A History of Christianity.* New York: Atheneum, 1985. An up-to-date and readable text by an English Roman Catholic. Based more on politics, economics, and social and cultural facts than on theology, it is a study of Christianity as it relates to the role of the Roman Catholic Church in world history.

Kee, Howard Clark. *The New Testament in Context: Sources and Documents.* Englewood Cliffs, N.J.: Prentice-Hall, 1984. An absorbing analysis of the political, cultural, religious, literary, and philosophical contexts of New Testament texts and documents.

————. *Understanding the New Testament.* 4th ed. Englewood Cliffs, N.J.: Prentice-Hall, 1983. In this new edition, Kee traces the history of the New Testament period, discusses the literary origins and content of each book, explains how Christianity was launched and spread, and reveals the variety of ways in which Jesus's message was received.

Lindbeck, George. *The Future of Roman Catholic Theology.* Philadelphia: Fortress Press, 1970. A systematic analysis of the basic theological trends that emerged from Vatican II, as organized around the theme of the mission of the Church. Lindbeck, a

Lutheran, is less interested as to where Catholicism is, but rather where it is going.

McKenzie, John L. *Dictionary of the Bible.* New York: Macmillan, 1965. Still an excellent guide to practically every important subject and event in both the Old and New Testament.

Moran, Gabriel. *Theology of Revelation.* New York: Herder and Herder, 1966. An analysis of the nature of divine revelation as taught in *The Dogmatic Constitution on Divine Revelation.*

Murray, John Courtney, ed. *Religious Liberty: An End and a Beginning.* New York: Macmillan, 1966. A wide-ranging collection of rather scholarly studies on church-state relations.

Oberman, Heiko. *Forerunners of the Reformation.* Trans. Paul L. Nyhus. New York: Holt, Rinehart and Winston, 1966. An overview of major themes of the fourteenth and fifteenth centuries such as conciliarism, curialism, mysticism, and the impact of Renaissance humanism. Helps place the Reformation and the Counter-Reformation in historical perspective.

Price, James L. *Interpreting the New Testament.* 2nd ed. New York: Holt, Rinehart and Winston, 1971. A fine presentation of recent New Testament scholarship that attempts to describe the uniqueness of each New Testament writing as significant literary and theological entities.

Rahner, Karl. *The Christian of the Future.* New York: Herder and Herder, 1967. A collection of essays on the situation of the Church in the conciliar and postconciliar period.

Schillebeeckx, Edward. *The Real Achievement of Vatican II.* Trans. H. J. Vaughn. New York: Herder and Herder, 1967. A presentation of the author's insights concerning changes in Catholicism's religious thinking occasioned by Vatican II.

Schoof, T. M. *A Survey of Catholic Theology: 1800–1970.* New York: Paulist Press, 1970. A somewhat difficult but rewarding analysis of the development of modern Catholic theology.

Part II

Catholicism Today: Key Issues

Bausch, William J. *A New Look at the Sacraments.* revised ed. Mystic, Conn.: Twenty-Third Publications, 1983. An excellent history of the development of the sacraments, together with a pastoral analysis of the role of each sacrament in Catholic life today.

Brown, Raymond. *Jesus, God and Man: Modern Biblical Reflection.* New York: Macmillan, 1967. Very readable and clear presentation of the biblical understanding of Jesus's divinity and humanity. Especially helpful regarding the fullness of Jesus's humanity.

Cooke, Bernard. *Sacraments and Sacramentality.* Mystic, Conn.: Twenty-Third Publications, 1983. A marvelous presentation of the role of the sacraments in the post-Vatican II Church. Shows that sacrament includes more than liturgical rituals and, in fact, touches everything in life that is distinctively human.

Curran, Charles E., Robert E. Hunt, et al. *Dissent in and for the Church.* New York: Sheed and Ward, 1970. An informative series of essays delineating the role of dissent in the Church.

Curran, Charles E. *Issues in Sexual and Medical Ethics.* Notre Dame, Ind.: University of Notre Dame Press, 1978. Addresses a number of current issues in sexual and medical ethics, including marriage and divorce, respect for life, and human experimentation and genetics.

————. *Toward an American Catholic Moral Theology.* Notre Dame, Ind.: University of Notre Dame Press, 1987. Contains essays that outline the development of moral theology with particular reference to the United States and other essays that treat social issues having a special meaning for American society such as the *United States Bishops' Pastoral Letter on the Economy.*

Fagan, Sean. *Has Sin Changed?* Garden City, N.Y.: Image Books, 1979. A well-balanced analysis of the confusion concerning sin, together with a critical look at those aspects of the common understanding of sin that need correcting and development. A clear look at Catholic morality.

Greeley, Andrew. *Sexual Intimacy.* New York: Seaburg Press, 1973. Not a manual of sexuality but a very healthy presentation of the light Christian symbols throw on the ambiguity and confusion of human sexuality.

Hannigan, James P. *What Are They Saying About Sexual Morality?* Ramsey, N.J.: Paulist Press, 1982. Useful and easily readable overview of recent developments in Catholic moral theology.

Kasper, Walter. *Jesus the Christ.* New York: Paulist Press, 1976. Among recent works on Jesus this is perhaps the most outstanding. A brilliant synthesis of biblical, philosophical, and traditional material that can be recommended without hesitation.

Kee, Howard Clark. *Jesus in History.* New York: Harcourt, Brace and World, 1970. An examination of the special aims of the Gospel writers and of the role of Jesus in history as presented by the evangelists.

Küng, Hans. *Eternal Life.* Garden City, N.Y.: Image Books, 1985. A discussion of life after death and the contemporary medical, philosophical, and theological problems that any consideration of this question engenders. Includes analysis of the present understanding of heaven, hell, and the "end of the world."

Küng, Hans. *On Being a Christian.* New York: Doubleday, 1976. Very readable and interesting presentation about the meaning of Jesus and the challenge of being a Christian in the modern world.

Kreeft, Peter J. *Everything You Ever Wanted to Know About Heaven, But Never Dreamed of Asking.* San Francisco: Harper and Row, 1982. Despite the rather bizarre title, an interesting and readable book on the meaning of heaven written in a mode akin to that of C. S. Lewis.

Link, Mark. *The Seventh Trumpet.* Niles, Ill.: Argus Communications, 1978. An excellent introduction to the life and basic teachings of Jesus. Useful as a class text and for adult discussion groups.

Maly, Eugene H. *Sin: Biblical Perspective.* Dayton, Ohio: Pflaum Press, 1973. An examination of the biblical aspects of sin, both from the perspective of Hebrew awareness and in the light of Christ's redemptive act.

Pelikan, Jaroslav. *Jesus Through the Centuries.* New Haven, Conn.: Yale University Press, 1985. Intriguing study of Jesus's place in the general history of culture. Analyzes the manner in which Jesus has been variously understood by Christians during the twenty centuries of Christian history.

Rahner, Karl. *Foundations of Christian Faith*. New York: Seaburg Press, 1978. The most comprehensive and systematic statement of Rahner's Christology. Though brilliant, the concepts are often difficult to understand.

————. *The Church and the Sacraments*. New York: Herder and Herder, 1966. Analyzes the relationship between the Church and the sacraments within the framework of the Church as the enduring presence of Christ in the world, the fundamental sacrament of Christ, and the source of all the sacraments.

Schillebeeckx, Edward. *Christ: The Sacrament of the Encounter with God*. New York: Sheed and Ward, 1963. A clear presentation of the sacramental relationship of Christ to the Father, of the Church to Christ, and of the seven sacraments to the life of the Church.

————. *Jesus: An Experiment in Christology*. New York: Seaburg Press, 1979. Difficult but worthwhile reading. Schillebeeckx seeks to discover the historical Jesus and to examine what is peculiar and unique about "this person Jesus."

Part III

The Future: Movements in the Church

Benested, J. Brian. *The Pursuit of a Just Social Order: Policy Statements of the U.S. Catholic Bishops, 1966–1980*. Washington, D.C.: Ethics and Public Policy Center, 1982. A rather critical study of the social teaching of American bishops during the fifteen-year period following Vatican II.

Boff, Leonardo, and Clodovis Boff. *Liberation Theology*. San Francisco: Harper and Row, 1986. An exposition and defense of liberation theology that constitutes a primer for understanding one of the most controversial movements of the century.

Brown, Raymond E. *Biblical Reflections on Crises Facing the Church*. New York: Paulist Press, 1975. An important examination of biblical criticism's impact on Roman Catholicism's understanding of catechetics, the ordination of women, the papacy, and the role of Mary, Jesus, and ecumenism.

Brown, Robert McAfee. *The Ecumenical Revolution.* Garden City, N.Y.: Anchor-Image Book, 1969. The definitive study of the ecumenical movement from its earliest beginnings to post-Vatican II.

Cunningham, Lawrence S. *The Catholic Heritage.* New York: Crossroad, 1985. An engaging book that weaves a tremendous tapestry of Catholic history and tradition. Excellent for an understanding of what it means and has meant to be a Catholic.

Curran, Charles E. *American Catholic Social Ethics: Twentieth Century Approaches.* Notre Dame, Ind.: University of Notre Dame Press, 1982. An excellent overview of the development of social ethics in the United States during the twentieth century.

Ferm, Deane William. *Third World Liberation Theologies: An Introductory Survey.* Maryknoll, N.Y.: Orbis, 1986. An excellent introduction to the writings of the more important liberation theologians.

―――. *Third World Liberation Theologies: A Reader.* Maryknoll, N.Y.: Orbis, 1986. A companion to Ferm's *Third World Liberation Theologies: An Introductory Survey.* Contains many selections from significant books and articles that allow liberation theologians to speak for themselves.

Gelpi, Donald L., S.J. *Pentecostalism: A Theological Viewpoint.* New York: Paulist Press, 1971. Traces the development of the Catholic charismatic experience and also explains the theological and biblical sources of such "spirit-filled" endeavors.

Laurentin, René. *Catholic Pentecostalism.* Trans. Matthew O'Connell. Garden City, N.Y.: Image Books, 1978. Originally written in French in 1974, the book explains the origin of Catholic "pentecostalism" and provides clear insights into various aspects of the charismatic movement such as Spirit-baptism and speaking in tongues.

MacNutt, Francis. *Healing.* New York: Bantam Books, 1974. Perhaps the most scholarly and comprehensive book yet written on the meaning of Christian healing.

McBrien, Richard P. *Caesar's Coin.* New York: Macmillan, 1987. A very readable and important guide for any reader perplexed by the issues of religion and politics in American society. Helps to clarify the fundamental ideas and historical background of the religion and politics debate.

————. *Catholicism.* Minneapolis: Winston Press, 1980. A two-volume introduction to Roman Catholicism written in a concise fashion for anyone interested in discovering the meaning of the present-day Church.

McDonell, Kilian, O.S.B. ed. *The Holy Spirit and Power.* Garden City, N.Y.: Doubleday, 1975. Excellent essays on the history and meaning of the Catholic charismatic renewal.

McGrath, Sr. Albertus Magnus. *What a Modern Catholic Believes About Women.* Chicago: Thomas More Press, 1972. A well-written effort to uncover the elements constitutive of the Church's attitude and legislation regarding the role of women in the ministry of the Church.

Pawlikowski, John T. *What Are They Saying about Christian-Jewish Relations?* New York: Paulist Press, 1980. An essential introduction to the Christian-Jewish dialogue.

Poliakov, Leon. *The History of Anti-Semitism.* Trans. Richard Howard. New York: Schocken Books, 1974. The most systematic treatment of the history of anti-Semitism from the time of Christ to the ghettoes of the sixteenth century.

Quebedeaux, Richard. *The New Charismatics, II.* San Francisco: Harper and Row, 1983. Possibly the best guide to the people, the history, and the theology of the charismatic movement, both Protestant and Catholic.

Swidler, Leonard, and Arlene Swidler, eds. *Women Priests: A Catholic Commentary on the Vatican Declaration.* New York: Paulist Press, 1977. A collaborative commentary by leading Catholic scholars on the Vatican's *Declaration on the Admission of Women to the Ministerial Priesthood* in 1976. The book helps focus the many diverse elements of this complicated issue.

Tetlow, Elisabeth M. *Women and Ministry in the New Testament.* New York: Paulist Press, 1980. Explores the role and ministry of women in Jesus' time and in the primitive Church set against the backdrop of the status of women in ancient Greece, the Roman Empire, and late Judaism.

Epilogue

The Church in the Year 2000

Buhlmann, Walbert. *The Church of the Future: A Model for the Year 2001.* Maryknoll, N.Y.: Orbis, 1986. A study of the Church in Africa, Asia, and Latin America that indicates how the Church as a whole can—as it prepares for the third millenium—benefit from the new values and forms of Christian living emerging from these churches.

Index